# Beginner's
# TURKISH

# Beginner's
# TURKISH

*Fuad A. Attaoullah, B.A., B.Sc.*

Hippocrene Books
*New York*

# AN APPRECIATION BY
# SIR WYNDHAM DEEDES

(who served the Ottoman Empire in the Imperial Gendarmerie
and in the Civil Inspectorate.)

It gives me great pleasure to welcome a book of this class. It is obviously the result of years of hard work, and its publication comes at a most propitious time. Turkey is to-day, standing side by side with the Allies, and it is essential that a means should be available whereby her language may be thoroughly and easily learnt, in order to appreciate better her ideals. The English language is being taught throughout Turkey, and the Turkish President himself, a very great friend of Britain, took up its study a few years ago, and now speaks it fluently.

I know that, owing to the lack of a really comprehensive and explanatory Grammar -Turkish has some points which need careful and detailed explanation because they are completely strange to the English mind- mastery of the language has been up to the present a matter of years; but I feel convinced that, by the publication of this book this difficulty has in great measure been overcome.

All the principal features of the language have been clearly expounded, two of them in particular the "Gerunds" and the form which the author has called the " Definitive Combination", being much enlarged upon. I am very pleased to note this for although they are part and parcel of the language, and correct Turkish phrasing is dependent on them, they have never been fully elucidated.

I was also very glad to see that the author has made a point of giving the literal English translation under each Turkish word in the example sentences throughout the Grammar, each English word being placed in the same succession as the Turkish particles. It has always been a matter of difficulty for the beginner to appreciate that all words are made up of the stem, to which are added suffixes representing the various aspects of the word in general, and that in the verb conjugation the personal pronoun is added to the end of the word in the form of a suffix instead of a separate word in front. This building up of the Turkish word has been very simply explained, and the method adopted by the author of showing the various suffixes in heavier print will enable it to be grasped with ease.

I think I may claim to speak with some knowledge on this subject, having been through the interesting, but at the same time arduous experience of learning Turkish many years ago. I have no doubt that if, at that time, I had had the advantage which this book offers I should have been saved much trouble. I wholeheartedly recommend the book to the English public, particularly at a time when it is so important for England and Turkey to know more of each other's life and culture.

TO THE MEMORY OF ATATÜRK
THIS BOOK IS AFFECTIONATELY AND GRATEFULLY DEDICATED.

THE name of the GHAZİ MUSTAPHA KEMAL PASHA, renamed by a grateful nation, KEMAL ATATÜRK or KEMAL FATHER OF THE TURKS, will always be intimately associated by all peoples with the constitution and progress of Modern Turkey. The measure of the reform introduced under his administration has wrought a marvellous change, which will be increasingly appreciated as Turkey takes her rightful place in the Commonwealth of Nations.

Among the foremost of these reforms was the nationalization of the language on a purely Turkish basis with its efficacy in stamping out illiteracy from among the nation.

The fate of his country had made a deep impression on his soul, for he was ever conscious of the gradual breaking up of the Turkish Empire. He could see the last flickering flame of the National Independence in danger of being totally extinguished.

Turkey must be saved. She must live to play the part for which Providence had cast her. He realized and appreciated the call to guide and lead her, and with prophetic vision, and conscious of the errors committed in the past, set himself to the gigantic task.

The extent and breadth of his outlook, and his experience of the horrors of war, together with his conviction of its utter futility, filled his heart with an unbounded, burning desire to see Turkey at peace with the rest of the world.

He laid the foundation for the re-rapprochement of the Democracies of the East with the Democracies of the West, and this happy position must now be maintained, for much good will emerge from this friendship which lies in the hearts of the Turkish people, ready to be bestowed on the offer of fellowship extended to them.

Animated with the desire to see the crystallization of this Anglo-Turkish understanding, and appreciating that peoples can more truly understand each other when they can speak together in each other's language, I have prepared this book in a humble endeavour to help achieve this end.

FUAD A. ATTAOULLAH.

# CONTENTS

References are to section numbers (unless shown with pn).

T.G.Where quoted refers to "Turkish Grammar"
PH. Where quoted refers to "Phonetics"

# PREFACE

For many years European and Ottoman Turkish linguists, as well as many Ottoman Turkish grammarians who had applied themselves to the close study of the Turkish language, were firmly under the impression that its harmony and fluidity was in a large measure due to the presence of Persian and Arabic words, and to the introduction of grammatical forms identified with these languages, and it was generally feared that if these were eliminated a purely Turkish language would severely suffer by the loss of these peculiar characteristics.

The controversy arising out of this belief resulted in a general lethargy and the postponement of serious attempts to reconstitute the language on a purely Turkish basis, the language meanwhile becoming more and more assailed by foreign elements. During this period a most eminent and learned scholar produced the first Turkish grammar, which has contributed largely to the creation of the present melodious and expressive language with its extensive vocabulary and rich variety of inflections so euphonically constituted as to produce the rhythm and cadence which has been the admiration of all linguists.

Unfortunately, however, from the Turkish Nationalist point of view, this was moulded on the Arabic grammar and this fact resulted in considerable linguistic confusion.

The language of the learned now became a more or less composite one, being made up of Turkish, Arabic, and Persian vocabularies, the influence of the latter two predominating, and at one time there were almost two distinct languages; that of the learned, and that of the ordinary man in the street, who for lack of State controlled and compulsory education could not learn the former, and was therefore unable to understand the cultivated tongue. At a later period another attempt was made to regulate and improve the grammar, again by a very well known authority, whose mastery of the Turkish language is indisputable. It was a very good lay-out of the Turkish language on a modern style, where a clearer explanation than hitherto was given, together with many illustrative examples, but it did not make any attempt at radical reform, although the author mentioned in his book that such a move was necessary. There were two other factors also which added to the confusion. One was the gradual introduction into the language of French and English words by pedantic scholars who had been educated in Europe, and perhaps did not possess full mastery of their mother tongue. The other was the influence the European literature had on the principles of phrase formation, this bringing about what might be termed a Turko-European style which was unintelligible and out of tune with the rules of the real Ottoman-Arabic-Persian style. The introduction of these outside elements naturally caused the language to deviate more and more from its true original and gradually the nucleus itself became effaced.

It is with distress that we note how superficially the reforms were approached. It was very obvious that the outstanding deficiency in the language, as then constructed, was the inability by means of its alphabet, which was severely lacking in vowel forms, to orthographically reproduce in a correct and easy manner the true sounds of the Turkish tongue, the existing four vowels being sadly insufficient for this purpose.

Two of these vowels, i and o, were used to represent several different sounds, which were determined by the quality and type of the consonant accompanying them. At one time a move was made to remedy this defect by creating the necessary letters to vowelize the Turkish word, but here again difficulty was encountered, for the movement was frustrated by the orthodox and reactionary feelings of the calligraphists, the orthographers, and the printers, the former priding themselves on the beauty of the style of which they were the authors and which was the result of years of painstaking toil, and the latter not wishing to have to undertake extra work in typesetting. Another important contributory factor was the prevailing method of teaching which at that time was very inefficient. Thus it can be seen that there were many obstacles to be surmounted and conflicting opinions to be conciliated before any satisfactory reform could be effected.

It was at this crisis that the language found in Atatürk, as did the nation in its larger and comprehensive sense, its saviour. In spite of the deep-rooted superstition and belief that it would be impossible ever to resuscitate the original mother tongue of the Turks, he, with his vast knowledge, most cleverly dug out of the depths of literary chaos the unsoiled original structure of the language. He also was able to explain in full detail all the intricacies of the working of the essential factors, and proved this structure to be in the nature of a mother tongue such as Sanskrit.

His decision, therefore, to drop entirely all the various existing methods, to eliminate all foreign words without distinction, and to bring back into use all Turkish vocabularies, to adopt the Latin characters generally, and to adapt them to the requirements of the language (where necessary creating new ones for the special sounds) was another proof of the genius of Atatürk. We can now understand why this reform was welcomed by the nation with such sincere feelings of appreciation and gratitude. When telling a large gathering of people present at a garden party, the benefit the language and the nation alike would reap from the change over from the Kufic script to Latin characters, the reassuring words of Atatürk, "I am sure of it and I want you also to be sure of it," were drowned in deafening applause.

Without the slightest hesitation, everyone, from the high official down to the man in the street, set himself to the task of learning the new alphabet. Atatürk in Ankara at his own experimental and training school, and İsmet İnönü in Malatya, both in front of the blackboard, conducted classes personally, thus taking the lead in this stupendous task which they had undertaken and which they had set their energies to bring to fruition. It was a great achievement, and it is entirely wrong to think that the change in the language was just a matter of discarding the old characters and substituting the Latin ones, with the idea of making it conform to Western standards. On the contrary, it was a radical reform, brought about by the desire to make the language once more Turkish by bringing back into use all Turkish grammatical rules and vocabularies, replacing the old m lée of adjunct and disjunct Arabic characters by a new Turkish alphabet composed of single consonants, and a complete set of vowels, all of adjunct character, and discarding all foreign words which had crept in (Turkicizing any for which there was no true Turkish equivalent), thereby making one national language, common to all classes. It brought to a happy conclusion the chaotic struggle which had been going on for the past century. In the words of Ismet Inönü : "With these new characters the great Turkish nation will enter a new world of enlightenment ... we believe therein with a true assurance and honest conviction"; we can read his approval and appreciation of the action of Atatürk, and his feelings of confidence were shared by the whole nation.

The Turkish language is particularly comprehensive for it provides all the necessary words including the most minute nuances, to express the deepest subtleties of the mind, the full vigour of the human feelings, and all the elements found in nature, by means of its word-building capacity. For instance, as will be observed in the Vocabularies and the Conversational Phrases, and as has been fully explained in the grammar, any one verb root can produce all the necessary words to express the possible qualifications of the subject in respect of the different phases of the action of the verb, such as its *manner, ability, capacity, inclination, profession*, etc., and all the words to express the various resultants of the action of the verb are obtained by the insertion of letters or syllables, or the affixing of specific suffixes, and so on, to the root word. Out of nouns, adjectives are obtained, out of adjectives and nouns verbs are created.

Through research carried out since the adoption of the Latin characters much has been achieved. To perfect the character of the language any words which had dropped out of use have been re-introduced, and all the grammatical rules are gradually being adopted. The vocabulary is rapidly increasing and true Turkish words are replacing the discarded foreign ones. After a close examination of the chapters on noun, adjective, and verb formation, one particular point of the language will stand out, and that is the ease with which all the various shades of meaning of the words are obtained.

A very careful study of the alphabet, the explanation of the division and working of the vowels and consonants, together with the graduation of sounds is of the utmost importance in obtaining the correct pronunciation.

In the various chapters certain expressions, have been used, which, though appropriate as illustrating certain grammatical features under immediate review, may not be the most felicitous renderings. Owing, however, to the peculiarity of the language it was essential to use them and it will be necessary for the student to put all thoughts of any other language out of his mind, and make every endeavour to grasp and understand what is meant by the varions explanations throughout the Grammar. Particular attention must also be paid to the chapter on "Phonetics" as this will help him to realize fully the logical euphonic principle underlying the varying vowel changes and make his studies considerably easier.

To obtain a correct Turkish pronunciation it is essential and imperative for the student to study and grasp the information given in the classification of vowels and consonants.

The language is very much in accordance with the modern science of phonetics. It is formed of sounds which are the natural result of the laws of position and inflection of the tongue, and the movements of the lips and jaws and no strain is put on any organ. There is only one way of pronouncing each letter. The letter "o", for instance, gives only one sound, not several as in the English " no, not, none ", etc. There are no diphthongs as in the English "phoenix, main, moon, bread, void, neither", etc. When two vowels come together they each retain their own individual sound. There are no digraphs, that is two letters put together to represent one sound as in "physic, bridge, church, north, rough," etc. There are no mute letters as in "spite, yellow, would, tongue, two, write, knit ", etc. Every letter in every word is sounded individually, and every word is pronounced exactly as it is written. Consequently the reading of the language is very easy once the student has acquainted himself thoroughly with the correct pronunciation, particularly of the vowels.

A very interesting and particular characteristic feature of the language is the predominance of soft and melodious tones. As will be seen this is entirely due to the balanced grouping together of the "hard" and "soft" sounds, the vowels A, I, O, U, being the "hard" ones, and E, İ, Ö, Ü, the "soft". The formation of words, of adjectives, of verbs, and of phrases, are all subject to this fundamental rule, and suffixes in formation of adjectives, of verbal nouns and others, post-positions, and inflection affixes, will all in their turn *be in pairs,* one being *soft* for the *soft words,* and the other *hard* for the *hard words.* The verb conjugation follows the same rule except in the present tense.

Consonants also are divided into groups, *sharp, flat,* and *neutral.* The neutral ones are often found together with the other two, where they serve to reduce to a certain extent any harshness in a word which might be found to be out of harmony with the euphony of the language as a whole, and which is so common with other languages.

The NOUN has a particular form which is interesting to note. Two nouns are placed side by side, in what is called a "Definitive Combination" (= ilgi hali), whereby the second one becomes the complement of the first one. Several of these "Definitive Combinations" can be linked together and used in one sentence, thereby enabling the speaker to make a clearer and more concise statement than would ordinarily be the case. This form of noun is very much used.

In the conjugation of the VERB the actual personal pronouns are not usually used but are replaced by an equivalent personal suffix, this being affixed to the end of the word after all the other suffixes, i.e. tense, mood, etc., have been added. The agglutination of the various particles to the noun or verb root is carried out in a very clear and concise manner.

Take a verb root for instance: this will first of all have the *tense* and *mood* suffixes added, *soft* ones for words containing the *soft* vowels, and *hard* ones for words containing the *hard* vowels. Should it now be necessary to make this newly formed word *negative,* the negative suffix, again hard or soft, will be inserted immediately after the verb root *before* the tense suffix. Should the word be put into the *interrogatory* form, the suffix of interrogation will be placed *after* the tense suffix, and *finally* the *personal suffix* will be affixed, this again being hard or soft as the case may be. It is quite easy and simple to know, out of a possible choice of several, which suffix to choose, once the fundamentals of the language have been learned.

In phrase formation the subject is usually placed at the beginning of the sentence, and the complete verbal form (with addition of other parts of speech as previously referred to) right at the end.

The method adopted of showing the stem word (noun or verb root), with all the various suffixes in *heavy type,* will, it is believed, prove to be very illuminating and instructive.

The GRAMMAR has been comprehensively dealt with, and although the space is limited, nothing of importance has been left out. Should the student not wish to take the language up seriously, however, or carry on his studies in the progressive method adopted, he can examine any one chapter independently of the others, as each one is so arranged that it contains the relevant general notes of interest and the necessary remarks for reference. Further, each rule has been furnished with more than one example, in order to illustrate the variations which are the result of the shape and form of the structure (*hard* and *soft*, *vowel* and *consonant ending*) of the word. Another feature is the literal English translation which has been given under each Turkish word, denoting at the same time the case into which the word has to be put, with the definite object of leading the mind of the student into the Turkish manner of thought expression, whilst the actual English meaning has in most cases also been given.

I sincerely trust that I have succeeded in my endeavour to make clear to the Anglo-Saxon mind the fundamentals and peculiarities of the Turkish language which have hitherto been so clumsily, albeit unwittingly, expounded. As stated previously there are many points which owing to lack of space, I could only touch upon lightly, but I feel that I have laid the foundation for further research into the unlimited resources of this very interesting language, and the student will be able to carry his studies further by taking a complementary course in actual Turkish books, which he will then be in a position to understand.

I trust that the vocabularies and phrases in the examples will be of great help to the student, and I look forward to the day when the study of the Turkish language will be in far larger measure taken up by the younger generation of the Commonwealth of the English-speaking peoples, and shall be happy to know that this work has helped the furtherance of that aim.

**F. A. ATTAOULLAH.**

THE TURKISH LECTURE AND READING ROOM,
62 CHANCERY LANE,
W.C. 2.

also at:

57 EDGWAREBURY LANE,
EDGWARE, MIDDX.

# KEY TO THE GRAMMAR

This Grammar contains a comprehensive expose of the rules governing the Turkish language, but, as in the ordinary way it would take the student some considerable time to go into each item I have prepared this key to show him which points should be studied first in order to fully grasp the rest of the grammar.

Reference to the numbers quoted throughout is not essential, as each part is complete in itself but they serve in some cases to refresh the memory, and in others to show the continuity of the fundamentals of the language.

After having acquired a fairly wide vocabulary and a clear conception of the phonetics the first step will be to memorize the various tenses of the verb "to be" conjugated with a noun or adjective, see 62s-v. This will enable the student to express in Turkish any of the elementary phrases as, for instance, "I am a tall man", noting in the meantime that the adjective is placed in front of the indefinite noun, see 3 and 27b; and the person, either 1st or 2nd, of the conjugated verb denoted by a suffix affixed to the end of the verb, which is itself at the end of the sentence.

When a noun, proper or common, or a pronoun in the 3rd person singular or plural, forms the subject of the verb, it is placed either at the beginning of the phrase, or in front of the verb (see examples 9 and 10). He can then memorize the Verbal Pronoun suffixes shown in chart 57e, ee, eee after which he will have the complete key to the verb conjugation. Now he should learn the Turkish equivalents to the various English tenses as set out in a practical manner in chart 109. He will also study the Transitive and Intransitive Verbs, with their appropriate verbal direct and indirect complements. This knowledge is essential, as, in the sentence, the object of the verb is always mentioned before the verb. This object is placed in one of the declension cases, see 16, 17, and 19, and for the reason mentioned above, when learning the verb its appropriate case must also be learnt, see 140c, 151, 154c.

The Definitive Combination, see 24, is of great importance. It is the particular peculiarity of the language, and must be carefully studied in full detail.

At this stage the Verbal Noun, see 12a, and the Relative Gerund, see 136, may be studied, after which the student will be in a position to follow the process of Phrase making explained in 190 with examples and make a clear and concise Turkish phrase. The study of the distinction between " olmak -to be", and "bulunmak -to be in a state of", the conjugation of the verbal noun in the simple and progressive forms, and finally the Gerunds will place him in a position to follow with ease and full understanding the remainder of the book.

# TURKISH GRAMMAR
# SELF-TAUGHT

## PHONETICS
## THE TURKISH ALPHABET

THE characters of the new Turkish alphabet have been adopted from the Latin alphabet, but only those letters suitable to the language have been taken, with the addition of a few special characters. It is composed of twenty-nine letters, twenty-one of which are consonants and eight vowels.

A, B, C, Ç, D, E, F, G, Ğ, H, I, İ, J, K, L, M, N, O, O, P, R, S, Ş, T, Ü, U, V, Y, Z. There are also three special characters "â, î, û", which are nothing but the same three letters in the alphabet but pronounced with a longer sound, this being denoted by the circumflex sign.

To acquire the exact and correct sounds of the letters in the Turkish alphabet I will ask the student to detach himself entirely from that of the English, French, or German, and read with great attention the following:

| Character | Name | Pronunciation | Phonetics Used |
|---|---|---|---|
| A a | A | as the sound of *u* in the English words *sun, up* | u |
| Â â | AA | (1) as the sound of *a* in the English words *car, father* | aa |
| | | (2) except when following a *k* or *g*, when the sound of an *i* is inserted before the *a*, making it sound as if written *kia* or *gia* (see also Ph. 3) | ia |

| Character | Name | Pronunciation | Phonetics Used |
|-----------|------|---------------|----------------|
| B b | BE(h) | as the sound of *b* in the English word *bat* | b |
| C c | JE(h) | as the sound of *j* in the English word *jump* | j |
| Ç ç | CHE(h) | as the sound of *ch* in the English word *church* | ch |
| D d | DE(h) | as the sound of *d* in the English word *dog* | d |
| E e | E(h) | as the sound of *e* in the English word *net* | e |
| F f | FE(h) | as the sound of *f* in the English word *fat* | f |
| G g | GE(h) | as the sound of *g* in the English word *gown* | g |
| Ğ ğ | GHE(h) | as the sound of *gh* in the English word *leghorn*. | gh |

(Alph. 1) This letter is always in the middle or at the end of a word, never at the beginning.

(Alph. 2) It is a very soft semi-mute consonant as in the Turkish word *dağ* (dugh). In the middle of a word it is almost lost in the throat, causing in the meantime a pause on the preceding vowel of the syllable, when followed by a consonant or vowel as in the words *sağlam* (sughlum), *ağıl* (ughi(r)l).

(Alph. 3) If following the consonant "n" (as in "sanğat") the pronunciation is stronger, almost as if written "sunghut".

(Alph. 4) Getting lost in the throat, causing the same pause on the preceding vowel, but merging into the succeeding vowel sound by way of changing into that vowel, or a *y*, when followed by a soft vowel, as in the Turkish words *yirmi*, *göğüs*, which are pronounced : yiyirmi, göyüs.

| Character | Name | Pronunciation | Phonetics Used |
|-----------|------|---------------|----------------|
| H h | HE(h) | as the sound of *h* in the English word *hat* | h |
| I ı | I(r) | as the sound of *er* and *ir* in the words *father, fir*. **Never takes acc.** ^ | i(r) |
| İ i | I | as the sound of *i* in the English words *mid, mince* | i |

| Î î | EE | as the sound of *ee* in the English word *weed*. **Actually printed î.** | ee |
| J j | JE(h) | as the soft sound of the *s* in the middle of the words *leisure, measure* or as the letter *j* in the French words *jour, jardin*. | j' |
| K k | KE(h) | as the sound of *k* in the English word *king* | k |
| L l | LE(h) | as the sound of *l* in the English word *lamb* | l |
| M m | ME(h) | as the sound of *m* in the English word *mug* | m |
| N n | NE(h) | as the sound of *n* in the English word *net* | n |
| O o | AU | as the sound of *au* in the English words *fault, vault* | au |
| Ö ö | EU | as the sound of *ur* in the English words *demur, further*; or as the sound of *eu* in the French word *peu* | eu |
| P p | PE(h) | as the sound of *p* in the English word *pin* | p |
| R r | RE(h) | as the sound of *r* in the English word *rock*. **It must always be sounded when it comes at the end of the word** | r |
| S s | SE(h) | as the sound of *s* in the English word *soap* | s |
| Ş ş | SHE(h) | as the sound of *sh* in the English word *shop* | sh |
| T t | TE(h) | as the sound of *t* in the English word *time* | t |
| U u | OO | as the sound of *u* in the English word *pull*, with the same length of stress; or as the sound of *oo* in the English word *stood* | oo |
| Û û | Û | as the long sound of *u* in the English word *rule*; or as the sound of *oo* in the English word *cool* with the same |  |

|   |   | length of sound (see Ph. 3) | û |
| Ü ü | EW | as the sound of *eu* in the English words *lieu*; or as the sound of *u* in the French words *tu, fût*; or as the sound of *ü* in the German word *über* | ew |
| V v | VE(h) | as the sound of *v* in the English word *violet* | v |
| Y y | YE(h) | as the sound of *y* in the English word *yellow*. | y |
| Z z | ZE(h) | as the sound of *z* in the English word *zebra*. | z |

(1) It is of great importance to make the distinction between *i* (i) and *ı* (i(r)); *ı* (i(r)) and *ö* (eû); *o* (au) and *u* (oo); *u* (oo) and *ü* (ew).

(1a) Great care must be taken to sound the letter "r" when it comes at the end of a word, as otherwise confusion will arise, especially when the "r" is the final letter of a suffix, as:

| | | | |
|---|---|---|---|
| *güzeldir* | = it is good | *bıçaklar* | = knives |
| *güzeldi* | = it was good | *bıçakla* | = with a knife |

(2) The three special characters **â, î,** and **û**, which appear, generally speaking, only in words of Arabic or Persian origin, are not harder than usual, but longer in the continuity of the sound, and great care must be taken in putting in this sign, as there are also other words which are spelt the same, but without the sign, and their meaning is entirely different. Examples:

| | | | | |
|---|---|---|---|---|
| *âdet* | = custom | and | *adet* | = number. |
| *âlem* | = world, universe | and | *alem* | = flag. |
| *hâlâ* | = as yet | and | *hala* | = auntie. |
| *dînî* | = religious | and | *dini* | = the religion (obj. case) |

(3) We shall learn as we go along of the importance of forming words in a euphonious manner, or in other words, of the juxtaposition of **hard** or **soft syllables** in the formation of words. There are, however, still words of Persian and Arabic extraction beginning with or including the letters **k, g, l** and s, which appear not to be governed by this rule, yet these words are not altogether out of place as far as the general euphony of

the language is concerned. In these cases the vowels are directly affected. They are lengthened, and the sound of the consonant is softened. For example: **kâ, gâ, kû, gû,** instead of being hard are pronounced softly as if an "i" were in front of the vowel. **To denote where this takes place a circumflex sign is placed over the vowel.** Examples:

| | |
|---|---|
| *kâr* | *is pronounced "kiar"* |
| *rüzgâr* | *is pronounced "rüzgiar"* |
| *kûfi* | *is pronounced "kiufi "* |
| *efkâr* | *is pronounced "efkiar"* |
| *zadegân* | *is pronounced "zadegian".* |

The letter "**l**" has a strong influence over the vowels particularly the HARD ones, which it SOFTENS. This effect is marked by placing the same circumflex sign over the vowel which precedes or follows the "**l**". Examples:

*lûzum, ilâveten, lâzım, mülâkat, suâl*

**NOTE:** Usually such words are of foreign origin.
**RULE:** When â or û follows immediately after k and l, and when â follows g they are pronounced as explained above; but any of these vowels with the circumflex sign, following any other letter except s, are pronounced only as long or broad vowels. When following s they are a little softer.

(4) In the pronunciation of Turkish words the syllables are, generally speaking, all of more or less the same length, slight emphasis being placed on the **last syllable**, or, in words of only one *syllable*, on the **last consonant**. Examples:

| | |
|---|---|
| *bal* (honey) | emphasis on the "*l*" |
| *kiremit* (tile) | emphasis on the "*mit*" |
| *salata* (salad) | emphasis on the "*ta*" |

(4a) When suffixes are added (in word formation, etc.), the accent is still on the last *syllable*, it being transferred from the last *syllable* of the original word to the **last syllable** of the **newly** formed word. Examples:

*baldan* (from honey)
*kiremitin* (of the tile)
*salatalık* (greens for salad purpose)

(5) This rule is broken with certain Arabic and Persian words taken into the language. In this case, the second syllable is separated from the first, the two syllables being pronounced separately with a very slight pause between, both parts being equally stressed. This separation is marked by an apostrophe between the syllables, as:

*kal'e, mes'ul, mes'ele, kat'iyet.*

(5a) Turkish words are uttered in an almost calculated breath, and as will be seen, when any suffix is to be added, the appropriate one will be one which is in harmony with the last syllable, this being one of the factors creating the "fluidity " of the word.

(5b) This fluidity, however, is broken by some foreign words similar to (5), except that the *emphasis* is on the *part preceding* the apostrophe, this latter coming after a *vowel*. Examples:

| | | | |
|---|---|---|---|
| *te'diye* | = payment | *müste'cir* | = tenant |
| *ru'yet* | = sight | *me'mur* | = official |

(5c) NOTE: This kind of word is gradually being changed, the apostrophe being dropped.

# SYLLABLES

(6) Turkish syllables are composed of **one vowel** with **one** or **two consonants** following it or **one consonant preceding it**, as:-

*al, ard, sa, nal, halt,* etc.
*el, ırk, da, kın, denk,* etc.
*ön, ört, ne, göz, dört,* etc.

Two consonants **preceding** a vowel are only found in foreign words taken into the language.

(6a) In words of two syllables or more only the last one can be of more than three letters, as:

*dördüncü,    köprü,    öldürt*

(6b) A vowel can form a syllable by itself only at the beginning of a Turkish word but can form a syllable by itself in the middle and at the end of foreign words taken into the language:

*evet, emek, daire, mânia*

# VOWELS

(7) The vowels are divided into two sections:

LIP vowels and TEETH vowels.

When the lip vowels are uttered, the teeth do not show and the lips protrude.

*o, u, ö, ü* (pronounced au, ou, eu, ew), are lip vowels as will be seen in the following examples:

| | | | | | |
|---|---|---|---|---|---|
| kol (kaul) | = "arm" | | gök (geuk) | = "sky" |
| pul (pool) | = "stamp" | | süt (sewt) | = "milk" |

(7a) The teeth vowels are obtained through drawing the lips back a very little and showing the teeth.

*a, e, ı, i* (u, e, i(r), i) are teeth vowels. Examples:

| | | | | | |
|---|---|---|---|---|---|
| dal (dul) | = *branch* | | yıl (yi(r)l) | = *year* |
| tel (tel) | = *wire* | | fil (fil) | = *elephant* |

(7b) These are again divided into sounds which we will call "wide" and "narrow".

(7c) When the mouth has to be opened widely to correctly pronounce the vowel it is called "wide".

*a, e, o, ö* (u, e, au, eu) are wide, as in:

| | | | | | |
|---|---|---|---|---|---|
| bal (bul) | = *honey* | | yol (yaul) | = *road* |
| bel (bel) | = *waist* | | köy (keuy) | = *village* |

25

(7d) If the mouth has only to be opened a little way the vowel will be narrow.

*ı, i, u, ü,* (i(r), i, oo, ew) are narrow, as in:

| | | | |
|---|---|---|---|
| k*ı*l (ki(r)l) | = *hair* | ç*u*l (chool) | = *haircloth* |
| d*i*l (dil) | = *tongue* | g*ü*l (gewl) | = *rose* |

(8) Vowels are again divided, into "hard", *a, ı, o, u,* as in:

| | | | |
|---|---|---|---|
| m*a*l (mul) | = *possession* | k*o*y (kauy) | = *bay* |
| k*ı*l (ki(r)l) | = *bristle* | k*u*l (kool) | = *servant* |

(9) and into "soft", *e, i, ö, ü,* as in:

| | | | |
|---|---|---|---|
| k*e*l (kel) | = *ringwormy* | g*ö*l (geul) | = *lake* |
| ç*i*l (chil) | = *bright* | g*ü*l (gewl) | = *rose* |

The latter two, the **"hard"** and **"soft"** vowels, are among the fundamentals of the language and must be memorized.

# CONSONANTS

(10) In the utterance of the consonants the lips either meet and remain closed, remain apart, or meet and open again, and in the meantime the position and movement of the tongue creates sounds of various tones. These sounds can be divided into four categories : –

| | |
|---|---|
| (11) LIP consonants | *b, p, m, f, v.* |
| (12) TEETH-GUMS consonants | *l, d, n, t.* |
| (13) FRONT PALATE consonants | *c, ç, j, r, s, ş, z.* |
| (14) REAR PALATE consonants | *g, h, k, y, ğ.* |

(15) The consonants are again divided into three classes : The SHARP, the FLAT, and the NEUTRAL.

(15a) A *flat* consonant is easily uttered, and when stress is put upon it, it becomes a "sharp" one, its equivalent.

(15b) A *sharp* consonant is produced under effort, is strong, and has an assimilatory power over a "flat" consonant.

(15c) A *neutral* consonant, irrespective of its condition at the time of utterance, has no power to effect, and is not subject to alteration.

| Flat | Sharp | Neutral |
|------|-------|---------|
| C | Ç | L |
| V | F | M |
| B | P | N |
| G | K | R |
| Z | S | Y |
| J | Ş | Ğ |
| D | T | |
| | H | |

(16) The student will notice by studying Turkish words that consonants of the same **class group** *themselves* **together**, as: *Baca, Paça, Koç, Peçe, Kesik, Sepet, Kepek, Kıskaç,* etc.

(16a) This division is of vast importance and wide application. Many rules in the formation of words, adjectives, etc., are directly controlled by it. Where the rule seems to fail, in that, between two consonants of one class, a consonant of the opposite class or a neutral one had been placed, it will be found that the sound position of the medial consonant had been influenced by the vowels in the word, as in *kabak, görücü, mercimek, taslak, kanat, yumurta,* etc.

# WORDS AND VERB ROOTS

(17) Turkish words and verb roots will either be hard (*a, ı, o, u*) or soft (*e, i, ö, ü*), according to the vowels they contain. In both cases of course, they will either end with a vowel or consonant, but when they do the latter it could either be a *sharp* consonant (*ç, p, t, k,* etc.), a *flat* one (*g, v, z, j,* etc.), (these are very few, see 31c and 31cc) or a *neutral* one (*l, m, n, r, y, ğ*), and it is most essential to take notice of the structure of the word or verb root so that the correct "endings" can be applied when forming the various "cases", etc., as will be seen later on.

| Verb Root (with Infin. end) | Words (nouns, etc.) | | |
|---|---|---|---|
| kana-mak | baba | = | hard (vowel ending). |
| dene-mek | dede | = | soft (vowel ending). |
| sok-mak | kabak | = | hard (sharp cons. end.). |
| küs-mek | kümes | = | soft (sharp cons. end.). |
| sav-mak | saylav | = | hard (flat cons. end.). |
| gör-mek | şeker | = | soft (neutral cons. end.). |

(18) Words, as we know, are composed of single sounds, or of several sounds in formation. In the Turkish euphony the sounds are divided into two groups, the "soft subdued" ones and the "hard strong" ones, the hard and soft vowels being the controlling factors. There is one prevailing rule and that is that a word is either all hard or hardish or all soft or softish (34a). A hard syllable is never put in direct contact with a soft syllable in any word which is of Turkish origin.

## ROOT WORDS AND SUFFIXES (OR ENDINGS)

(18a) There is always graduation of sound, no sudden fall nor rise from hard to soft or vice versa as explained a little further on. This rule is the natural result of the mouth work, according to the latest scientific research in the sphere of phonetics, that is, that some particular vowels force the utterance of some particular consonants, and vice versa. In the Grammar the student will learn that for all the various cases, for adjective formation, etc., there are hard and soft endings, both, of course, meaning exactly the same, so that, to a word composed of soft syllables he will add a soft ending, and to a hard word, a hard ending, *the vowel in the LAST syllable determining the one to be used.*

| Hard word with hard ending | Soft word with soft ending. |
|---|---|
| ara-*lık* = space | iyi-*lik* = kindness |
| balık-*çı* = fisherman | ekmek-*çi* = baker |
| kur-*untu* = delusion | süpür-*üntü* = rubbish |
| tabak-*lar* = plates | teneke-*ler* = tins |

(This rule, however, does not apply in the terminations of the present tense in the verb conjugations, but of this we will speak later on.)

# GRADUATION OF SOUNDS

(19) The Turkish vowels comprise all the natural fundamental sounds which are produced by the vocal cords. These sounds, as we have already mentioned, are produced according to natural laws. Examples:

| | |
|---|---|
| *kapı* and not *kapi* | *konak* and not *konek.* |
| *sıkıntı* and not *sikinti* | *sürme* and not *sürma.* |

It is only by the well-proportioned balance that the most melodious harmony in the sounds of the language has come forth. It is really the natural result of the smooth working of the laws of phonetics.

There are, however, some combinations of vowels, *a-i, u-i, a-e, u-e*, which appear, in some foreign words, to deviate from this rule (see 34a).

The subject is very vast, and I will just give the very elementary points which it is necessary for the student to know to enable him to grasp the process of word formation. To help him to understand what is about to be explained I will put the sounds under two headings, "rise" and "drop".

(20) The *wide* vowel sounds *a, e, o, ö* will be the *rise* and the *narrow* vowel sounds *ı, i, u, ü* will be the *drop*, irrespective of where they appear in the word.
NOTE: *Rise* and *drop* cannot really be definitely defined, but to put it in a simple way we can say that when two sounds come together the weaker one will be the *drop* and the stronger one the *rise*.

(21) These sounds may be *grouped* together either in a *consecutive* or in an *alternate* manner (see 22-23).

(22) The basis of the sounds in word formation is repetition that is that each of the sounds *a, ı, u* ("hard") and *e, i, ü* ("soft") is followed by itself. Examples for repetition:

| | | |
|---|---|---|
| *tapa* (stopper) | *sıkı* (tight) | *kılıf* (cover) |
| *kuru* (dry) | *sene* (year) | *cici* (pretty) |
| *sini* (tray) | *sallanma* (swinging) | *çalkalama* (shaking) |
| *kırıntı* (piece) | *kuruntu* (delusion) | *zemberek* (latch) |
| *kertenkele* (lizard) | *silinti* (erasion) | *süprüntü* (sweepings) |

(23) Where a sound is not followed by itself it is followed by one of the other sounds in its own group, forming a "variation". When there is variation there are, generally speaking, no more than two vowel sounds in one word.

(23a) These are either in the form of a "drop" from a high tone, as:

*arı* (bee)                           *boru* (tube)
*tabur* (battalion)                   *barut* (gunpowder)

(23b) or a "rise" from a low tone, as:

*kısa* (short)                        *sıcak* (warm)

(23c) or, in both cases, rise or drop, afterwards reverting to the first sound, as:

*saluncak* (swing)                    *sarımtrak* (yellowish)
*kırlangıç* (swallow)                 *sıcaklık* (warmth)

**NOTE:** There are a few words which have more than two vowel sounds of a kind, but these are of foreign origin.

(24) Then again we find the two processes brought together in the form of a repetition of the first sound, followed by a "drop" or "rise", as:

Repetition and drop        :        *kenevir* (hemp seed)
Repetition and rise        :        *girişken* (pushful)

(25) Or, again, from a drop to a rise with the repetition of the latter, as:

*yıkanmak* (to bathe)                 *sıvamak* (to plaster)

(26) The two sounds *o* and *ö* have a special feature in the formation of words. They do not repeat themselves. Where there would be repetition in other words, in the case of a word containing either *o* or *ö* this letter will be followed by *u* and *ü*, as:

| | | | |
|---|---|---|---|
| *koku* (odour) | *kötü* (bad) | *soğuk* (cold) | *gönül* (affection) |
| *topuk* (heel) | *köprü* (bridge) | *doğru* (straight) | *körük* (bellows) |

(27) In the case of variation in words containing *o* and *ö* the drop is made with the sounds *u* and *ü* respectively, instead of *ı* and *i*, and a rise with *a* and *e*, Examples:

*konak* (residence)　　　　*kötek* (thrashing)
*sokak* (street)　　　　　　*börek* (pastry)

The same principle applies to the longer words, **repetition** and **rise** or **drop**, etc. Examples:

*Zonguldak* (town of that name)
*Safranbolu* (town of that name)
*korkuluk* (scarecrow)
*İnebolu* (town of that name)

# MUTATION

(28) The most outstanding point to be borne in mind is that in the Turkish language there are **two main divisions**, i.e. **hard** words and **soft** words. The application of this fundamental law, i.e. by the grouping together of the **hard sounds** and the grouping together of the **soft sounds**, is very far reaching. It controls the process of word formation, the verb conjugation, the declension cases of the noun, etc. In other words it actually brings about the law of Mutation. For instance, **when a suffix commencing with a consonant** (*ci, ki, li, kun, lık, süz,* etc.) is added to a word, either consonant or vowel ending, **the vowel in the suffix must be in harmony with the last vowel in the word.** Examples:

*kir-li* (dirty)　　　　　　*coş-kun* (excited)
*temiz-lik* (cleanliness)　　*sür-üm-süz* (unsaleable)
*şapka-cı* (hat-maker)　　　*koru-cu* (keeper)
*günde-lik* (daily pay)

(28a) **When a suffix commencing with a vowel,** (*ik, ak, in, un,* etc.) is added to a word, **the vowel of the suffix must be in harmony with the last vowel in the word.** Examples:

*kır-ık* (broken)　　　　　*kork-ak* (coward)
*kesim-in* (of the cut)

(28b) Suffixes are, in their turn, divided into two main groups:

(a) those containing a *wide* vowel, and
(b) those containing a *narrow* vowel (see Ph. 7c and d).

(a) As out of the four *wide* vowels, *a, e, o, ö,* only *two* are used, *a* and *e*, these are used in **pairs, the hard *a* for hard words**, and **the soft *e* for soft words**, as for instance, *ca* (hard), and *ce* (soft), *lar* (hard), and *ler* (soft), etc.

(b) Of the *narrow* vowels, *all four are used*, as for instance, *lık, lik, luk, lük,* and from these the one which harmonises most accurately with the last vowel in the word will be chosen.

(28c) When a suffix is in the form of a single letter (*k, m, s,*) a vowel in harmony with the last vowel in the word is inserted between the root word and the suffix, as some consonants cannot be pronounced together. (This will be better understood if the student studies the English word "sarcasm" where, between the "s" and "m" there is a sound as if a vowel were there.) Examples:

| | |
|---|---|
| *yaz-ı-ş* (manner of writing) | *bak-ı-m* (maintenance) |
| *dil-i-m* (a slice) | *dik-i-m* (sewing) |
| *gör-ü-m* (sight) | *yür-ü-k* (nomad) |

# ASSIMILATION

This successiveness of natural sounds, which is called "fluidity" plays a great part in the Turkish words.

(29) When two consonants come together, one being the ending letter of the root word, and the second one the beginning letter of an "ending" (such as *-dan* and *-den* of the ablative case) a "sharp" consonant will assimilate in sound the "flat" one, and change it to its equivalent "sharp" one, as explained further on (Ph. 15b). Examples:

| | | | | | |
|---|---|---|---|---|---|
| *kap-dan* | becomes | *kap-tan* | *kaş-dan* | becomes | *kaş-tan* |
| *ağaç-dan* | becomes | *ağaç-tan* | *raf-dan* | becomes | *raf-tan,* |
| etc. | | | | | |

Taking the two (ablative case) endings -*dan* for hard and -*den* for soft words again as an example, I would point out the fact that these actually are the two real endings and the student would not be exactly wrong if he used only these, but here again comes the matter of more euphonious pronunciation. It was found that *d* was not easy to say directly following t as *tokat-dan* and *iskelet-den*, and so, in such words, the *d* was changed to *t* thus making the words *tokat-tan* and *iskelet-ten*. Even if this letter had not been changed the student will find that in the ordinary quickness of conversational speech the *d* would sound very much like a *t*.

(30) The words to which the -*tan* will be added will be HARD words, i.e. containing the vowels *a, o, ı,* or *u*, ending in *k, t, p, s, ş, ç, f, h* Examples:

| | | | |
|---|---|---|---|
| *konak-tan* | *kaput-tan* | *çorap-tan* | *yulaf-tan* |
| *makas-tan* | *savaş-tan* | *tıkaç-tan* | *Allah-tan* |

(30a) The -*ten* will be added to SOFT words, i.e. containing the vowels *e, i, ö, ü*, ending in the same consonants. Examples:

| | | |
|---|---|---|
| *böbrek-ten* | *süt-ten* | *çöp-ten* |
| *kümes-ten* | *çiriş-ten* | *pirinç-ten* | *Şeref-ten* |

(30b) The actual endings -*dan* and -*den* will be added to all the other letters. (*ğ, l, m, n, r, y,* 15c) (*v, g, z, j,* 15a).

(30c) Verb roots and tense suffixes in verb conjugation etc., are also subject to Graduation, Mutation, and Assimilation rules.

(30d) In some cases, the harmony causes one of the consonants to be dropped altogether, but this does not happen very often (see 33c).

(31) Again, when the "sharp" consonants, *p, t, ç, k,* are at the end of the root word and come in contact with any suffix *commencing with a vowel* (in word forming and declension cases) they are changed to *b, d, c, ğ,* which are their equivalents in the "flat" and "neutral" groups (see also 31cc-32, 36, 37). Examples:

| | | | |
|---|---|---|---|
| *Çorap* | becomes | *Çorabın* | (Gen. case) |
| *Kabak* | becomes | *Kabağa* | (Dat. case) |
| *Kireç* | becomes | *Kireci* | (Obj. case) |

33

This only happens if the word had originally ended with a FLAT consonant, and had been made SHARP when brought into the language (see also 31cc to 32).
An up-to-date dictionary must be consulted when conjugating, as this will show the required letter.

(31a) The above rule (Ph. 31), with the exception of the verbs *etmek* (to do), *gitmek* (to go), *gütmek* (to bear), does not apply to verb roots in the formation of the Present, Indefinite, and Future tenses, the Optative Mood, and the gerundial moods. Examples for *itmek* = to push, and *kaçmak* = to run away:

| (Pres.) | *Ediyor* | *Gidiyor* | *Güdüyor* | *İtiyor* | *Kaçıyor* |
|---|---|---|---|---|---|
| (Ind.) | *Eder* | *Gider* | *Güder* | *İter* | *Kaçar* |
| (Fut.) | *Edecek* | *Gidecek* | *Güdecek* | *İtecek* | *Kaçacak* |
| (Opt.) | *Ede* | *Gide* | *Güde* | *İte* | *Kaça* |

uuuuu(31b) When a suffix commencing with (*c, g, b, d*) is to be added to a word ending with a sharp consonant (*ç, k, p, t, f, h, s, ş*) (Ph. 15b) the latter will force the former to change to (*ç, k, p, t*).

(31c) The **graduation of sounds, assimilation, mutation,** and the insertion of *y, n,* and *s,* between the **main word** and the **suffixes** (expl. in the Grammar) are great factors in the maintenance of the fluidity of the language. This fluidity and the fact of the **accent being laid on the last syllable** necessitates that **when a word ends in a consonant** this latter should be a "**sharp**" one.

(31cc) This will be found to be the case in most Turkish words, and should any foreign word taken into the language end in a "flat" consonant, this will be changed to its equivalent "sharp" one. This is incidental, however, when the word is modified (declension, etc.) for the original letter is put back, see Ph. 31. Examples:

| *çorab* | becomes | *çorap* | *kiremid* | becomes | *kiremit* |
|---|---|---|---|---|---|
| *kitab* | becomes | *kitap* | *Ahmed* | becomes | *Ahmet* |

(31d) When foreign words ending with **sharp consonants** are taken into the language they are not altered at all, and are not subject to alteration, their consonants having all the power of a Turkish sharp consonant.

(32) Rule 31cc has an exception when the words are of only one syllable, as:

*Ok* . . . . . *Okun, Oka, Oku*          *Sap* . . . . *Sapın, Sapa, Sapı*
*At* . . . . . *Atın, Ata, Atı*          *Saç* . . . . *Saçın, Saça, Saçı*

Thus we can see that the ending letters of words (nouns, adjectives, and others) are subject to direct vowel and consonant influence, and undergo changes. We must also remember, as we have mentioned before, that the utterance of certain vowels forces the utterance of certain consonants (Ph. 18-18a).

(32b) NOTE: There are now very few Turkish words ending in *c, b, d, v, z, j, g.*

## INFLUENCE OF HARD AND SOFT SOUNDS ON FOREIGN WORDS

(33) The fundamental rule of "*hard*" and "*soft*" sounds has, throughout the life of the language, exercised its assimilatory power in the matter of shaping into the Turkish mould of word formation, by way of everyday common usage, every foreign word brought into the language. Thus, in a word where a hard sound had existed together with two soft sounds, one sound had influenced the other and made it conform to the rule. For instance:

| | | | |
|---|---|---|---|
| *Hoce* | (Persian) | became | *Hoca* |
| *Çarçive* | (Persian) | became | *Çerçeve* |
| *Çiharşenbe* | (Persian) | became | *Çarşamba* |
| *Station* | (French) | became | *İstasyon* |
| *Mehmed* | (Arabic) | became | *Memet* |
| *Fire up* | (English, Nautical) | became | *Fayrap*, etc. |
| *Ma'den* | (Arabic) | became | *Mağden* |

(34) Any exceptions to this rule will also be found to be of foreign origin, and even their pronunciation has been more or less Turkicised. Although they have retained their structure they have lost their original pronunciation and are today subject to the Turkish euphony. For example:

| | | | | | |
|---|---|---|---|---|---|
| *i'mar* | or | *İimar* | (Arabic) | became | *îmar* |
| *ma'rifet* | or | *maarifet* | (Arabic) | became | *mârifet* |
| *mi'de* | or | *müide* | (Arabic) | became | *mîde*, etc. |

**NOTE:** There is a tendency to drop the signs wherever possible, and eventually they will be written in the simple manner, as: *imar, marifet, mide.*

(34a) A divergence of sound is sometimes caused by the hard vowels *a* and *u* coming in contact with the soft *e* and *i*, as in:

| | | | | | |
|---|---|---|---|---|---|
| *şimal* | = | north | *şamil* | = | comprise |
| *kitap* | = | book | *kâtip* | = | clerk |
| *İrak* | = | Irak | *rakip* | = | rival |
| *merak* | = | anxiety | *sadet* | = | boundary |
| *suret* | = | copy | *mebus* | = | M.P. |

On the surface it might appear that they are forming an exception, but in reality they have been Turkicised in all respects, for the *l* in *şimal*, the *p* in *kitap*, the *k* in *İrak* and *merak*, the *ş* in *şamil*, the *k* in *kâtip*, *the r* in *rakip, and the s* in *sadet* have in their turn softened the *a*, and the *s* in *suret and mebus*, the *u*.

In vowel-ending words of this type, or words where the last syllable contains a soft vowel, these *soft* vowels *e* and *i* have a softening effect on the *hard* ones *a* and *u*, thereby making the word almost as soft as an original soft one, as in:

| | | | | | |
|---|---|---|---|---|---|
| *nümune* | = | sample | *rutubet* | = | damp |
| *sühulet* | = | ease | *duhuliye* | = | entrance fee |

These words form the "hardish" and "softish" groups mentioned in (18).

A rule, which applies to these foreign words only, is that when the word ends with *l* it is considered to be "soft" irrespective of its vowel sounds, and will therefore take the various "soft" suffixes, as in:

| | | | |
|---|---|---|---|
| *misâl* | *misâller* | *resûl* | *resûller* |

# LETTERS K, Ğ

(35) There are no guttural sounds in the language. All such sounds have gradually changed into " back palate sounds " which makes them a shade softer, and this would be where the previously mentioned "hardish" sounds would apply. Should this softening not

be reverted to, the pronunciation would be too hard and cause a strain on the throat.
Examples:

| | | | | | |
|---|---|---|---|---|---|
| *yigirmi* | becomes | *yiğirmi* | *egri* | becomes | *eğri* |
| *saglam* | becomes | *sağlam* | *igne* | becomes | *iğne* |
| *dogru* | becomes | *doğru* | | | |

In these cases the *ğ* becomes almost mute and lost in the throat of the pronouncer, not heard by the listener, yet it is felt by the pronouncer. The words given above could almost be pronounced as if they were spelt:

| | | | | | |
|---|---|---|---|---|---|
| *yürmi* | or | *yûrmi* | *eeri* | or | *éri* |
| *saalam* | or | *sâlam* | *iine* | or | *îne* (Alphabet 2, 4). |
| *dooru* | or | *dôru* | | | |

(36) The sound represented by the letter *k* is one which is subject to several changes. It retains its original sound when it is at the beginning or in the middle of the word, but is subject to "softening" when being at the end of the word, and **preceded by a vowel,** it comes in contact with a suffix or termination beginning with a vowel. It then changes to a *ğ* in hard words (see Alph. 1). For example:

| | | |
|---|---|---|
| *kuyruk* | becomes | *kuyruğu* (Obj. case) |
| *kabak* | becomes | *kabağı* (Obj. case) |

(37) In soft words where this seems to be still too hard it changes in the pronunciation to a very soft *ğ* or almost to the sound of *y* although still written *ğ*. Examples:

| | | | | |
|---|---|---|---|---|
| *ördek* | becomes | *ördeği* | and is pronounced as if written | *ördeyi* |
| *beşik* | becomes | *beşiği* | and is pronounced as if written | *beşiyi* |

(37a) The *k* can actually be written "*y*" when subject to changes, but it is more correct to keep to *ğ*.

(37aa) When at the end of a word, hard or soft, and **preceded by a consonant,** the letter *k* changes to *g* and not to *ğ* when coming in contact with a suffix commencing with a vowel. Examples:

| *âhenk* | = | harmony | *âhenge* | = | *to the harmony* |
|---------|---|---------|----------|---|------------------|
| *künk* | = | earthenware pipe | *künge* | = | *to the e. pipe* |

In conclusion I must reiterate the following points:

The Turkish word is a built-up structure consisting of the *stem* and *various suffixes*. In the case of *verbs*, the *verb root acts as the stem*.

This stem is either *hard* or *soft*, and ends in either a *consonant* or a *vowel*.

The suffixes, in their turn, are either *"wide"*, *in which case they are only in pairs, one for hard words and one for soft words,* or *"narrow"*, *in which case they will contain any one of the four narrow vowels, the one harmonizing most accurately with the last vowel in the word to which it is being added, being chosen.* Finally, in the pronunciation, great care must be taken to *sound every letter in every word individually*. This is particularly necessary in the case of the letters *"r"*, *"n"*, and *"h"* when they come at the end of a word, as otherwise, for reasons already explained, confusion will arise.

# TURKISH GRAMMAR

**Note:** Every sentence and phrase in the Grammar is numbered, the numbers running consecutively throughout, and when referring to any part, its number is quoted to enable the student to look back and refresh his memory, should he wish to.

The *"endings"* or *"suffixes"* are printed in bolder type to help the student to get a quicker grasp of the word formation.

Where a word has several suffixes, for instance, tense, plus mood, plus personal pronoun, etc., they are separated from each other by a slight space so that each stands out distinctly, and one or other of them shown in heavy type to illustrate the construction.

## MAIN EUPHONIC RULES

As already mentioned in the Preface, and as shown in the chapters on Phonetics, the Turkish word is either a simple word, or else a stem word to which has been added one, two, or several particles, called suffixes.

There are certain fundamental rules concerning the affixing of these suffixes, and it is essential that the student keep them in mind all the time, as they have to be applied with great frequency, and in fact form the pivot of all the euphonic changes.

In certain circumstances the end letter of the stem, or of the compound stem, and the first letter of the suffix will affect each other, causing one or other to change (see Ph. 29-31b).

Although I have given these rules in their respective places in the Grammar, I am hereunder giving a summary of them with the idea of impressing them on the mind of the student.

When adding SUFFIXES to words or verb roots the VOWEL of the suffix must be adjusted to be in HARMONY with the last vowel of the word (see Ph. 28).

Consonant-ending Turkish words invariably end with SHARP or NEUTRAL consonants, not FLAT, and the consonants of consonant-commencing suffixes are generally FLAT or NEUTRAL.

There will be no change (assimilation, etc.), should the word end or the suffix begin, with a NEUTRAL consonant.

When, however, SUFFIXES beginning with the FLAT CONSONANTS *b, d, g, c,* are being added to *SHARP CONSONANT* ending words or verb roots, these *FLAT CONSONANTS* are changed to their equivalent SHARP ones, *p, t, k, ç* (see Ph. 31b).

When a *SUFFIX* commencing with a *VOWEL* is being added to "made" *SHARP CONSONANT* ending words (made sharp when brought into the language) this *SHARP CONSONANT* is forced back to its original *FLAT CONSONANT* (see Ph. 31).

If the *SHARP CONSONANT* is an "original" one (not a "made" one) there is no change (see Ph. 31d 32).

When a *SUFFIX* commencing with a *VOWEL* is being added to a *VOWEL* ending word or verb root a servile letter *y, n,* or *s,* is inserted between the *word* and the *suffix.*

*When a SUFFIX* in the form of a *single consonant* is to be added to a *CONSONANT* ending word a VOWEL (or sound letter) in harmony with the last vowel in the word is inserted (see Ph. 28c).

When, however, this suffix is in the form of a *syllable,* as for instance *"lar"* it is joined straight on to the word (except the PRESENT TENSE suffix *"yor"* in front of which a "sound" letter is placed).

# GENDER

(1) Turkish nouns, adjectives and personal pronouns have no gender. Should the

necessity be felt for expressing the sex of human beings the word *erkek* is put in front of the noun to denote male and *kız* or *kadın* to denote female, and, in the case of animals, *erkek* to denote male, and *dişi*, female.

(1a) *Personal Pronouns* (50), the *Definitive Personal Pronoun suffixes* (50h) and the *Personal Verbal Pronoun suffixes* (57e) have no gender at all. Examples:

| (man or woman) | my book | = | *kitabım* |
| (its, her, his) | work | = | *işi* |
| (it, she, he) | goes | = | *gidiyor* |
| (man or woman) | I go | = | *gidiyorum* |

## ARTICLE

(2) There is no article in Turkish (see 15, 16, 37, 142c, d, 143, & 144).

## SIGNS OF PLURALITY

(3) The plural signs follow the basic rule (see Ph. 28b), a hard ending for hard words and a soft ending for soft words.

*-lar* is added to the end of hard nouns, as:

| *insan* = man | *insanlar* = men |
| *şapka* = hat | *şapkalar* = hats |

*-ler* is added to the end of soft nouns, as:

| *elbise* = dress | *elbiseler* = dresses |
| *kalem* = pen | *kalemler* = pens |

## POSITION OF "*lar*", "*ler*" IN THE OBLIQUE CASES

(4) Once this termination, *lar* or *ler*, is added to the noun or compound noun, etc. it forms part of the word and both together as one word are subject to inflection; in

41

other words the plural sign comes directly after the noun and any suffixes follow after. Examples:

(GEN. Case) *adamın* = of the man      *adamların* = of the men
(DAT. Case) *eve* = to the house      *evlere* = to the houses

## POSITION OF "*lar*", "*ler*" IN VERB CONJUGATION

(5) In verb conjugation the endings *lar* and *ler* are also added to the third person singular in all the four forms of any tense, to form the third person plural. Their position in all forms (affir., neg., inter., int.-neg.) is the same, and they are not subject to any shifting, as:

*gidiyorlar* = they are going      *gitmiyorlar* = they are not going
*gidiyorlar mı?* = are they going?      *gitmiyorlar mı?* = are they not going?

## THE NOUN

(6) The noun in Turkish is divided into "Proper", "Common", "Abstract" "Compound", and "Collective", as:

Proper      : *Kemal Atatürk, İstanbul*
Common      : *kadın* (woman), *okul* (school)
Collective      : *donanma* (navy), *takım* (team)
Abstract      : *mutluluk* (happiness), *dürüstlük* (honesty)
Compound      : *diş fırçası* (tooth brush), *yemek odası* (dining room)

**NOTE:** These latter will be treated under a separate heading owing to their different style of construction.

(7) The gender of the noun is usually determined by the object it represents, otherwise it is qualified (see (1)).

(8) Common, collective compound, and abstract nouns are made plural by affixing *lar* to hard words and *ler* to soft (see (3)).

(9) Proper nouns are also made plural on certain occasions: When emphasis is to be placed on the action of the "doer", as:

| | |
|---|---|
| *Türkler, Napolyonları* hatta *Cengizleri* *kıskandıracak fetihler yapmışlardır.* | The Turks have achieved conquests which might make the Napoleons and the Genghis (men such as) envious. |

(9a) When mention of several persons of one family is made, as:

*İngiltere George'lardan çok hizmet görmüştür.*
England has had much service from the Georges.

(9b) When comparison is made between an ordinary and a public figure, as:

*Türk gençliği daha nice Atatürkler, İsmet İnönüler yetiştirir.*
The Turkish youth will yet provide many Atatürks, and İsmet İnönües.

(9c) When mention of historical families, or one member of the family is made, as:

*Tepedelenliler* = The Tepedelenlis

(9d) When denoting nations, as:

*Türkler ve İngilizler doğuştan centilmendirler.*
The Turks and the English are gentlemen by nature.

## STATE AND FUNCTION OF THE NOUN

(10) The function of the noun in the sentence is either that of the subject of the verb, when it will be in the Nominative Case or that of any one of the verbal cases when it determines or completes the action of the verb. It is generally considered to be *definite* when it is not qualified by any adjective or preposition denoting *indefiniteness*. Examples:

*Bebek* (nom. case) *ağlıyor.* = Baby cries.
*Bebeği* (obj. case) *gördün mü?* = Have you seen the baby?

43

# NOUN FORMATION

(11) Apart from the ordinary nouns there are nouns constructed by way of adding suffixes to adjectives, to other nouns, and also to verb roots.

## NOUNS Formed From VERBS

(12) A verb in the infinitive can also be a noun, and as such, the meaning is rendered as the *act* of the *action*. It is then subject to all the various cases of declension, like a noun. Examples:

| | |
|---|---|
| *okumak* | = to read |
| *Bu kitabı okumak* (verb) *isterim.* | = I wish to read this book. |
| | |
| *okumak* | = reading |
| *Kitap okumayı* (noun) *severim.* | = I love book reading. |

(12a) Nouns are also obtained from verbs by dropping the verbal ending *mak* and *mek* and adding various suffixes to the verb root, these invariably following the rule (Ph. 8, 9, 18, and 18a) of adjusting the vowel of the suffix to harmonize with the vowels contained in the word to which the suffix is being affixed, as follows. By adding *ma* and *me* to denote the action of the verb, as:

| | |
|---|---|
| *koşmak* = to run | *koşma* = running |
| *yürümek* = to walk | *yürüme* = walking |

(12aa) *This verbal noun* (12a) *plays a very important part as a Gerund.*

*(12b) By adding the suffixes lık, (lik, luk, lük) to the verb* (root and ending) to denote "condition of doing" or "state of action". These, however, are scarcely ever used. It is an emphatic form of the action and is used when it is desired to lay stress on this action. Usually (12a) is used:

| | |
|---|---|
| *koşmak* = to run | *koşmaklık* = the state of running |
| *yürümek* = to walk | *yürümeklik* = the state of walking |

44

(12c) By adding the suffix *ış, yış (iş, uş, üş, yiş, yuş, yüş)* to the root, to denote a kind of action, manner, and style. As:

| | |
|---|---|
| *bakmak* = to look | *bakış* = glance |
| *uçmak* = to fly | *uçuş* = flight |
| *görmek* = to see | *görüş* = view |
| *çiğnemek* = to trample | *çiğneyiş* = trampling |
| *yürümek* = to walk | *yürüyüş* = gait |

(12d) By adding the letter *k* to vowel-ending verb roots and the necessary "sound" letter (*ak, ık, uk, ek, ik, ük,*) to consonant-ending verb roots of the verb to denote the state of permanency of the result of the action or an instrument of the action, as:

| | |
|---|---|
| *kapamak* = to close | *kapak* = lid |
| *yanmak* = to burn | *yanık* = scorch |
| *delmek* = to pierce | *delik* = hole |
| *döşemek* = to spread | *döşek* = bed |

(12e) By adding *ım, im, um, üm,* as a final to a primitive verb root it forms a noun of action:

| | |
|---|---|
| *almak* = to take, to buy | *alım* = taking, buying |
| *satmak* = to sell | *satım* = selling |
| *katılmak* = to participate | *katılım* = participation |
| *basmak* = to print | *basım* = printing |
| *seçmek* = to select | *seçim* = selection |
| *kesmek* = to cut | *kesim* = cutting |
| *içmek* = to drink | *içim* = drinking |
| *yapmak* = to make | *yapım* = making |

(12f) By adding *gı, kı (gi, gu, gü; ki, ku, kü)* to denote the instrument used to achieve the action or the result of the action:

| | |
|---|---|
| *karmak* = to sting | *kargı* = pike |
| *sarmak* = to bind round | *sargı* = binder |
| *saymak* = to respect | *saygı* = respect |
| *burmak* = to twist | *burgu* = gimlet |

| | |
|---|---|
| *duymak* = to feel | *duygu* = feeling |
| *bilmek* = to know | *bilgi* = knowledge |
| *sevmek* = to love | *sevgi* = affection |
| *içmek* = to drink | *içki* = drink |
| *süzmek* = to strain | *süzgü* = strainer |
| *görmek* = to see | *görgü* = experience |

(12g) By adding *ç*, to the root of the verb to denote an actor, or an instrument, holding the quality or permanent state of the verb:

| | |
|---|---|
| *kazanmak* = to gain | *kazanç* = gain |
| *kıskanmak* = to be jealous | *kıskanç* = jealous |
| *tıkamak* = to stop up a hole | *tıkaç* = stopper |
| *çekmek* = to draw | *çekiç* = claw-hammer |
| *sevinmek* = to rejoice | *sevinç* = joy |

(12h) By adding *gaç, kaç (geç, keç)* etc., to denote an actor, or instrument, with special capacity, ability, speciality of the quality of the verb:

| | |
|---|---|
| *kısmak* = to squeeze | *kıskaç* = pincers |
| *yüzmek* = to swim | *yüzgeç* = a clever swimmer |
| *süzmek* = to strain | *süzgeç* = colander |
| *dalmak* = to dive | *dalgıç* = a diver |

(12i) By adding *ı, i (u, ü)* to obtain abstract nouns:

| | |
|---|---|
| *korkmak* = to be frightened | *korku* = fright |
| *batmak* = to sink | *batı* = west (where the sun sets) |
| *yarmak* = to split | *yarı* = half |
| *savmak* = to count | *sayı* = count |
| *sağmak* = to milk | *sağı* = milking |
| *dizmek* = to string (beads) | *dizi* = string (beads) |

(12j) By the addition of *ıntı, inti (untu, üntü)*, to denote the completed action of the verb:

| | |
|---|---|
| *çıkmak* = to go out | *çıkıntı* = projection |

| | |
|---|---|
| *sıkmak* = to press | *sıkıntı* = confusion |
| *girmek* = to enter | *girinti* = recess |
| *süpürmek* = to sweep | *süpürüntü* = rubbish |

(12k) By adding *tı (ti, tu, tü)* to denote the passive state of the verb:

| | |
|---|---|
| *kararmak* = to grow black | *karartı* = the growing black, obscuration |
| *ağarmak* = to grow white | *ağartı* = the growing white |
| *kızarmak* = to grow red | *kızartı* = the growing red |

## NOUNS MADE FROM NOUNS

(13) Nouns are also obtained by adding certain suffixes to other nouns, changing their meaning. By adding *cı, ci, cu, cü (çı, çi, çu, çü)* (Ph. 31b), to nouns to denote profession or speciality, as:

| | |
|---|---|
| *hamam* = bath-house | *hamamcı* = bath attendant |
| *kahve* = coffee | *kahveci* = coffee seller or café owner |
| *kuyu* = well | *kuyucu* = one who digs wells |
| *üzüm* = grapes or raisins | *üzümcü* = one who sells grapes or raisins |
| *bıçak* = knife | *bıçakçı* = maker of knives |

The above are actually adjectives, but are used as nouns (see 28j).

(13a) By adding *lık (lik, luk, lük)*, to form abstract nouns, nouns of locality, comparative nouns, etc. Examples:

| | |
|---|---|
| *arkadaş* = companion | *arkadaşlık* = companionship (Abs.) |
| *mezar* = tomb | *mezarlık* = cemetery (Loc.) |
| *çam* = pine tree | *çamlık* = pine grove |
| *buz* = ice | *buzluk* = ice-box |

## NOUNS FORMED FROM ADJECTIVES

(13b) By adding *lık, (lik, luk, lük)* to adjectives to form nouns, where the quality of the adjective becomes the "state" of that quality:

47

| | |
|---|---|
| *tatlı* = sweet | *tatlılık* = sweetness |
| *çirkin* = ugly | *çirkinlik* = ugliness |
| *güzel* = beautiful | *güzellik* = beauty |
| *görgüsüz* = inexperienced | *görgüsüzlük* = inexperience |

# DIMINUTIVE NOUNS

(14) A Diminutive noun is obtained by the addition of *cık, cuk, cağız,* to hard nouns, and *cik, cük, ceğiz,* to soft nouns. Examples:

| | |
|---|---|
| *dükkâncık* = little shop | *tepecik* = little hill |
| *avcık* = little game (bird) | *kedicik* = small cat |
| *kuzucuk* = little lamb | *köycük* = small village |
| *pantoloncuk* = little trousers | *sürücük* = small flock |

| | |
|---|---|
| *dükkâncağız* = little shop | *tepeceğiz* = little hill |
| *avcağız* = little game (bird) | *kediceğiz* = small cat |
| *kuzucağız* = little lamb | *köyceğiz* = small village |
| *adamcağız* = little man | *sürüceğiz* = small flock |

(The two hard endings *cık, cağız,* etc., both bear exactly the same meaning, as will be seen by the above examples. The same applies to the soft endings.)

The meaning of a diminutive noun is not always "smallness in size", but more or less "fine in stature" and "pleasant in effect", as:

| | |
|---|---|
| *heykelcik* = dainty little statue | *şapkacık* = dainty hat |

It is also used when affection is to be understood, as:

| | |
|---|---|
| *annecik* = dear mother | *kadıncağız* = dear woman |

Before adding the diminutive suffix to words ending with *k*, the *k* is dropped, as:

| | |
|---|---|
| *benek, benecik* = little mole | *yanak, yanacık* = little cheek |

48

# DECLENSION (VERBAL CASES) OF THE NOUN

In a sentence the noun completes or limits the action of the verb, both transitive and intransitive.

This relationship of the noun to the verb is marked by the affixing of certain prepositions (more correctly called postpositions) to the end of each word. Throughout the Grammar we shall refer to them as "suffixes".

This is known as the case of the noun. There are nine cases of the noun (clauses, sentences, etc.) in relation to the verb. They are:

|  | Cons. end. | Vowel end. |
|---|---|---|
| (15) THE NOMINATIVE CASE | adam | oda |
| (16) THE OBJECTIVE CASE | adamı, etc. | odayı, etc. |
| (17) THE DATIVE CASE | adama, etc. | odaya, etc. |
| (18) THE LOCATIVE CASE | adamda, etc. | odada, etc. |
| (19) THE ABLATIVE CASE | adamdan, etc. | odadan, etc. |
| (20) THE INSTRUMENTATIVE CASE | adamla, etc. | odayla, etc. |
| (21) THE CAUSATIVE CASE | adam için, etc. | oda için, etc. |
| (22) THE VOCATIVE CASE | adam! | baba! |
| (23) THE POSSESSIVE CASE | adamın, etc. | odanın, etc. |

## THE NOMINATIVE CASE (YALIN DURUM)

(15) When the noun, single or qualified or as part of a sentence, is in its primary structure, it is in the *NOMINATIVE CASE*.

In *A SENTENCE* the subject is always in the *nominative case*, and always comes before the VERB. Examples:

*çocuk oynuyor* = the child plays
*her adam bunu yapabilir* = every man can do this

When the object of the verb is indefinite it is placed in the nominative case, by itself or preceded by *bir* (a). Example:

*bir adam gördüm* = I saw a man

49

# CONSONANT ENDING NOUNS IN THE NOMINATIVE CASE

Neutral consonants: *l, m, n, r, y, ğ,* (Ph. 15c)

| Hard *(a, ı, o, u)* (Ph. 8) | Soft *(e, i, ö, ü)* (Ph. 9) |
|---|---|
| *dam* = roof | *yem* = bait |
| *kan* = blood | *beden* = body (human) |
| *hamal* = porter | *reçel* = jam |
| *tabur* = battalion | *kömür* = coal |
| *yay* = spring (steel) | *güvey* = bridegroom |

Sharp consonants: *ç, f, h, k, p, s, ş, t* (Ph. 15b)

| Hard *(a, ı, o, u)* (Ph. 8) | | Soft *(e, i, ö, ü)* (Ph. 9) | |
|---|---|---|---|
| *aç* = hungry | *yulaf* = oats | *geç* = late | *hedef* = target |
| *tas* = bowl | *arkadaş* = friend | *ses* = voice | *keşiş* = hermit |
| *kap* = dish | *katık* = relish | *sebep* = cause | *değnek* = stick |
| *kat* = floor | *silah* = fire-arm | *demet* = bunch | *tesbih* = chaplet |

Flat consonants: *b, c, d, g, j, v, z* (Ph. 15a)

(15a) ORIGINAL TURKISH words ending in *b, c,* and *d* are very few. Foreign words ending with *b, c,* and *d* are, when introduced into the language, changed to *p, ç,* and *t* (Ph. 32b).

| Hard *(a, ı, o, u)* | Soft *(e, i, ö, ü)* |
|---|---|
| *ad* = name | *cep* = pocket |
| *av* = game | *ev* = house |
| *sınav* = exam | *söylev* = speech |
| *yavuz* = inflexible | *öküz* = ox |
| *topuz* = knob | *körfez* = bay |

# VOWEL ENDING NOUNS IN THE NOMINATIVE CASE

Hard *(a, ı, o, u)* (Ph. 8)          Soft *(e, i, ö, ü)* (Ph. 9)

*baba* = father          *dede* = grandfather
*dadı* = nurse           *keçi* = goat
*palto* = coat           *köprü* = bridge
*kuyu* = well            *sürgü* = bolt

## THE OBJECTIVE CASE
## (BELİRTME DURUMU)

(16) A noun is in the "*OBJECTIVE*" case when, single or qualified, or as part of a sentence it is directly governed by the verb. (See Transitive verb, 142)

The *OBJECTIVE* case is the *direct case* of the *transitive verb* and *makes definite* the object represented by the noun.

In *A SENTENCE* it precedes the VERB, and in some instances is followed by another case. Examples:

*Ahmet'i* gördüm          = I have seen Ahmet
*Selime odayı* süpürdü          = Selime swept the room

The *OBJECTIVE* case is obtained by affixing:

(16a) *ı, i, u, ü* to words ending with all consonants (Hard Ph. 8, Soft Ph. 9), *ç, k, p,* and *t* being subject to changes (Ph. 31-2).

(16b) A "*y*" (*yı, yi, yu, yü*) is inserted between the noun and the suffix when the noun ends with a vowel (Hard Ph. 8, Soft Ph. 9).

# CONSONANT-ENDING NOUNS IN THE OBJECTIVE CASE

Neutral Consonants: *ğ, l, m, n, r, y* (Ph. 15c)

Hard *(a, ı, o, u)* (Ph. 8)

*hamal - hamalı* = the porter
*hamam - hamamı* = the bath house
*saman - samanı* = the straw
*damar - damarı* = the vein
*alay - alayı* = the regiment
*dağ - dağı* = the mountain
*son - sonu* = the end
*pul - pulu* = the stamp

Soft *(e, i, ö, ü)* (Ph. 9).

*temel - temeli* = the foundation
*kesim - kesimi* = the cut
*çimen - çimeni* = the turf
*kemer - kemeri* = the belt
*güney - güneyi* = the south
*çiy - çiyi* = the dew
*göl - gölü* = the lake
*kül - külü* = the ash

Sharp Consonants: *f, h, s, ş* (Ph. 15b)

Hard *(a, ı, o, u)* (Ph. 8)

*yulaf - yulafı* = the oats
*günah - günahı* = the sin
*makas - makası* = the scissors
*savaş - savaşı* = the battle
*muz - muzu* = the banana
*baykuş - baykuşu* = the owl
*ruh - ruhu* = the soul

Soft *(e, i, ö, ü)* (Ph. 9)

*şeref - şerefi* = the honour
*tesbih - tesbihi* = the chaplet
*kümes - kümesi* = the hen coop
*güneş - güneşi* = the sun
*küf - küfü* = the mildew
*örs - örsü* = the anvil
*gümüş - gümüşü* = the silver

(16c) Sharp Consonants *(ç, p, k, t)* change to *(b, c, d, ğ)* (Ph. 31-32) in words of foreign origin, when the suffixes are added, if the ending letter in the word had already undergone a phonetic change from *(b, c, d, ğ)* to *(ç, p, k, t)* when brought into the language.

For these an up-to-date dictionary must be consulted (see also 16d).

Hard *(a, ı, o, u)* (Ph. 8)

| original | when taken into the language | Obj. Case | |
|---|---|---|---|
| *ağac* | *ağaç* | *ağacı* | = the tree |
| *kabag* | *kabak* | *kabağı* | = the marrow |
| *dolab* | *dolap* | *dolabı* | = the cupboard |
| *kanad* | *kanat* | *kanadı* | = the wing |

Soft *(e, i, ö, ü)* (Ph. 9)

| | When taken into the language | Obj. Case | |
|---|---|---|---|
| | *kireç* | *kireci* | = the lime |
| | *köpek* | *köpeği* | = the dog |
| | *müsebbip* | *müsebbibi* | = the causation |
| | *simit* | *simidi* | = the cake |

(16d) When the end letter of a Turkish or foreign word is *(ç, k, p, t)* (Ph. 31d) and is of a primary character it is not subject to alteration. An up-to-date dictionary must be consulted with regard to the character of the letter and the inflection to which it will be subjected. It is usually shown in one of the oblique cases with the appropriate letter.

Some examples are given below:

| *koç* | - | *koçu* | = the ram (Ph. 32) |
|---|---|---|---|
| *ak* | - | *akı* | = the white (Ph. 32) |
| *ok* | - | *oku* | = the arrow (31d) |
| *sap* | - | *sapı* | = the handle (Ph. 32) |
| *ip* | - | *ipi* | = the rope (31d) |
| *süt* | - | *sütü* | = the milk (Ph. 32) |
| *it* | - | *iti* | = the dog (31d) |

Flat Consonants: *b, c, d, g, j, v, z* (Ph. 15a)

| ad | - | adı | = the name | leb | - | lebi | = the lip |
|------|---|--------|------------------|---------|---|----------|---------------|
| and | - | andı | = the vow | kod | - | kodu | = the code |
| garaj | - | garajı | = the garage | brifing | - | brifingi | = the briefing |
| manav | - | manavı | = the fruiterer | ev | - | evi | = the house |
| buz | - | buzu | = the ice | göz | - | gözü | = the eye |

## VOWEL-ENDING NOUNS IN THE OBJECTIVE CASE

Hard *(a, ı, o, u)* (Ph. 8)

| salatayı | = the salad |
|----------|----------------|
| çarpıntıyı | = the palpitation |
| orduyu | = the army |
| paltoyu | = the overcoat |

Soft *(e, i, ö, ü)* (Ph. 9)

| keresteyi | = the timber |
|-----------|--------------|
| tilkiyi | = the fox |
| örgüyü | = the plait |
| üzüntüyü | = the worry |

Some phrases:

| Odayı süpürdüm. | = I swept the room. | (objective case definite) |
|-----------------|----------------------|---------------------------|
| Mektubu aldım. | = I received the letter. | (objective case definite) |

The OBJECTIVE case of a *compound noun* (25, 25k) or of two nouns in juxtaposition (Def. Com., see 24 and 24n) is obtained by inserting an "*n*" between the word and the suffix *(ı, i, u, ü)*. Examples:

| Hanımelini severim. | = Lady's Hand (Honeysuckle) I love. |
|---------------------|-------------------------------------|
| Gecesefasını severim. | = Night's Delight (Evening Primrose) I love. |
| Odanın kapısını kapadım. | = The door (object. case) of the room I shut. |
| Kapının anahtarını kaybettim. | = The key (object. case) of the door I lost. |

# THE DATIVE CASE (YÖNELME DURUMU)

## ("To," and sometimes "on" or "at" in Eng. Trans.)

(17) A noun is in the "*DATIVE*" case when it marks the direction of the action of the *VERB*. *This case forms the direct verbal case of an Intra-Transitive verb* (see 154c).

It is formed by affixing:

(17a) *a* (Hard Ph. 8) and *e* (Soft Ph. 9) to all consonant-ending words. The consonants (*ç, k, p, t*) are then subject to changes (Ph. 31 and 32).

(17b) A "*y*" (*ya, ye*) is inserted between the noun and the suffix when a noun ends with a vowel (Hard and Soft).

## CONSONANT-ENDING NOUNS IN THE DATIVE CASE

Neutral Consonants: *ğ, l, m, n, r, y* (Ph. 15c)

Hard *(a, ı, o, u)* (Ph. 8)    Soft *(e, i, ö, ü)* (Ph. 9).

| Hard | | Soft | |
|---|---|---|---|
| *hamala* | = to the porter | *tele* | = to the wire |
| *hamama* | = to the wash house | *biçime* | = to the shape |
| *samana* | = to the straw | *çimene* | = to the turf |
| *damara* | = to the vein | *mermere* | = to the marble |
| *alaya* | = to the regiment | *kuzeye* | = to the north |
| *dağa* | = to the mountain | *güneye* | = to the south |
| *koyuna* | = to the sheep | *düğüne* | = to the wedding feast |

**NOTE:** There are many words in the Turkish language ending with *y, n,* and *s,* and care must be taken not to confuse these with the *y, n,* and *s* inserted when adding a *vowel-beginning* suffix, to a *vowel-ending* word.

Hard *(a, ı, o, u)* (Ph. 8)                    Soft *(e, i, ö, ü)* (Ph. 9)

| | | | | |
|---|---|---|---|---|
| *çarşaf - çarşafa* | = to the sheet | *selef - selefe* | = to the predecessor |
| *günah - günaha* | = to the sin | *tesbih - tesbihe* | = to the chaplet |
| *makas - makasa* | = to the scissors | *kümes - kümese* | = to the hen coop |
| *savaş - savaşa* | = to the battle | *güneş - güneşe* | = to the sun |
| *kılıf - kılıfa* | = to the case (pillow) | *gümüş - gümüşe* | = to the silver |

(17c) *SHARP* CONSONANTS *(ç, k, p, t)* revert back to *(b, c, d, ğ)* (Ph. 31, 31cc and 32) in words of foreign origin when the suffixes are added, if the ending letter in the word had already undergone a phonetic change from *(b, c, d, ğ)* to *(ç, k, p, t)* when brought into the language.

For these an up-to-date dictionary must be consulted (see 16c and d).

Hard *(a, ı, o, u)* (Ph. 8)

| original | when taken into the language | Obj. Case | |
|---|---|---|---|
| *ağac* | *ağaç* | *ağaca* | = to the tree |
| *kabag* | *kabak* | *kabağa* | = to the marrow |
| *dolab* | *dolap* | *dolaba* | = to the cupboard |
| *kanad* | *kanat* | *kanada* | = to the wing |

Soft *(e, i, ö, ü)* (Ph. 9)

| | | | |
|---|---|---|---|
| *kirec* | *kireç* | *kirece* | = to the lime |
| *yüreğ* | *yürek* | *yüreğe* | = to the heart |
| *müsebbib* | *müsebbip* | *müsebbihe* | = to the causation |
| *simid* | *simit* | *simide* | = to the cake |

When the end letter of a Turkish or foreign word, introduced into the language, is *(ç, k, p, t)* (Ph. 31d) and is of a primary character it is not subject to alteration. An up-to-date dictionary must be consulted to find out the nature of the ending letter.

Some examples are given below:

| Hard (*a, ı, o, u*) (Ph. 8) | | | Soft (*e, i, ö, ü*) (Ph. 9) | |
|---|---|---|---|---|
| *koç - koça* | = to the ram | | *et - ete* | = to the meat |
| *ak - aka* | = to the white | | *çit - çite* | = to the fence |
| *saç - saça* | = to the hair | | *süt - süte* | = to the milk |
| *karbonat - karbonata* | = to the carbonate | | | |

Flat Consonants: *b, c, d, g, j, v, z* (Ph. 15a)

| Hard (*a, ı, o, u*) (Ph. 8) | | | Soft (*e, i, ö, ü*) (Ph. 9). | |
|---|---|---|---|---|
| *garaj - garaja* | = to the garage | | *cip - cipe* | = to the jeep |
| *manav - manava* | = to the fruiterer | | *ev - eve* | = to the house |
| *buz - buza* | = to the ice | | *göz - göze* | = to the eye |

**There are very few soft words ending in flat consonants.**

## VOWEL-ENDING NOUNS IN THE DATIVE CASE

| Hard (*a, ı, o, u*) (Ph. 8) | | | Soft (*e, i, ö, ü*) (Ph. 9) | |
|---|---|---|---|---|
| *salataya* | = to the salad | | *keresteye* | = to the timber |
| *çarpıntıya* | = to palpitation | | *tilkiye* | = to the fox |
| *orduya* | = to the army | | *örgüye* | = to the plait |
| *paltoya* | = to the overcoat | | *üzüntüye* | = to the worry |

Some phrases:

| | |
|---|---|
| 1. *Masaya kitabı koydum.* | = I placed the book on the table. |
| 2. *Pazara gidemedim.* | = I could not go to the bazaar (or market). |
| 3. *Pazara gitmedim.* | = I did not go to the bazaar (or market). |
| 4. *Pencereye bir taş attı.* | = He/she threw a stone at the window. |

(Note slight difference between the verbs in phrases 2 and 3.)

# THE LOCATIVE CASE (KALMA DURUMU)
("In", and sometimes "on" or "at" in Eng. trans.)

(18) A noun is in the "LOCATIVE" case when it designates where the action takes place. It is one of the verbal cases *common to all verbs.*

In the sentence it is placed directly in front of the objective or dative case.

The "*LOCATIVE*" case is obtained by affixing:

(18a) *da* (Hard, Ph. 8) and *de* (Soft, Ph. 9) when the word ends with a VOWEL or the NEUTRAL consonants (Ph. 15c) *ğ, l, m, n, r, y* and some of the *FLAT* consonants (Ph. 15a) *g, j, v, z,*

(18b) The "*d*" is changed to "*t*" (*ta* and *te*) when the word ends with any one of the *SHARP* consonants *ç, f, h, k, p, t, s, ş* (Ph. 15b).

## VOWEL-ENDING NOUNS IN THE LOCATIVE CASE

Hard *(a, ı, o, u)* (Ph. 8)

| | |
|---|---|
| *ortada* | = in the middle |
| *burada* | = in here |
| *kıyıda* | = on the side |
| *boruda* | = in the pipe |

Soft *(e, i, ö, ü)* (Ph. 9)

| | |
|---|---|
| *ötede* | = therein (there) |
| *beride* | = herein (here) |
| *tepede* | = on the hill |
| *sürüde* | = in the herd |

## CONSONANT-ENDING NOUNS IN THE LOCATIVE CASE
Neutral Consonants: *ğ, l, m, n, r, y* (Ph. 15c)

Hard *(a, ı, o, u)* (Ph. 8)

| | |
|---|---|
| *hamamda* | = in the bath house |
| *koyunda* | = on the sheep |
| *solda* | = on the left |
| *karda* | = in the snow |
| *bağda* | = in the vineyard |
| *yayda* | = on the spring |

Soft *(e, i, ö, ü)* (Ph. 9)

| | |
|---|---|
| *biçimde* | = in the shape |
| *çimende* | = on or in the grass |
| *temelde* | = at the foundation |
| *kemerde* | = in the belt |
| *güneyde* | = in the south |

Flat Consonants: *b, c, d, g, j, v, z* (Ph. 15a)

Hard *(a, ı, o, u)* (Ph. 8)                    Soft *(e, i, ö, ü)* (Ph. 9)

*kazda* = on the goose                    Very few words end in flat
*garajda* = in the garage                 consonants
*manavda* = at the dry-fruiterer          *evde* = in the house
*tozda* = in the dust                     *gözde* = in the eye

Sharp Consonants: *ç, f, h, k, p, t, s, ş* (Ph. 15b)

Hard *(a, ı, o, u)* (Ph. 8)                    Soft *(e, i, ö, ü)* (Ph. 9)

*ağaçta*    = on the tree              *çekiçte*   = in the hammer
*parkta*    = in the park              *köşkte*    = in the villa
*şarapta*   = in the wine             *sebepte*   = in the cause
*saatta*    = in the hour             *demette*   = in the bunch
*kanatta*   = on the wing             *dertte*    = in mentioning
*sarrafta*  = at the money changer    *şerefte*   = in the honour
*silahta*   = in the fire-arm         *teslihte*  = in arming
*tasta*     = in the bowl             *kümeste*   = in the hen coop
*taşta*     = in the stone            *beşte*     = at five (o'clock)

*da* "in" has various meanings. Please study examples:

*Evde kimse yok.*                = There is nobody at home.
*Israrda fayda yok.*             = There is no benefit in insisting; or
*Israr etmekte ne fayda olabilir?* = What benefit could there be in insisting?
*Bunun üzerinde durmayalım.*     = We shall not dwell on this.
*Bunun hakkında söz söyleyemem.* = I cannot say a word about this.
*Bu işteki fikriniz nedir?*      = What is your opinion on this matter?
*Buradaki kitap kimindir?*       = Whose is the book on here?
*(Orada) ne var?*                = What is there (therein)?
*Sözde yarın gelecek.*           = In word (verbal) (according to his statement)
                                   he will be coming to-morrow.

# THE ABLATIVE CASE (ÇIKMA DURUMU)
## (Usually "from" or "of" in Eng. Trans.)

(19) A noun is in the "*ABLATIVE*" case when it designates the source, commencement, or point of departure of the action.

It is the direct verbal case of the *Intransitive* verb.

The "*ABLATIVE*" case is obtained by affixing:

(19a) *dan* (Hard, Ph. 8) and *den* (Soft, Ph. 9) when the word ends with a vowel or the NEUTRAL consonants (Ph. 15c) *ğ, l, m, n, r, y* and some of the FLAT consonants (Ph. 15a) *g, j, v, z.*

(19b) The "*d*" is changed to "*t*" *(tan, ten)* when the word ends with any one of the SHARP consonants (*ç, f, h, k, p, t, s, ş*) (Ph. 15b).

### VOWEL-ENDING NOUNS IN THE ABLATIVE CASE

Hard *(a, ı, o, u)* (Ph. 8)

Soft *(e, i, ö, ü)* (Ph. 9)

| | |
|---|---|
| *ortadan* = from the middle | *öteden* = from that part |
| *buradan* = from here | *beriden* = from here |
| *kıyıdan* = from the side | *tepeden* = from the hill |
| *borudan* = from the pipe | *sürüden* = from the herd |
| *kafadan* = from the head | *deriden* = of leather |

### CONSONANT-ENDING NOUNS IN THE ABLATIVE CASE

#### Neutral Consonants: *l, m, n, r, y, ğ* (Ph. 15c)

Hard *(a, ı, o, u)* (Ph. 8)

Soft *(e, i, ö, ü)* (Ph. 9)

| | |
|---|---|
| *hamamdan* = from the bath house | *biçimden* = from the shape |
| *koyundan* = from the sheep | *çimenden* = from the turf |
| *soldan* = from the left | *temelden* = from the foundation |
| *kardan* = from the snow | *kemerden* = from the belt |

*bağdan* = from the vineyard  *çiyden* = from the dew
*yaydan* = from the spring  *güneyden* = from the south

Flat Consonants: *b, c, d, g, j, v, z* (Ph. 15a)

Hard *(a, ı, o, u)* (Ph. 8)  Soft *(e, i, ö, ü)* (Ph. 9)

*yazdan* = from summer  Very few words in *g* and *j*
*garajdan* = from the garage  *evden* = from the house
*manavdan* = from the fruiterer  *gözden* = from the eye
*tozdan* = from the dust  *sözden* = from word

Sharp Consonants: *ç, f, h, k, p, t, s, ş* (Ph. 15b)

Hard *(a, ı, o, u)* (Ph. 8)  Soft *(e, i, ö, ü)* (Ph. 9)

*ağaçtan* = from the tree  *çekiçten* = from the hammer
*parktan* = from the park  *köşkten* = from the villa
*şaraptan* = from the wine  *sebepten* = from the cause
*bir hattan* = from a line  *demetten* = from the bunch
*kanattan* = from the wing  *dertten* = from mentioning
*sarraftan* = from the money-changer  *şereften* = from the honour
*silahtan* = from the fire-arm  *kadehten* = from the glass
*tastan* = from the bowl  *kümesten* = from the hencoop
*taştan* = from the stone  *beşten* = from five

Some Phrases:

1. *Sarraftan*  *aldım.*  = I have had it from the
money-changer.
(the money changer *from*  have taken I)

2. *Uzaktan*  *gördüm.*  = I have seen it from a distance.
(distance *from*  have seen I)

3. *Yazdan*  *beri*  *burada*  *yım.* = I have been here since the summer.
(summer *from*  since  here at  am *I*)

(Note: Turkish mode of expression in phrase 3. present tense used.)

61

"**dan**" has several meanings. Please study the examples:

| | | | |
|---|---|---|---|
| *Arkadan* | *yetişti.* | | = He caught up from behind. |
| behind from | caught up he | | |

| | | | |
|---|---|---|---|
| *çamurdan* | *yapılmış* | *duvar* | = a wall made of mud |
| mud from | made | wall | |

| | | |
|---|---|---|
| *benden* | *uzak* | = far from me |
| I from | far | |

| | | |
|---|---|---|
| *benden* | *iyi* | = better than me |
| I from | good | |

| | | | |
|---|---|---|---|
| *Benden* | *önce* | *geldi.* | = He came before me. |
| I from | before | he came | |

| | | | | |
|---|---|---|---|---|
| *Saat* | *beşten* | *sonra* | *gelecek.* | = He will come after five o'clock. |
| hour | five from | after | will come he | |

| | | | |
|---|---|---|---|
| *Beşten* | *beri* | *bekliyorum.* | = I have been waiting since five. |
| five from | since | am waiting I | |

| | | |
|---|---|---|
| *küsmekten* | *ise* | = instead of getting angry |
| to get angry from | if | |

| | | | |
|---|---|---|---|
| *Bundan* | *dolayı* | *gelemem.* | = Owing to this I cannot come. |
| this from | owing | come cannot I | |

| | | | | |
|---|---|---|---|---|
| *Ekmekten* | *başka bir* | *şey* | *yok.* | = There is nothing but bread. |
| bread from | else a | thing | there is not | |

# THE INSTRUMENTATIVE CASE (ARAÇ DURUMU)
## ("With" or sometimes "by" in English translations)

(20) A noun is in the "*INSTRUMENTATIVE*" case when it designates *with whom* or *with what* instrument the action is carried out.

It is unlike the other cases, for it is obtained not by the addition of a suffix but by placing separately the post-position *ile* = *WITH* or *BY* after the noun, both Hard and Soft, the noun being left in the *"NOMINATIVE"* case. Examples:

| | | | |
|---|---|---|---|
| *bir adam ile* | = with a man | *el ile* | = by hand (with hand) |
| *kâr ile* | = with profit | *emek ile* | = with hard work |

(20a) It has been found, however, that it is easier to pronounce it as if joined on, and therefore, generally speaking, the "*i*" is dropped and the abbreviated ending, i.e. *la, le*, added to the word, when the word ends with a consonant.

(20b) A "*y*" (*yla, yle*) is inserted between the noun and the suffix when the noun ends with a vowel.

### CONSONANT-ENDING NOUNS IN THE INSTRUMENTATIVE CASE
Neutral, Sharp and Flat Consonants

| Hard *(a, ı, o, u)* (Ph. 8) | | Soft *(e, i, ö, ü)* (Ph. 9) | |
|---|---|---|---|
| *uçakla* | = by plane | *emekle* | = with hand work |
| *çarşafla* | = with the sheet | *güneşle* | = with the sun |
| *alayla* | = with the regiment | *benimle* | = with me |
| *kalburla* | = with a sieve | *kömürle* | = with coal |
| *sazla* | = with music | *gözle* | = with the eye |
| *odunla* | = with wood | *düzenle* | = by intrigue |

### VOWEL-ENDING NOUNS IN THE INSTRUMENTATIVE CASE

| *parayla* | = with money | *dedeyle* | = with grandfather |
|---|---|---|---|
| *radyoyla* | = with the radio | *tilkiyle* | = with a fox |
| *kamçıyla* | = with the whip | *sürüyle* | = with a herd |

## THE CAUSATIVE CASE (ETTİRGEN DURUMU)
("For" or sometimes "to" in English translations)

(21) A noun is in the *"CAUSATIVE"* case when it gives reason for the realization of the action.

The "*CAUSATIVE*" case is obtained by placing the word *için* after the noun, both consonant and vowel ending.

It is not subject to any change and is always written separately.

## CONSONANT-ENDING NOUNS IN THE CAUSATIVE CASE
### Neutral, Sharp and Flat Consonants

Hard *(a, ı, o, u)* (Ph. 8)                                  Soft *(e, i, ö, ü)* (Ph. 9)

| | | | | |
|---|---|---|---|---|
| *katık için* | = for relish | | *tef için* | = for the tambourine |
| *yulaf için* | = for oats | | *kümes için* | = for the hen coop |
| *top için* | = for the ball | | *etek için* | = for the skirt |
| *insan için* | = for man | | *kireç için* | = for the lime |
| *kıral için* | = for the king | | *sis için* | = for the fog |
| *bakkal için* | = for the grocer | | *küp için* | = for the earthen jar |
| *kır için* | = for the countryside | | *temel için* | = for the foundation |
| *buz için* | = for the ice | | *fil için* | = for the elephant |
| *havuz için* | = for the swimming pool | | *deniz için* | = for the sea |

## VOWEL-ENDING NOUNS IN THE CAUSATIVE CASE

Hard *(a, ı, o, u)* (Ph. 8)                                  Soft *(e, i, ö, ü)* (Ph. 9)

| | | | | |
|---|---|---|---|---|
| *para için* | = for money | | *deve için* | = for the camel |
| *bacı için* | = for nurse | | *kedi için* | = for the cat |
| *salata için* | = for the salad | | *köprü için* | = for the bridge |
| *kuzu için* | = for the lamb | | *gürültü için* | = for the noise |

Some Phrases:

| | | | | |
|---|---|---|---|---|
| *Seni* | *korkutmak için* | | *söylüyor.* | = He says that to frighten you. |
| you (obj. case) | to frighten for | | says (he) | |

| | | | | |
|---|---|---|---|---|
| *Seni* | *almak* | *için* | *geldi.* | = He came to take you. |
| you (obj. case) | to take | for | came (he) | |

| | | | |
|---|---|---|---|
| *Para* | *için* | *yaptı.* | = He did it for money. |
| money | for | did (he) | |

# THE VOCATIVE CASE (SESLENME DURUMU)

(22) The *"vocative"* case is formed by placing words of *address* or *interjections* either in *front* of the noun, *after* the noun or at *the end* of the sentence, *after the verb*.

Some examples are given hereunder:

| | |
|---|---|
| *A kardaşım* (address) | = O my brother |
| *Bay, baksana* (address) | = I say, Sir or Mr. |
| *Ah öğlum ah* (complaint) | = My dear child |
| *Dersine çalışmalısın ha* (notice) | = See that you do learn your lesson |
| *Behey adam* (anger) | = O you man |
| *Yahu, Bay Ahmet* | = Hey, Mr. Ahmet |
| *Türk! Öğün, çalış, güven* | = Turk! Have pride, work, be self reliant |
| *(K. Atatürk)* | |

# THE POSSESSIVE/GENITIVE CASE (İYELİK/TAMLAYAN DURUMU)
("of" and "'s" in English translations)

(23) A noun or pronoun is placed in the possessive case when it denotes possession. It is formed by adding:

(23a) *ın, (in, un, ün)* to hard and soft words (Ph. 8-9) ending with all consonants, the sharp consonants *ç, k, p, t* changing to *b, c, d, ğ* (Ph. 31, 32).

(23b) An *n (nın, nin, nun, nün)* is inserted between the word and the suffix when the word ends with a vowel (Hard, Ph. 8) or (Soft, Ph. 9).

### CONSONANT-ENDING NOUNS IN THE POSSESSIVE CASE
Neutral Consonants: *l, m, n, r, y, ğ* (Ph. 15c)

| Hard *(a, ı, o, u)* (Ph. 8) | | Soft *(e, i, ö, ü)* (Ph. 9) | |
|---|---|---|---|
| *sakalın* | = of the beard | *kesimin* | = of the cut |
| *bayramın* | = of the bayram | *düğünün* | = of the wedding feast |

| | | | |
|---|---|---|---|
| *zamanın* | = of the time | *semerin* | = of the saddle (donkey) |
| *gururun* | = of the vanity | *kuzeyin* | = of the north |
| *sarayın* | = of the palace | | |

## Sharp Consonants: *f, h, s, ş* (Ph. 15b)

**Hard *(a, ı, o, u)* (Ph. 8)**

| | |
|---|---|
| *sarrafın* | = of the moneychanger |
| *günahın* | = of the sin |
| *elmasın* | = of the diamond |
| *baykuşun* | = of the owl |

**Soft *(e, i, ö, ü)* (Ph. 9)**

| | |
|---|---|
| *keşfin* | = of the invention |
| *tesbihin* | = of the chaplet |
| *kümesin* | = of the hen coop |
| *gümüşün* | = of the silver |

(23c) The Sharp Consonants (*ç, k, p, t*) change to (*c, b, d, ğ*). This change will not take place unless the word has undergone a phonetic change when first brought into the language.

| original | when taken into the language | Possessive Case | |
|---|---|---|---|
| *ağac* | *ağaç* | *ağacın* | = of the tree |
| *kabag* | *kabak* | *kabağın* | = of the marrow |
| *dolab* | *dolap* | *dolabın* | = of the cupboard |
| *kanad* | *kanat* | *kanadın* | = of the wing |
| *kirec* | *kireç* | *kirecin* | = of the lime |
| *köpeğ* | *köpek* | *köpeğin* | = of the dog |
| *merkeb* | *merkep* | *merkebin* | = of the donkey |
| *kiremid* | *kiremit* | *kiremidin* | = of the roofing tile |

(23d) When the end letter of a Turkish or foreign word is *ç, k, p, t* and is of a primary character it is not subject to alteration. An up-to-date dictionary must be consulted (see 16d). Examples:

| | | | |
|---|---|---|---|
| *suç* | = misdeed | *suçun* | = of the misdeed |
| *top* | = the ball | *topun* | = of the ball |

| | | | |
|---|---|---|---|
| *saç* | = the hair | *saçın* | = of the hair |
| *ok* | = the arrow | *okun* | = of the arrow |
| *karbonat* | = carbonate | *karbonatın* | = of the casbonate |
| *saadet* | = happiness | *saadetin* | = of the happiness |
| *sepet* | = the basket | *sepetin* | = of the basket |

(23e)                **VOWEL-ENDING NOUNS**

Hard *(a, ı, o, u)* (Ph. 8)

| | | | |
|---|---|---|---|
| *yuva* | = nest | *yuvanın* | = of the nest |
| *baca* | = chimney | *bacanın* | = of the chimney |
| *boru* | = pipe | *borunun* | = of the pipe |
| *bu* | = this | *bunun* | = of this |

Soft *(e, i, ö, ü)* (Ph. 9)

| | | | |
|---|---|---|---|
| *teneke* | = tin | *tenekenin* | = of the tin |
| *tilki* | = fox | *tilkinin* | = of the fox |
| *köprü* | = bridge | *köprünün* | = of the bridge |

Some words form an exception to this rule. Example:

| | | | |
|---|---|---|---|
| *su* | = water | *suyun, sunun* | = instead of |

(23f) Certain Arabic and Turkish words of two syllables are reduced to one by the elimination of the last vowel, when placed in the Objective, Dative, and Possessive cases (see also 68u). Examples:

*vakit* = time

(change)                                    (no change)

| | |
|---|---|
| *vak.ti* (Obj.) | *vakitten* (Abl.) |
| *vak.te* (Dat.) | *vakitte* (Loc.) |
| *vak.tin* (Poss.) | *vakit* için (Caus.) |

# TWO NOUNS OR DEF: COMBINATIONS JOINED BY *VE* = AND

(23g) **NOTE:** When two *nouns* joined by a *conjunction* are to be put in any one of the *"Declension"* cases, or form the *first* or the *second* part of a *"Definitive Combination"*, or where two *"Definitive Combinations"* are both in the same verbal case to a verb, the *second one only* is put in the *required case,* the first one being left in the *nominative* case (see also 24g, iii). *There is a tendency, however, to adhere to the original rule.*

**Note:** The dots show where the alteration has been omitted.

Examples:

> *Ayşe*    *ve*     *Güven'e*     *selam*     *söyle.*
> Ayşe    and    to Güven    salutation   say
> = Give my regards to Ayşe and Güven.

The above would, in the ordinary way, have been:
*Ayşe'ye ve Güven'e selam söyle.*

> *İstiklâl*         *ve*      *Cumhuriyetin*     *Müdafaası*
> the Independence   and    of the Republic   the defence
> = the defence of the Republic and the Independence

The above, in the ordinary way, would have been
*İstiklâlin ve Cumhuriyetin müdafaası*

> *İstiklâl*       *ve*     *Cumhuriyetin*   *Muhafaza*    *ve*    *Müdafaası*
> the Independence   and    the Republic    safeguard    and    the defence
> = the safeguard and the defence of the Republic and the Independence

The above would, in the ordinary way, have been:

*İstiklâlin ve Cumhuriyetin Muhafazası ve Müdafaası*

# THE DEFINITIVE COMBINATION (İLGİ HALİ)

*This form of sentence is very much used in Turkish.*

*It will be found that several words, or several phrases can be condensed into one concise sentence, which can then be placed in the respective verbal case, according to the verb to which it is related. It is therefore essential that the greatest attention be paid to this chapter.*

*It will be seen also that in the chapter on GERUNDS it plays no less important a part.*

(24) Two nouns, placed next to each other, form a *DEFINITIVE COMBINATION,* when:

The *SECOND ONE* determines-
- (a) the general, or
- (b) the possessive function of the first one.

Examples:

| | | |
|---|---|---|
| (i) *adamın biri* | [of the man the one] | = a man (indefinite) |
| (ii) *adamın beygiri* | [of the man the horse] | = the man's horse |

or when

(c) the *FIRST ONE* describes the state of the second one in relation to the first one,
or
(d) the *FIRST ONE* limits or completes the meaning of the second one.

Examples:

(i) *hastalığın şiddeti* [of the illness the gravity] = the gravity of the illness.
(ii) *çocukların dördü* [of the children the four] = four of the children -the four children

The first noun is placed in the *"GENITIVE"* or *"POSSESSIVE"* case. The second noun is placed in the *"ACCUSATIVE"* case.

(24a) I have intentionally made a distinction between the *"OBJECTIVE"* case and the *"ACCUSATIVE"* case, although they are usually understood to be identical in English.

I have reserved the term of *"Objective"* case for the object of the verb only and have used "*Accusative*" for the second word forming the "*Definitive Combination*" (where the first one is in the "*Possessive*" case and the second one becomes the object possessed which means that it is under the direct control of the first noun).

(24aa) **NOTE:** *I shall call the first formation of a Definitive Combination, i.e., the first word in the Genitive case, and the second word in the Accusative case, the "Simple" or "Nominative" form and, as such, it can only be the subject of the verb. When it is to play any other part in the sentence it will be placed in the required Verbal case, and the suffix denoting that case added to the second word (already in the Accusative case) without interfering with the "simple" structure.*

(24b) For consonant-ending words in the "*DEFINITIVE COMBINATION*" the ACC. case suffix is the same as the OBJ. case, i.e. *ı (i, u, ü,)*, but for vowel-ending words an "*s*" *(sı, si, su, sü)* is inserted before the suffix in the ACC. case, whereas in the OBJ. case a "*y*" is inserted. Examples:

Objective Case of a Simple Noun

| Consonant-ending | : *duvarı* | = the wall |
| Consonant-ending | : *odaları* | = the rooms |
| Vowel-ending | : *odayı* | = the room |

of the second noun of a "*definitive combination*"

| Consonant-ending | : *(evin) duvarı* | = (of the house) the wall |
| Consonant-ending | : *(evin) odaları* | = (of the house) the rooms |
| Vowel-ending | : *(hizmetçinin) odası* | = (of the servant) the room |

### ACCUSATIVE CASE (Tamlanan)

It is of great importance to make a distinction between the two forms of the word, to know when the word forms part of an "*OBJECTIVE*" case of a verb, and when it is the second noun (or word) of a "*Definitive Combination*" and therefore in the "*Accusative*" case.

It is easy to detect this when the word ends with a vowel but it is not so easy when the word ends with a consonant, particularly if the first word of the "*Definitive Combinations*" has been omitted (see 24q).

(24bb) Furthermore, when two nouns become, as a whole, a verbal case to a transitive verb and when as such they are jointly put in the *"Objective Case"* (24n) an *n*, not the ordinary Obj. case servile letter *y*, is inserted between the last letter of the second noun and the suffix *ı (i, u, ü)*. *This letter "n" is the clue whereby it will be understood that there is a Def. Combination formation (ilgi hali) which has been placed in another verbal case. This clue is especially helpful when the 1st word of the Def. Com. has been omitted (see 24q)*. Examples:

"Objective" Case (see 16) of a word qualifying the direct action of the verb in an ordinary sentence.

| | | |
|---|---|---|
| Consonant-ending | : *duvarı gördüm* | = the wall have seen (I) |
| Consonant-ending | : *odaları gördüm* | = the rooms have seen (I) |
| Vowel-ending | : *odayı gördüm* | = the room have seen (I) |

"Accusative" Case (see also 24e) of the second noun of a "definitive combination"

Cons.-ending : *(evin) duvarı yüksektir* / [(of the house) the wall high is]
  = the wall of the house is high

Cons.-ending : *(evin) odaları büyüktür* / [(of the house) the rooms large are]
  = the rooms of the house are large

Vowel-ending : *(hizmetçinin) odası temizdir* / [(of the servant) the room clean is]
  = the servant's room is clean

"Objective" Case (see 24n) of a "definitive combination" in its simple form

Cons.-ending : *(evin) duvarını gördüm* / [(of the house) the wall have seen (I)]
  = I've seen the wall of the house

Cons.-ending : *(evin) odalarını gördüm* / [(of the house) the rooms have seen (I)]
  = I've seen the rooms of the house

Vowel-ending : *(hizmetçinin) odasını gördüm* / [(of the servant) the room have
              seen (I)]
  = I've seen the servant's room

NOTE: When we refer to the "1st and 2nd" noun we mean in Turkish, not in English, for as the student will have realized by now from our various examples, and without necessarily having thoroughly gone into "Phrase Formation" the sequence of words in a Turkish sentence is the reverse of English.

## Formation of the Definitive Combination (İlgi Hali)

(24c) The "*GENITIVE*" case is obtained in the exact manner as the "*POSSESSIVE*" case (see 23a), except for 1st p. Pers. Pro. (50f).

(24d) When the first noun is to be placed in the "*GENITIVE*" case and it ends with a vowel, a letter *n* is placed between the word and the suffix *ın, (in, un, ün)*. Examples:

*yumurta* = egg *beyaz* = the white     *yumurtanın beyazı* / [of the egg the white]
                                     = the white of the egg

*kasa* = safe    *anahtar* = the key     *kasanın anahtarı* / [of the safe the key]
                                     = the key of the safe

*sürü* = flock    *çoban* = the shepherd    *sürünün çobanı*/[of the flock the shepherd]
                                     = the shepherd of the flock

(24e) The "*ACCUSATIVE*" case is obtained by affixing *ı, (i, u, ü)* to words ending with all consonants.

An "s" *(sı, si, su, sü)* is inserted when the word ends with a vowel. Examples:

*adamın beygiri*       = [of the man the horse] the man's horse
*sepetin içi*           = [of the basket the inside] the basket's inside
*külün üstü*          = [of the ash the surface] the ash's surface
*kursun sonu*        = [of the course the end] the course's end
*adamın cüzdanı*    = [of the man the wallet] the man's wallet
*tarlanın kuyusu*     = [of the field the well] the field's well
*çocuğun küçüğü*    = [of the child the small] the small of the child
                         = the small child from among the children
*elmanın güzeli*      = [of the apple the nice] the nice of apple
                         = the nice apple from among the apples

(24f) When the noun to be placed in the *Genitive* or in the *Accusative* case ends with consonants *ç, k, p, t* (Ph. 31) in both cases these letters are changed into *b, c, d* (Ph. 31, 32) and *k* to *ğ* or *y* (Ph. 37). Examples:

| | | |
|---|---|---|
| *kuyruk* = tail | *kemik* = bone | *kuyruğun kemiği* / [of the tail the bone]<br>= the bone of the tail |
| *oğlak* = kid | *kuyruk* = tail | *oğlağın kuyruğu* / [of the kid the tail]<br>= the kid's tail |
| *kulak* = ear | *kıkırdak* = cartilage | *kulağın kıkırdağı* / [of the ear the cartilage]<br>= the cartilage of the ear |
| *kabak* = marrow | *acılık* = bitterness | *kabağın acılığı*/[of the the bitterness marrow]<br>= the bitterness of the marrow |
| *erik* = plum | *ekşilik* = sourness | *eriğin ekşiliği* / [of the plum the sourness]<br>= the sourness of the plum |

(24g) The *DEFINITIVE COMBINATION* (**ilgi hali**) may also be formed of:

(a) A Noun and an Adjective (or vice versa).
(b) A Pronoun and a Noun.
(c) A *verb* or a *verbal noun* and a noun (or vice versa).

Examples:

(i) *adamın iyisi* / [the man *of* the good]        =the good man from among men

(ii) *bunun sebebi* / [this *of* the cause]        = the cause of this

(iii) *Cumhuriyetin    müdafaası  mecburiyetine    düşersen*
    [the Republic of     defence    to the obligation    if you will be faced with]
= if you are called upon to defend the Republic

When the second word is an *adjective* it has a qualificative function.

(24h) A single or many nouns may form the first or the second part of the *Combination* of *Nouns.* Examples:

73

*İstanbul'un     havası, manzarası, kısaca     her şeyi     güzeldir.*
[Istanbul of     the air, the scenery in short     everything     is beautiful]
= The air, the scenery in short everything of Istanbul is beautiful.

*tavanların,     duvarların     boyası     pek fena     yapılmış.*
[the ceilings of,     of the walls     the paint     much bad     has been done]
= The paint-work of the ceilings and the walls has been very badly done.

The *DEFINITIVE NOUNS* can be made plural as follows:

(24i) *The first one only. (tamlayan).* Examples:

*adamların görgüsü* / [of the men the experience] = the men's experience
*okulların tatili* / [the schools *of* the vacation] = the vacation of the schools
*köpeklerin havlaması* / [the dogs *of* the barking] = the barking of the dogs

(24j) *The second one only. (Tamlanan)* Examples:

*adamın gözleri* / [the man *of* the eyes] = the man's eyes
*insanın ayakları* / [the man *of* the feet] = the man's feet
*evin duvarları* / [the house *of* the walls] = the walls of the house

(24k) *Both at the same time.* Examples:

*orduların topları* / [the armies *of* the guns] = the guns of the armies
*gazetelerin makaleleri* / [the papers *of* the articles] = the articles of the papers

**NOTE: The English of these examples is shown in this form to illustrate the agglutination in Turkish of word and suffix.**

(24l) A further *Noun or Adjective* can determine the function or describe completely the state of the two first *DEFINITIVE NOUNS (DEFINITIVE COMBINATION).* This word is always placed in the *Accusative Case* and the second of the two definitive nouns placed as it is, in the *"GENITIVE"* case. Example:

*(adamın     beygiri)nin     ayakları*
[(of the man     the horse) of the     the feet]
= the feet of the man's horse

74

(24m) A *DEFINITIVE COMBINATION*, as such (the Simple or Nominative form, see Note 24aa), is, in a sentence, the subject of the verb. Examples:

*Yumurtanın beyazı güzeldir.* / [of the egg, the white, delicious is]
= The white of the egg is delicious.

*Bahçenin kapısı sarıdır.* / [of the garden, the gate, is yellow]
= The garden gate is yellow.

(24n) A *DEFINITIVE COMBINATION*, as such, may be the "*OBJECTIVE*" case of a transitive verb.

An "*n*" *(nı, ni, nu, nü)* is inserted between the "*Accusative*" case suffix and the "*Objective*" case suffix *ı, (i, u, ü)*. Examples:

*Yumurtanın beyazını isterim.* / [of the egg the white I want]
= I want the white of the egg.

*Bahçenin kapısını açtılar.* / [of the garden the gate they opened]
= They opened the garden's gate.

(24p) While retaining their suffixal structure, i.e. the first word in the "*GENITIVE*" case and the second in the "*ACCUSATIVE*" case, the "*DEFINITIVE COMBINATION*" as such can be put in any of the verbal cases.

When it is to be put in one of the other four cases *DATIVE, ABLATIVE, LOCATIVE* or *POSSESSIVE*, owing to the fact that the last word is already in the *Accusative case (ı, i, u, ü; sı, si, su, sü)* and ends with a vowel, an "*n*" is inserted between the last suffix (*Accusative*) of the last word and the suffix of the new case (DATIVE, ABLATIVE, LOCATIVE, or POSSESSIVE) (see also 24n) In the other three cases the last word remains unchanged.

## THE DATIVE CASE (TO, AT, or ON)

*adamın ayağına*     = to the man's foot
*adamın beygirine*   = to the man's horse
*beygirin kuyruğuna* = to the horse's tail

| | |
|---|---|
| *külün üstüne* | = to the surface of the ash |
| *memleketin havasına* | = to the climate of the country |
| *adamın kesesine* | = to the man's purse |
| *tarlanın kuyusuna* | = to the well of the field |
| *çobanın sürüsüne* | = to the shepherd's flock |

## THE ABLATIVE CASE (FROM, OF)

| | |
|---|---|
| *adamın ayağından* | = from the man's foot |
| *adamın beygirinden* | = from the man's horse |
| *beygirin kuyruğundan* | = from the horse's tail |
| *külün üstünden* | = from the surface of the ash |
| *memleketin havasından* | = from the climate of the country |
| *adamın kesesinden* | = from the man's purse |
| *tarlanın kuyusundan* | = from the well of the field |
| *çobanın sürüsünden* | = from the shepherd's flock |

## THE LOCATIVE CASE (IN, AT, or ON)

| | |
|---|---|
| *adamın ayağında* | = in the man's foot |
| *adamın beygirinde* | = in the man's horse |
| *beygirin kuyruğunda* | = in the horse's tail |
| *külün üstünde* | = in the surface of the ash |
| *memleketin havasında* | = in the climate of the country |
| *adamın kesesinde* | = in the man's purse |
| *tarlanın kuyusunda* | = in the well of the field |
| *çobanın sürüsünde* | = in the shepherd's flock |

## THE POSSESSIVE CASE (OF)

| | |
|---|---|
| *adamın ayağının* | = of the man's foot |
| *adamın beygirinin* | = of the man's horse |
| *beygirin kuyruğunun* | = of the horse's tail |
| *külün üstünün* | = of the surface of the ash |
| *memleketin havasının* | = of the climate of the country |
| *adamın kesesinin* | = of the man's purse |
| *tarlanın kuyusunun* | = of the well of the field |
| *çobanın sürüsünün* | = of the shepherd's flock |

## THE INSTRUMENTATIVE CASE (WITH)

*çobanın sürüsüyle*                          = with the shepherd's flock

## THE CAUSATIVE CASE (FOR)

*çobanın sürüsü için*                        = for the shepherd's flock

(24q) The first word in the "DEFINITIVE" COMBINATION can be omitted, if the omission does not create ambiguity. This is invariably done when the first word is a personal pronoun in the Poss. case (see 501d) or when the second word is an Indef. adjective (see 54). Examples:

| | |
|---|---|
| *Atatürkün sabrı* | = (proper noun - noun) (the patience of Atatürk) |
| *onun cesareti* | = (pronoun-noun) (his courage) |
| *herkesçe malumdu* | = (verb) (was known to every one) |
| *... dehası* | = (pronoun omitted - noun) (his) genius |
| (50ll) *nı* | = (objective case) through this suffix *dehası* becomes the verbal objective case of the verb that follows |
| *cihan teslim etmişti.* | = (subject - verb) (the world had recognized) |

| | | |
|---|---|---|
| *adamın* | *biri* | = some man *(......) biri* = someone) |
| man the of | the one | |

### The Compound Noun (Definitive Complex)

(25) The "*Compound Noun*" (Definitive Complex) in the Turkish language has a particular structure. It is derived from the "*DEFINITIVE COMBINATION*" explained in (24), the difference being that the relationship between the two nouns is modified as the case may be.

The "*Compound Noun*" (DEFINITIVE COMPLEX) is formed as follows:

(25a) The first noun is reduced to the Nominative, and the second noun is left in the Accusative case, when the first noun designates:

CLASSIFICATION as in the examples:

| | |
|---|---|
| *kapı tahtası* | = wood for making doors (door wood) |
| *çini fabrikası* | = factory for making tiles (tile factory) |
| *halk evi* | = house of the people (party club) |

(25b) SPECIFICATION as in the example:

| | |
|---|---|
| *hamam kubbesi* | = a dome special for a Turkish bath (bath house dome) |

(25c) POSITION as in the examples:

| | |
|---|---|
| *İstanbul valisi* | = the governor of Istanbul |
| *okul öğretmeni* | = school teacher |

(25d) SITUATION as in the examples:

| | |
|---|---|
| *Ayasofya Meydanı* | = the square situated near the mosque of St. Sophia |
| *Sultan Hamamı* | = a place called by that name |

(25e) NOMINATION as in the examples:

| | |
|---|---|
| *hanımeli* | = lady hand (Turkish name for honey-suckle) |
| *çobanpüskülü* | = shepherd tassel (holy -plant name) |
| *horozibiği* | = cock's comb (a plant) |

**NOTE:** The meaning of any of the above examples would be different were we to apply to them rule (24), thereby making them Def. Combinations. For example:

| | |
|---|---|
| *hanımın eli* | = the hand of the lady |
| *çobanın püskülü* | = the tassel of the shepherd |
| *horozun ibiği* | = the comb of the cock |

(25f) The plural of this "*Compound Noun*" is made by adding *lar, ler* to the last word.

Great care must be taken, that when adding the plural suffix the word is first reduced to its primary form, i.e. the "*NOMINATIVE*" case, the plural suffix affixed, and then the suffix for the accusative case re-affixed (without the servile letter "*s*" (see 24b) as the word now ends with a consonant). Examples:

| | | | |
|---|---|---|---|
| *yemek odası* | = dining room | *gül reçeli* | = rose-petal jam |
| *yemek odaları* | = dining rooms | *gül reçelleri* | = rose-petal jams |

(25g) The second word can be an adjective. Examples:

| | | | | | |
|---|---|---|---|---|---|
| *asker* | = soldier | *kaçak* | = fugitive | *asker kaçağı* | = deserter |
| *insan* | = man, mankind | *âşık* | = lover | *insan âşığı* | = lover of man/mankind |
| *gül* | = rose | *pembe* | = pink | *gül pembesi* | = rose pink |
| *gök* | = sky | *mavi* | = blue | *gök mavisi* | = sky blue |
| *kanarya* | = canary | *sarı* | = yellow | *kanarya sarısı* | = canary yellow |

**NOTE: A very important point to note is that in a compound noun (as 25g) the adjective comes after the noun, whereas the adjective in the ordinary way comes before the noun:**

(25h) The first word can be a verb in the INFINITIVE and the second word a NOUN. Examples:

| | | |
|---|---|---|
| *yaşamak* | *arzusu* | = the desire to live |
| to live | the desire | |
| *evlenmek* | *fikri* | = the idea to get married |
| to get married | the idea | |

(25i) Another noun or an adjective can determine the general function of the Compound Noun (Def. Complex) and together they will form a "*DEFINITIVE COMBINATION*". The last word of the Compound Noun is then placed in the "*Genitive*" case and the added noun in the "*Accusative*" case. Examples:

| | |
|---|---|
| *hanımelinin kokusu* | = the scent of the honeysuckle (lady's hand) |
| *çobanpüskülünün güzelliği* | = the beauty of the flower called çobanpüskülü |
| *Sapanca gölünün büyüklüğü* | = the vastness of the lake of Sapanca |

**NOTE:** The difference between (24) and (25) is that in the first one the articles represented by the nouns are definitely explained whereas in the second case though the quality of the article is specified it still remains indefinite.

(25j) The first part can be composed of two nouns. Examples:

| | |
|---|---|
| *ana baba günü* | = mother father day (a day when one needs the care of a mother or father - used to denote panic) |
| *kedi köpek kavgası* | = fight of a dog and cat (fighting like cats and dogs) |
| *çoluk çocuk sözü* | = child's talk |

(25k) A *COMPOUND NOUN* (Def. Comp.) can be placed in all the verbal cases.

When put in the *"OBJECTIVE"*, *"DATIVE"*, *"ABLATIVE"*, *"LOCATIVE"* or *"POSSESSIVE"* case an *"n"* is inserted before adding the respective suffixes to the last word. Examples:

| | | | |
|---|---|---|---|
| *hanım* | *elinin* | *kokusunu* | *severim* |
| lady | the hand of | the scent | love I |

(I love the scent of lady-hand (honeysuckle).)

| | | |
|---|---|---|
| *yemek* | *odasına* | *girdim* |
| food | the room to | entered (I) |

(I entered the dining room.)

The same two sentences parsed

| | |
|---|---|
| *hanım* | = lady / nominative case / <br> first word of compound noun *"hanımeli"* = honeysuckle. |
| *eli* | = the hand / accusative case / <br> second word of compound noun *hanımeli* in accusative case. |
| *nin* | = of the / genitive case / <br> suffix for genitive case of compound noun *hanımeli* which is now first of two words of a definitive combination (*hanımelinin kokusu*) |
| *kokusu* | = the scent / accusative case / <br> second word of definitive combination in the accusative case (*su*) |
| *nu* | = the / objective case / <br> suffix for objective case of definitive case, being the verbal case of the transitive verb *severim* |
| *severim* | = I love / <br> first person singular of indefinite tense |

| | |
|---|---|
| *yemek* | = food / nominative case / |
| | first word of compound noun *yemek odası* |
| *odası* | = the room / accusative case / |
| | second word of compound noun *yemek odası* in accusative case (*sı*) |
| **na** | = to the / dative case / |
| | suffix for dative case of compound noun *yemek odası* which is now the |
| | verbal case of the intransitive verb *girdim* |
| *girdim* | = I entered / |
| | 1st person singular of past tense attestative |

(251) Compound nouns and Def. Combinations made according to the *Arabic and Persian rules* are no more made, but there are a few of them which are still in use, and I have therefore found it necessary to reproduce the two rules in the simplest way. In both cases the word in the *Acc. case* is placed *first* and the other word left in the Nominative. I have shown this in the Conversational Phrases by placing the accusative suffix separate from the word. According to the Persian rule the Acc. case is obtained by adding *ı, i,* or *y,* and the Arabic rule by adding *u, ü, ul,* or *ül.* Examples:

| | | |
|---|---|---|
| (Persian) | *derecei hararet* | = the degree of the heat |
| (Turkish) | *hararetin derecesi* | = the degree of the heat |
| | | |
| (Arabic) | *darül aceze* | = the home of the poor |
| (Turkish) | *acezenin darı* | = the home of the poor |

## THE COMPOUND NOUN (SIMPLE)

(26) The "*Compound Noun*" (simple) is formed of two nouns in the "*NOMINATIVE*" case placed side by side, the first being explanatory or descriptive of the essence or manufacture of the second one. Examples:

| | | |
|---|---|---|
| *tahta kapı* | (wood door) | = wooden door |
| *saç ayak* | (black iron foot) | = iron kettle stand |
| *pırlanta yüzük* | (diamond ring) | = diamond ring |
| *taş köprü* | (stone bridge) | = stone bridge |
| *kırkayak* | (forty feet) | = centipede |
| *çelik bıçak* | (steel knife) | = steel knife |
| *kurşunkalem* | (lead pen) | = pencil |

(26a) The plural of this compound noun is made by adding (*lar*, hard *ler*, soft) only to the last word. Examples:

| | | | |
|---|---|---|---|
| *altın kolye* | = gold necklace | *altın kolyeler* | = gold necklaces |
| *gümüş bilezik* | = silver bangle | *gümüş bilezikler* | = silver bangles |

(26b) When a compound noun represents a proper noun it cannot be made plural. Examples:

| | | |
|---|---|---|
| *Kadı Köy* | (Priest Village) | = a district known by that name |
| *Tahta Kale* | (Wood Fort) | = a district known by that name |

(26c) A *Compound noun* (simple) is placed in all the verbal cases according to the general rules.

(26d) There are certain proper nouns which are used in the plural form, but these are made under (25). Example:

*Toros Dağları* = the mountains of Toros

# THE ADJECTIVE

(27) There are various kinds of adjectives in the Turkish language. Some of them are adjectives by structure, but, with these, there is no definite sign to guide the student as to the classification; one has to know the meaning, and this must be learnt from a teacher, or the dictionary. These are called "irregular". Examples:

| | | |
|---|---|---|
| *güzel* = pretty | *hafif* = light | *ağır* = heavy |

(27a) There are also adjectives which are made from nouns, verb roots, and other words by adding specified suffixes. These are called "regular" as without necessarily knowing the meaning, the student can see at a glance the nature of the word, by its ending. Examples:

| | |
|---|---|
| aç*ık* | (open) is formed from the verb root *açmak* (to open) |
| uğur*lu* | (lucky) is formed from the noun *uğur* (luck) |
| tat*sız* | (tasteless) is formed from the noun *tat* (taste) |

(27b) **THE ADJECTIVE IS PLACED BEFORE THE NOUN.** It neither takes the plural sign nor the suffix of the different declension cases, only the noun it qualifies in both cases, being subject to the various changes. Examples:

| | |
|---|---|
| *güzel kadın* | = beautiful woman |
| *iyi adamlar* | = good men |
| *uzun sokaktan* | = from the long street |
| *kırmızı şapkanın* | = of the red hat |
| *güzel bahçeye* | = to the beautiful garden |

# ADJECTIVES FORMED FROM NOUNS

(28) By the addition of the suffixes *la, lı, li,* and *lü* to a noun the meaning of "containing" or "possessing" is given. Examples:

| | | | |
|---|---|---|---|
| *kâr* = profit | | *kârlı* = profitable | |
| *biçim* = shape | | *biçimli* = shapely | |
| *suç* = guilt | | *suçlu* = guilty | |
| *görgü* = experience | | *görgülü* = experienced | |

(28a) The same suffixes affixed to geographical nouns give the meaning of "belonging to that place". Examples:

| | | | |
|---|---|---|---|
| *İstanbul* = Istanbul | | *İstanbullu* = Native of Istanbul | |
| *Kap* = the Cape | | *Kaplı* = of the Cape | |
| *Londra* = London | | *Londralı* = Londoner | |
| *dağ* = mountain | | *dağlı* = mountaineer | |
| *şehir* = town | | *şehirli* = townsman | |
| *köy* = village | | *köylü* = villager | |

(28aa) When affixed to a town name it designates "origin of birth". Examples:

*Köprülü Mehmet Paşa* = Mehmet Pasha of Köprü
*Kavalalı Muhammed Ali Paşa* = Muhammed Ali Pasha of Kavala
*Hoşnavalı Emir Süleyman* = Emir Süleyman of Hoshnava

(28b) It can also be used without the mention of the noun it qualifies, and as a proper noun, when a historically or otherwise well-known person or member of such family, or a person, is mentioned. Examples:

*Köprülülerin hizmeti unutulamaz.*
The services of the Koprulues could not be forgotten.

*Kavalalılar Mısırı (bu kez de) yeniden canlandırmışlardır.*
The house of the Kavalas have revitalized Egypt (this time too).

(28bb) It is also applied to a family or a member of a family; known more by their birth-place or the district wherein they reside. Examples:

*Aksaraylı Ahmet ile Osman geldi (geldiler).*
Ahmet with Osman of Aksaray have come.

*Aksaraylı Bay Ahmet'in ailesi geldi.*
The family of Mr. Ahmet of Aksaray has come.

These can be expressed simply by *Aksaraylılar geldiler*, meaning (9a) "The people from Aksaray have come".

(28c) Of these suffixes *lu* only is affixed to nouns of quality such as "virtue, honour, intelligence, etc.", to denote "degree and rank with specific qualification". (This form is only found in old script and is no more in use.) Examples:

| | |
|---|---|
| *hamiyet* = zeal | *hamiyetlu* = title to inferior officials |
| *dirayet* = understanding | *dirayetlu* = a title |
| *fazilet* = virtue | *faziletlu* = a canonical title |

(28d) Note that these same nouns could be made ordinary qualitative adjectives by the application of the first rule. (28a)

| | |
|---|---|
| *hamiyet* = zeal | *hamivetli* = zealous |
| *dirayet* = intellect | *dirayetli* = intelligent |
| *fazilet* = virtue | *faziletli* = virtuous |
| *kaygu* = worry | *kaygulu* = worried |

(28e) To nouns of space and volume denoting "connection with". Examples:

*okul* = school                        *okullu* = from the school
*alay* = regiment                  *alaylı* = from the regiment

(28f) The suffixes *sız* and *siz* (*suz and süz*) are affixed to denote "absence" or "lack" of the quality of the noun. Examples:

*para* = money                     *parasız* = without money
*kâr* = profit                      *kârsız* = without profit
*yol* = road                        *yolsuz* = roadless
*alkol* = alcohol                  *alkolsüz* = nonalcoholic

(28ff) The suffixes *sızın* (hard) and *sizin* (soft) are affixed to verbal nouns (12), giving the meaning of *"without the action being enacted"*. Examples:

*anlamak* = understanding         *anlamaksızın* = without understanding
*çalışmak* = working                  *çalışmaksızın* = without working
*bilmek* = knowing               *bilmeksizin* = without knowing
*görmek* = seeing                 *görmeksizin* = without seeing

It is only used to negative the *"instrumentative"* case, and it is a modifying case of the *verb*. Examples:

*uğraşmakla* = by endeavouring        *bilmekle* = by knowing
*uğraşmaksızın* = without making an effort    *bilmeksizin* = without knowing
*çalışmaksızın insan ileri gidemez* = working without man forward can go not
(man cannot progress while he is not working)
*görmeksizin bir şey söyleyemem* = seeing without a thing cannot say I
(I cannot say anything unless I see (it))

(28ff) An adjective of Arabic or Persian origin is made negative by placing *gayri* and *na* before the adjective. Examples:

*tamam* = complete               *natamam* = incomplete
*hoş* = pleasant                   *nahoş* = unpleasant
*kâfi* = sufficient                *gayri kâfi* = insufficient
*mümkün* = possible             *gayri mümkün* = impossible

(28g) The suffixes *lık (lik, luk, lük)*, are added to denote purpose, proprietorship, speciality. Examples

| | |
|---|---|
| *turşuluk (lahana)* | = pickling (cabbage) |
| *damızlık (hayvan)* | = for breeding purpose (beast) |
| *gelinlik (elbise)* | = bridal (dress) |
| *elbiselik (kumaş)* | = suitable for dresses (material) |

(28h) *ca, ce (ça, çe)* are affixed to a noun to denote "manner relation". "*c*" is changed to "*ç*" when the word ends with a sharp consonant. Examples:

*insanca* = humane            *arkadaşça* = friendly

**NOTE:** These adjectives have also an adverbial function (see Adv. 56-56b).

(28hh) When added to a word denoting country or nationality it becomes a proper noun. Examples:

*Türkçe* = (Turkish) meaning the Turkish language
*İngilizce* = (English) meaning the English language
*Arapça* = (Arabic) meaning the Arabic language

(28hhh) When *ca, ce (ça çe)* are added to **Proper** or **Common** nouns *in the plural* it is translated as "according to" or "by". Examples:

*İngilizlerce* = According to the English
*Türklerce* = According to the Turks
*İnsanlarca* = According to man (men)

(28i) *msı, msi, msu, msü, (umsı, imsi, umsu, ümsü* according to endings) are affixed to nouns to denote "likeness, similarity", as:

*köyümsü bir yer* = a place like a village
*kırımsı bir yer* = a country-like place

These could also be expressed in a different way, i.e. with *gibi* meaning "like"

*köy gibi bir yer* = a place like a village
*bahçe gibi bir yer* = a place like a garden

NOTE: The former style, however, is more generally used.

(28j) *cı, (ci, cu, cü), çı (çi, çu, çü)* are affixed to nouns to denote occupation, specialization. Examples:

| | |
|---|---|
| *koru* = forest land | *korucu* = a keeper |
| *boza* = a Turkish drink | *bozacı* = seller of boza |
| *davul* = drum | *davulcu* = drummer |
| *teneke* = tin | *tenekeci* = tinsmith |

(28jj) When these suffixes are added to words ending with a sharp consonant the "flat" consonant *c* of the suffix is changed into its equivalent "sharp" consonant *ç*. Examples:

| | |
|---|---|
| *kalafat* = caulking | *kalafatçı* = caulker |
| *ekmek* = bread | *ekmekçi* = baker |
| *çorap* = sock | *çorapçı* = seller of socks |
| *kireç* = lime | *kireççi* = seller of lime |

(28k) *kâr, şinas* to nouns only of Arabic and Persian origin, and *daş,* to Turkish or foreign nouns, to form other adjectives or nouns, denoting habit profession and speciality. *No new words are now being formed.* Examples:

| | |
|---|---|
| *hürmetkâr* = respectful | *kadirşinas* = appreciative |
| *taktirkâr* = appreciative | *hakşinas* = righteous |
| *hizmetkâr* = servant | *nimetşinas* = grateful |
| *bestekâr* = composer | *musikişinas* = musician |
| *arkadaş* = friend | *yoldaş* = companion |

(28l) *î, ığ, iğ,* to nouns of Arabic origin. Examples:

| | |
|---|---|
| *kanun* = law | *kanunî* = legal |
| *insan* = man | *insanî* = human |

# ADJECTIVES FORMED FROM VERBS

(29) *To change a verb into an adjective* the infinitive ending *mak (mek)* is taken away and the following suffixes affixed: *ık, (ik uk, ük)*, to denote the resulting state of the action of the verb. For vowel-ending verb roots the vowel of the suffix is dropped, and just the "*k*" added. Examples :-

| | |
|---|---|
| *açmak* = to open | *açık* = open |
| *yırtmak* = to tear | *yırtık* = torn |
| *basmak* = to press | *basık* = flat |
| *kırmak* = to break | *kırık* = broken |
| *bozmak* = to spoil | *bozuk* = spoilt |
| *çözmek* = to undo | *çözük* = loose |

(29a) *k* is added to denote "the essence" of the verb in a permanent state. For consonant-ending verb roots a sound letter (*ı, i, u, ü*) is placed in front of the "*k*". Examples:

| | |
|---|---|
| *toparlamak* = to gather in a heap | *toparlak* = round |
| *yumuşamak* = to yield | *yumuşak* = soft |
| *büyümek* = to grow | *büyük* = big |
| *oynamak* = to play | *oynak* = frisky |
| *işlemek* = to work | *işlek* = busy |
| *soğumak* = to get cold | *soğuk* = cold |

NOTE: (29) and (29a) have only a shade of difference in their meaning.

(29b) *gın (gin, gun, gün, gan), kın, (kin, kun, kün, kan)* to denote "permanency", "continuity", or "specialization" of the action in the actor. Examples:

| | |
|---|---|
| *girmek* = to enter | *girgin* = pushful |
| *coşmak* = to get elated | *coşkun* = elated |
| *bozmak* = to destroy | *bozgun* = destroyed |
| *uymak* = to fit | *uygun* = agreeable, fitting |
| *çalışmak* = to work | *çalışkan* = laborious |
| *kesmek* = to cut | *keskin* = sharp |
| *küsmek* = to get angry | *küskün* = sulky |

(29c) *ıcı (ici, ucu, ücü) yıcı (yici, yucu, yücü)*, to denote profession, habit, or qualification of the verb, of a permanent nature and continuous in time. There is a difference between this adjective and No. 30. Examples:

| | |
|---|---|
| *yırtmak* = to tear | *yırtıcı* = predaceous |
| *kırmak* = to break | *kırıcı* = one who breaks, destructive |
| *soymak* = to strip | *soyucu* = one who strips (steals) |
| *sürmek* = to drive | *sürücü* = driver |
| *temizlemek* = to clean | *temizleyici* = cleaner |

(29d) *man, men, dar, der* is added to verb roots, and nouns to form adjectives or other nouns, denoting habit, profession and state of the action. Examples:

| | |
|---|---|
| *şişmek* = to expand | *şişman* = fat (adjective) |
| *yarmak* = to divide in pointed section | *yarman* = pointed, steep (adjective) |
| *öğretmek* = to teach | *öğretmen* = teacher (noun) |
| *göçmek* = to wander | *göçmen* = nomad (noun) |
| *diş* = tooth | *dişmen* = dentist (noun) |
| *köle* = slave | *kölemen* = slave trained as a soldier(noun) |
| *ön* = front | *önder* = leader |
| *kıymet* = value | *kıymetdar* = valuable |

(29e) *a, e,* to verb roots ending with a consonant to denote that from the commencement the doer has been a free and willing agent in the execution of the action. A "y" (*ya, ye*) is inserted between the verb root ending with a vowel and the suffix. (It also forms the OPTATIVE MOOD of the verb). Examples:

| | |
|---|---|
| *geçmek* = to pass | *geçe* = that passes<br>that has passed<br>passing |
| *kalmak* = to remain | *kala* = that remains<br>that has remained<br>remaining |
| *vermek* = to give | *vere* = that gives<br>that has given<br>giving |

| *batmak* = to sink | *bata* = that sinks |
|---|---|
| | that has sunk |
| | sinking |

Examples:

| *saat üçü beş geçe* | = five past three |
|---|---|
| *dörde beş kala* | = five remaining to four (five to four) |

*lı, li* is added to the above to denote that the author has *achieved* the aim with his own desire as a free agent. The meaning is *indefinite* or *comprehensive* of all time.

| *geleli* | = one who has come |
|---|---|
| *kalalı* | = one who has remained |

| *(ben) buraya* | *geleli* | *yarım* | *saat* | *oldu* |
|---|---|---|---|---|
| I here to | has arrived | half | hour | has been |

(It is half an hour since I arrived here.)

It is not necessary to put *"ben"* - *"I"*. The form of construction of the phrase will imply the person. Example:

| *geleli* | *yarım* | *saat* | *oldu mu?* |
|---|---|---|---|
| has arrived | half | hour | has it been? |

No. 2 (Is it half an hour since you arrived?)

| *geleli çok olmadı* | = It has not been much that I arrived. |
|---|---|
| | (It is not long since I arrived). |

NOTE: Phrase No. 2 cannot be put into Turkish expressing the same meaning, the reason being that after half an hour, that half an hour having lapsed into the past, the question must be in the past tense.

(29f) *sı, si, sıya, siye*. These suffixes are also affixed to this adjective (29e), to form another kind of adjective. Examples:

| *veresiye* | = on credit (free will on the part of the giver) |
|---|---|

This word implies free delivery of the goods without payment.

| *bu eşyaları veresiye aldım* | = I bought these goods on credit. |
|---|---|

(30) *an, en,* to root words ending with a consonant and *yan, yen,* to root words ending with a vowel to denote that the action is locally active.

This form of adjective is actually the present participle form of the verb (110 and 124). *It is also used, sing. or plural, as a noun.* Examples:

| | |
|---|---|
| *koşmak* = to run | *koşan* = which or who runs (runner) |
| *bilmek* = to know | *bilen* = which or who knows (knower) |
| *geçmek* = to pass | *geçen* = which or who passes (passer) |
| *gelmek* = to come | *gelen* = which or who comes (comer) |
| *yürümek* = to walk | *yürüyen* = which or who walks (walker) |
| *korumak* = to protect | *koruyan* = which or who protects (protector) |

Examples:

| | |
|---|---|
| *gelen vapur Türk vapurudur* | = the coming boat is a Turkish boat |
| *işleyen demir parıldar* | = the working iron shines |
| *koşan kimdir?* | = who is the running person? |

(30a) The same suffixes are affixed to verbs in the passive voice (NON-APPARENT), giving the same meaning, in the passive sense. Examples:

| | |
|---|---|
| *kuşatılmak* = to be surrounded | *kuşatılan* = surrounded |
| *geçilmek* = to be passed | *geçilen* = passed |

Examples:

*Kuşatılan kale dün teslim (alındı).*
= The surrounded fort (had been taken) yesterday.

*Demincek geçilen köy çok küçük idi or (küçüktü)*
= The village just passed was very small.

*Görünen köye kılavuz istemez*
= There is no need for a guide when the village is seen (in sight).

(30b) These adjectives have the negative meaning when the suffix of negation (*ma* or *me*) is added. Examples:

*unutulmamak* = not to be forgotten
*unutulmayan* = which or who is not forgotten

**Example:**

*(unutulmayan) günler saadet günleridir*
= days (which are not forgotten) are days of happiness

**NOTE:** Both suffixes (*an, en*) and (*yan, yen*) when affixed to the root word after the negation suffix become (*yan, yen*).

(31) *mış, miş, muş, müş* to denote that the action has been enacted by the author, the author retaining the quality of the action.

This suffix also represents in verb conjugation a tense and a mood. Examples:

*gün görmek* = to live comfortably          *gün görmüş* = worldly-wise
*tecrübe görmek* = to have experience       *tecrübe görmüş* = experienced
*geçmek* = to pass                          *geçmiş* = that has passed

*Baban gün görmüş bir adamdır.*
= Your father is a man who had lived in riches (a worldly-wise man).

*Geçmiş günleri hatırlamak istemem.*
= I do not wish to remember the days past.

*Tecrübe görmüş adam değildir.*
= He is not an experienced man.

(31a) The same suffixes to verbs in the passive voice or any other voice will give to the adjective the passive sense or the respective sense the verb may be in. Examples:

*Görülmüş (158) rüyaların hatırlanması güçtür.*
= The remembering of the dreams dreamt is difficult.

*Söylenmiş (158a) sözlerin tekrarı gereksizdir.*
= The repeating of the words said is unnecessary.

(31b) These adjectives are made NEGATIVE by inserting the suffix of NEGATION (*ma* or *me*) between the verb root and the suffix *mış* etc. Examples:

*Gün görmemiş insana benziyor.*
= He looks like a person who did not have a comfortable life.

*Para görmemiş adam gibi hareket ediyor.*
= He behaves like a man who had not seen any money.

(31c) An adjective is formed from primitive or reflex. verbs (175a, b) by taking the negative form of the past attestative, 1st person plural (obtained by inserting *ma* (hard) and *me* (soft) between the root and tense and person suffixes) and placing it before a noun. Examples:

| *Sokakta* | *sormadık* | *kimse* | *kalmadı.* |
|-----------|------------|---------|------------|
| (street in | asked not we | nobody | remained not) |

= There was not one person in the street we did not ask.

| *Görülmedik* | *şeyler* | *vardı.* |
|--------------|----------|----------|
| (we have not | things | there were been seen) |

= There were things (not yet seen) (rare).

**NOTE:** The adjectives formed under (31c and 32, *cak, cek*) have a very wide field of application in the language. They also in the form of nouns replace the verb, and form the very much used Relative Gerund.

(32) (*ar-er, ır-ir, ur-ür*), (*cak-cek*) to denote the possession of the quality of the action by the doer giving the sense of respective time of the tense and mood represented by these suffixes (see also 73 and 74). Examples:

| *çalar saat* | = chiming clock (indefinite) |
|--------------|------------------------------|
| *teper at* | = kicking horse |
| *görür göz* | = seeing eye |
| *akacak kan* | = blood that will run (future) |

| *(gider ayak) konuşmayı sever* | (going food) to talk (objective case) he likes |
|--------------------------------|------------------------------------------------|
| | = he likes to talk when he is about to leave |

| | |
|---|---|
| *(Gelecek) vapurla gideriz.* | with the boat (that will arrive) we will go |
| | = We will go with the next boat. |
| *(Gelecek sene) okula gideceğim.* | (the coming year) to the school |
| | = I will go. (I will go to school next year.) |

(32a) The same suffixes can be added to verbs in other voices giving adjectives with meanings of the respective senses of the verbs. Examples:

| | |
|---|---|
| *Bu anlaşılır iş değil.* | = It is not an affair that is comprehensible |
| *Ahmet (söz dinler) bir çocuktur.* | = Ahmet is an (obedient) child. |

(32aa) These adjectives are also used in the negative sense. Examples:

| | |
|---|---|
| *anlaşılmaz bir söz* | = an incomprehensible word |
| *Söz dinlemez bir adamdır.* | = He is a disobedient man. |

(32b) These *adjectives* are also conjugated with the verb *Olmak* in the *Past tense attestative*, where the sense of *actuality (Indef.)* and *anticipation (Future)* is brought into the action. Examples:

| | |
|---|---|
| *görür* (Ind.) *oldum* | = I saw (I could see) |
| *gidecek* (fut.) *oldum* | = I was going (I had intended to go) |

(32c) The part these verbal adjectives play in phrase construction is peculiar to the language, and great attention must be paid to the particular meaning obtained by this manner of phrasing. They are usually distinguished from a verb by being placed next to and in front of a noun, whereas a verb is always at the end of the phrase.

(32d) (*lı, li*) is added to the future tense (3rd person singular) to form an adjective.

| | |
|---|---|
| *alacak* = he (she) shall take | *alacaklı* = creditor |
| *verecek* = he (she) shall give | *verecekli* = debtor |

(The "debtor" in the above example being the one who is *to give* his money and the "creditor" to take the money for his goods.)

Some of these adjectives are not used at all. A dictionary or a teacher must be consulted.

# ADJECTIVES FORMED FROM OTHER ADJECTIVES

(33) *ca, ce, (ça, çe)* (only) are affixed to adjectives to denote "diminutiveness", "depreciation", and "reduction" (*c* changes to *ç*, see Ph. 31b). Examples:

| | |
|---|---|
| *güzelce bir kadın* | = a rather pretty woman |
| *uzunca bir değnek* | = a rather long stick |
| *çokça bir zaman* | = a rather long time |
| *azca bir para* | = rather little money |
| *ziyadece bir ağırlık* | = a somewhat excessive weight |

(33a) *ı, i, u, ü (ms)ı, i, u, ü; ı, u (mtrak); i, ü (mtrek)*, etc., are affixed to adjectives of colour and taste to denote "depreciation, reduction, weakness". Examples:

| | | | |
|---|---|---|---|
| *beyazımsı* = whitish | | *mavimtırak* = bluish (Ph. 34a) | |
| *yeşilimsi* = greenish | | *sarımtırak* = yellowish | |
| *tatlımsı* = sweetish | | *acımtırak* = slightly bitter | |
| *ekşimsi* = sourish | | *yeşilimtırak* = greenish | |

(33b) *cık, cik, cuk, cük*, are affixed to adjectives to denote "thoroughness", "quantity", "excess", "inspiring wonder ". "attachment", "admiration". Examples:

| | | |
|---|---|---|
| *taze* = young woman | | *tazecik* = very young woman |
| *ihtiyar* = old lady | | *ihtiyarcık* = respectable old lady |

(33c) When added to words ending with *k the k* is dropped as it is a "sharp" and guttural letter and *c* is "flat". As:

| | | |
|---|---|---|
| *ufak* = small | | *ufacık* = very small |
| *küçük* = small | | *küçücük* = fairly small |
| *yüksek* = high | | *yüksecik* = rather high |
| *alçak* = low | | *alçacık* = rather low |
| *yumuşak* = soft | | *yumuşacık* = rather soft |

# COMPOUND ADJECTIVES

(34) There are also adjectives known as "compound adjectives" formed of an adjective and a noun, where each word, being in a special case, is different from the usual adjective qualifying a noun. The two together form an adjective describing the state or quality of another noun. These compound adjectives may bear a different or modified meaning from that of the ordinary combination as already explained (see 25g). The meaning is metaphoric, figurative, and sometimes similar to that of the descriptive one. They are formed in three ways, as shown hereunder, and are placed in front of the noun they qualify:

(34a) By selecting a suitable descriptive adjective followed by the noun it qualifies, as:

| descriptive adjective and noun | actual meaning | as a compound adjective |
|---|---|---|
| boşboğaz | empty throat | gossiping (person) |
| pisboğaz | dirty throat | gluttonous |
| açıkgöz | open eye | sharp, wide awake |
| yalınayak | bare foot | being "down on one's uppers" |

(34b) By using the 2nd word of a definitive combination of a Pronoun and a noun (in the Acc. Case, the 1st word, i.e. the Pronoun, in the Gen. Case being omitted) followed by:

(a) an explicatory or qualitative adjective, as:

| Omitted (Pers. Pro. in Gen. case) | Noun and adjective | Actual meaning | As a compound adjective |
|---|---|---|---|
| (onun) | bağrı yanık | his chest burnt | heartbroken |
| (onun) | başı kabak | his head marrow | bare-headed |
| (onun) | alnı açık | his forehead open | free from shame |
| (onun) | sözü doğru | his word just | upright and honest |
| (onun) | kalbi temiz | his heart clean | straightforward |
| (onun) | eli sıkı | his hand tight | niggardly |

96

**(b)** another noun in the Acc. case plus the Locative case (see 50k-50lll).

| *(onun)* | *aklı* | *(onun)* | *başında* |
|----------|--------|----------|-----------|
| omitted | nominal | omitted | nominal accusative |
| possessive | accusative | possessive | and locative |

| *actual meaning* | = his intelligence in his head |
|------------------|-------------------------------|
| *as a compound adjective* | = intelligent |

| *(onun)* | *eli* | *(onun)* | *cebinde* |
|----------|-------|----------|-----------|
| omitted | nominal | omitted | nominal accusative |
| possessive | accusative | possessive | and locative |

| *actual meaning* | = his hand in his pocket |
|------------------|--------------------------|
| *as a compound adjective* | = open-handed |

**NOTE:** I have put *onun* (his) in front of the two nouns to show the actual formation before the omission.

**(34c)** By adding *lı (li, lu, lü)* to the noun preceded by its adjective in the Nominative case, or, by selecting a suitable adjective (noun made adjective by the addition of the suffix *lı (li, lu,* and *lü)* preceded by a noun or another adjective qualifying the second adjective. Examples:

| *dik kafalı* | (with an upright head) | = obstinate |
|--------------|------------------------|-------------|
| *keskin dilli* | (with a sharp tongue) | = shrewish |
| *kaz kafalı* | (with the head of a goose) | = silly |
| *kuş beyinli* | (with the brains of a bird) | = nitwit |

**NOTE:** The above are typically Turkish expressions and should be learnt by heart. There are quite a number of others.

# EMPHASIZING ADJECTIVES

(35) Adjectives of colour, and abstract adjectives are made more assertive and more explicative by taking the first sound or syllable (consonant and vowel) of the word and adding to it a *p, s, r,* or *m,* and placing this sound in front of the adjective. This will denote "extreme density", "completeness", "unlimitedness". Examples:

*BEmBEyaz* = dead white
*masmavi* = intense blue
*kapkara* = jet black
*yemyeşil* = green all over
*kıpkırmızı* = vividly red
*dosdoğru* = straight on
*dopdolu* = chock full
*büsbütün* = entirely
*sırsıklam* = wet to the bones
*tertemiz* = spotlessly clean
*dimdik* = unquestionably upright
*koskoca* = huge (tremendously)
*sımsıkı* = quite tight
*sipsivri* = sharply pointed

*BEsBElli* = absolutely evident
*mosmor* = definitely purple
*simsiyah* = pitch black
*bambaşka* = entirely different
*tamtakır* = totally empty
*bomboş* = quite empty
*kupkuru* = bone dry
*apaçık* = wide open
*çarçabuk* = quick as lightning
*basbayağı* = simply, just
*kaskatı* = hard as granite
*kıskıvrak* = tightly twisted

The above would not be translated as "very white" or "very open", etc., as their equivalents in Turkish would be *çok beyaz* or *pek açık,* etc. They are all definite expressions used, and as the rule as to where either the *s, p, r,* or *m* is added is rather complicated, I have given this list, as, out of the many, these are in the most general use. The student should therefore memorize them.

(36) There are some adjectives, not the ordinary ones, which are not made according to these rules and they should be learned by heart from a teacher. The following are a few examples:

| | |
|---|---|
| *sapasağlam* | = totally sound |
| *güpegündüz* | = broad daylight |
| *yamrı yumru* | = uneven and lumpy |
| *cambur cumbur* | = with a hollow rumbling sound |
| *eğri büğrü* | = gnarled and twisted |
| *çırılçıplak* | = stark naked |
| *takır tukur* | = tapping, knocking sounds |

# REPETITIVE ADJECTIVES

(36a) *Emphasis or explicatory need* is expressed by using another word completing the meaning of the first one. Examples:

| | | |
|---|---|---|
| *delik* = hole | *deşik* = rent, incised | *delik deşik* = tattered and torn |
| *derme* = gathered | *çatma* = stacked | *derme çatma* = jerry built |
| *kırık* = broken | *dökük* = fallen | *kırık dökük* = dilapidated |
| *etme* = doing | *bulma* = finding | *etme bulma* = retribution |

(36b) Where, perhaps, no explicatory word could be found, emphasis is created by replacing the first consonant of the first syllable by an "*m*", or by placing an "*m*" in front of the vowel, when the first syllable commences with a vowel. Examples:

*giden*          ***miden***          *yok*
(who goes      (who goes)      there is not)
= there is nobody going

*alay*          ***malay***          *gidiyorlardı*
(procession      procession      they were going)
= they were all going in a procession

*küçük **müçük** ama çok becerikli*
= he/she is small but he/she is very clever

*şaka*          ***maka***          *herifi*          *dövdü*
(joke          joke          the man          he gave a beating)
= on the quiet (with jests and jokes) he gave the man a beating

(36c) **NOTE:** It is interesting to see the power *repetition* has in the Turkish language. It is usual to use two words, one completing the meaning of the other one. Examples:

| | | |
|---|---|---|
| *kadir kıymet* | = value-price | or kadir ve kıymet |
| *devir teslim* | = to turn over-to deliver | or devir ve teslim |

(36d) *Repetition* is also used with the verb. (See also 172-174.) Examples:

99

| O | durur | durur | da | sonra | (öyle bir) | koşar ki. |
|---|-------|-------|-----|-------|-----------|-----------|
| he | would stay | would stay | and | afterwards | like that one | he runs that |

= He would stay and (suddenly behold) afterwards he would run in such a manner (as to astound you).

| Yürüye | yürüye | nihayet | eve | vardık. |
|--------|--------|---------|-----|---------|
| tramping | tramping | at last | house | to arrived we |

= We tramped and tramping and eventually arrived home.

## THE INDEFINITE ADJECTIVE

(37) We shall see in the chapters on verbs that some *objects* of the verb are *definite* and some are *indefinite*. This state of indefiniteness of the noun or sentence is determined by the adjective placed in front of the noun. The indefinite adjectives are printed in heavy type and marked in the examples given hereunder by the sign (i) immediately following:

| | |
|---|---|
| *bir (i) adam geldi* | = A (i) man came |
| *birkaç (i) söz söyle* | = say a few (i) words |
| *birkaç (i) gün bekleyelim* | = let us wait a few (i) days |
| *hiçbir şey (i) istemem* | = I don't want anything (i) (= nothing (i)) |
| *dün (i) de (ii) aynı şeyleri söyledi* | = yesterday (i) also (ii) he said the same things |
| *elmadan başka (i) bir şey (ii) istemem* | = I do not want anything (ii) but (i) apples |
| *diğer (i) adamı bulunuz* | = find the other (i) man |
| *her gün (i) işime giderim* | = every day (i) I go to my work |
| *herhangi (i) tramvayla gidebilirsiniz* | = you can go by any (i) tram |
| *başka bir şey (i) ister misin* | = would you like to have anything else (i) |
| *filan (i) yere gitmiş* | = he has gone to such and such (i) a place |
| *hangi (i) gün gittimse bulamadım* | = whichever (i) day I went I did not find him |
| *her defa (i) sordum* | = I asked him every time (i) |
| *öyle (i) hareket etmeyiniz* | = don't behave like that (i) |
| *şöyle (i) oturunuz* | = sit down like this (i) |
| *böyle (i) iş iyi sonuç vermez* | = such work as this (i) would not give a good result |
| *aynı (i) yoldan gidelim* | = let us go from the same (i) road |

(37a) Some of these adjectives have a dual function. They may be placed in front of a singular or a plural noun.

(37b) Some, again, may be used only with nouns in the plural, or collective nouns.

(37c) Some again are formed of more than one word. These are called compound indefinite adjectives. Some examples:

*birtakım (i) adamlar yalnız kendilerini düşünürler*
= some (i) people would only think of themselves

*birçok (i) sözler söylendi*
= many (i) words were said

*bazı (i) hallerini beğenmem*
= I don't like some (i) of his ways

*onların bütün (i) işlerini yaptım*
= I have done all (i) their work

*diğer (i) işler hakkında fikriniz nedir*
= what is your opinion about the other (i) affairs

*bütün (i) dünya her gün (ii) dinlenmeye çekilir*
= the whole (i) world retires (goes) to rest every day

*bütün (i) kitapları okudum*
= I read all (i) the books

*bütün (i) insanlar güneşi severler*
= all (i) men (mankind) love the sun (sunshine)

## ADJECTIVES OF COMPARISON (SUPERIORITY AND INFERIORTY)

(38) The quality of an adjective is increased or doubled by certain adjectives denoting "quantity", "density", "excess", and "unlimitedness", being placed in front of them as:

| | |
|---|---|
| *pek* = very | *pek güzel* = very beautiful |
| | *pek fena* = very bad |
| | |
| *çok* = much | *çok fena* = much bad (Turkish exp.) |
| | *çok güzel* = much beautiful |
| | |
| *pek çok* = very much | *pek çok para* = very much money |
| | |
| *fazla* = exceedingly, too | *fazla tatlı* = exceedingly or too sweet |
| | |
| *pek fazla* = much too much | *pek fazla para* = much too much money |
| | |
| *gayet* = to an excessive degree | *gayet güzel* = beautiful to an excessive degree |
| | |
| *son derece* = extremely | *son derece tehlikeli* = extremely dangerous |

(39) Adjectives are made *stronger* by qualifying them with the following:

| | |
|---|---|
| *daha* | = more |
| *çok daha* | = much more |
| *daha ziyade* | = much more |
| *daha fazla* | = exceedingly more |

The construction of sentences including these adjectives is carried out as follows:

The Substantive qualified is in the Nominative Case, and is put first. The Adjective is in the Nominative Case and is placed last, just before the verb. The Object of Comparison is in the Ablative Case and follows the substantive qualified.

The Adjective of Comparison is placed third, preceding the qualitative adjective, as shown in the third example. Examples:

*güzel* = beautiful          *daha güzel* = more beautiful

| Bu | adam | o | adamdan | daha | iyidir. |
|---|---|---|---|---|---|
| This | man | that | man from (than) | more | good is. |

102

| *Türkiye* | *daha* | *güzeldir.* |
|-----------|--------|-------------|
| Turkey | more | beautiful is. |

| *Bu kâğıt* | *o tebeşirden* | *çok daha* | *beyazdır.* |
|------------|----------------|------------|------------|
| This paper | that chalk from (than) | much more | white is. |

(This paper is much more white (whiter) than that chalk.)

(39a) By means of Superiority over the other objects, such as:

| *en* | = most |
|------|--------|
| *en fazla* | = most exceedingly |
| *en çok* | = much most |
| *en ziyade* | = to a most excessive degree |

The construction of a sentence with these adjectives is as follows:

The Object of Superiority is placed first and in the Nominative Case, the Object in comparison and in opposition in the Genitive Case and the Predicate (adjective qualifying the first word) in the Accusative Case. *(The Object in comparison and the Predicate together form a Definitive Combination.)* Examples:

*Kadın yaratıkların en güzelidir*
Woman of creatures the most beautiful is.

*Arı böceklerin en çalışkanıdır.*
Bee the insects of most laborious is.

(40) *Equality of the adjective with another qaalified noun is* shown by the addition of:

| *kadar* (quantity) | = as much |
|--------------------|-----------|
| *gibi* (quality) | = as |

Examples:

| *Bu* | *çocuk* | *öteki* | *çocuk* | *kadar* | *akıllıdır.* |
|------|---------|---------|---------|---------|--------------|
| This | child | the other | child | as much | intelligent is. |

(This child is as intelligent as the other one.)

| Burası | orası | **gibi** | güzeldir. |
|--------|-------|----------|-----------|
| This place | that place | as | beautiful is. |

(This place is as beautiful as that one.)

**(41) To denote inferiority:**

| az | = little |
|----|----------|
| pek az | = very little |
| çok az | = much little |
| daha az | = more little (less) |
| en az | = least |

(41a) The Object of inferiority is placed first and in the Nominative Case, the Object to which the inferiority is opposed and compared with, in the Ablative Case, and the predicate in the Nominative Case. Examples:

*Kedi tavşandan daha az faydalıdır.*
The cat is less useful than the rabbit.

| Yağ | sudan | daha az | ağırdır. |
|-----|-------|---------|----------|
| Oil | water **from** (than) | less | heavy is. |

| Bal | reçelden | pek az | farklıdır. |
|-----|----------|--------|-----------|
| Honey | jam **from** | very little | different is. |

NOTE: *Daha* is generally used in comparison, and *en* to mark superiority or inferiority.

| İnsan | hayvandan | daha | akıllıdır. |
|-------|-----------|------|-----------|
| Man | animal *from* | more | intelligent is. |

(Man is more intelligent than animal)

and examples of (39a).

I have purposely given the literal English translation of the above sentences, and the student must carefully study the way in which Turkish sentences are phrased. In other examples I have given only the English meaning, and the student must split up the words as an exercise.

# NOMINAL ADJECTIVES

(42) There are certain adjectives which, by the nature of their meaning, the object they qualify is generally understood, and, in that case, the noun is left out, *and these adjectives used as nouns*. Examples:

| | |
|---|---|
| *kel* = ringworry | *ekmekçi* = baker etc. |
| *topal* = lame | *dilsiz* = dumb |
| *kör* = blind | *solak* = left handed |
| *sütçü* = milkman | |

*Ekmekçi* (the baker) is understood to be *ekmekçi adam* (the baker man).
*Topal* (lame) is understood to be *topal insan* (lame man).
*Sütçü* (milkman) is understood to be *sütçü Mehmet* (Mehmet the milkman).

They are then treated as nouns, and are subject to all the variations of a noun, but when they are placed together with a noun they are adjectives as in the examples already mentioned: *topal insan* (lame man).

(42a) When such adjectives are without their respective substantives they are treated as nouns and can also be made plural. Example:

*zenginler (zengin adamlar) fukaralara (fukara insanlara)*
the rich (rich people) the poor to (to the poor people)

(43) Certain adjectives are sometimes used as abstract nouns, as:

| | |
|---|---|
| *sıcak* | = warm, but used also as "warmth" |
| *soğuk* | = cold, but used also as "the cold" |
| *zor* | = difficult, but used also as "difficulty" |

Examples:

| | |
|---|---|
| *Sıcaktan hoşlanırım.* | = From the heat I feel pleased. |
| | (English: I like the heat). |
| *Sıcağı çok severim.* | = The heat (obj.) very much I like. |
| | (English: I like the heat very much). |

| *Soğuktan korkarım.* | = From the cold I fear.<br>(English: I fear the cold). |
| *Zora gelemem.* | = To violence I cannot come.<br>(English: I can't tolerate violence). |
| *Kolayına bakınız.* | = Look to its easiness.<br>(English: Find the easiest way out). |

## THE DEMONSTRATIVE ADJECTIVE

(44) Demonstrative adjectives are actually definite adjectives, that is to say, they show the position of the noun.

Like adjectives they are placed in front of nouns.

*Bu* (this, or these) placed in front of the noun represents the thing nearest the speaker, as:

*bu adam* = this man

*İşbu* (this, or these) is same as above, but is now seldom used. It is found in old literature, as:

*işbu ferman* = this imperial sanction

*Şu* (that or those) used to denote an object placed a little further than the one nearest the speaker, as:

*şu ev* = that house

*O* (that or those) used to denote an object placed furthest away.

*o memlekette* = in that country

(45) *Bu, şu,* and *o,* are also placed in front of nouns in the plural in their singular form but bearing the meaning of plurality, as:

| | | | |
|---|---|---|---|
| *bu adamlar* | = these men | *işbu fermanlar* | = these imperial sanctions |
| *şu evler* | = those houses | *o memleketler* | = those countries |

They are also placed in front of any verbal case, whether the noun is in the singular or the plural.

# THE NUMERAL ADJECTIVE

**(46) Cardinal Numbers:** The cardinal numbers are definite quantitive adjectives. They are placed in front of the noun.

The noun is not made plural (with *lar* or *ler*) as:

| | | |
|---|---|---|
| *on adam* = ten men | | *yirmi kadın* = twenty women |

They are also placed after the noun, in Def. Combination form, when they establish a numerical relationship. The first word is generally omitted and the second word only, in the Accusative case, used.

When the number determines *selection* the first word, instead of being omitted, is placed in the Ablative case, as:

| | | |
|---|---|---|
| *Çocuklardan* | *dördü*(subject) | *geldi.* |
| (The children from) | the four (acc. c) | arrived. |
| = (Four of the children arrived.) | | |

| | | |
|---|---|---|
| *Arkadaşlarımdan* | *üçünü* (obj. c) | *gördüm.* |
| (Friends my from) | the three (acc. c) | seen have I. |
| = (I have seen three of my friends.) | | |

There are certain cases where the noun takes the plural sign (*ler* and *lar*) when the things cited are very well known, or when emphasis is meant. Examples:

| | | | |
|---|---|---|---|
| (Emph.) | *otuz* | *yıllar* | *savaşları* = the known thirty years |
| | thirty | years | the wars |

| (Known) | iki | dünyalar = the known two worlds |
|---|---|---|
| | two | worlds |

| (Known) | on | iki | adalar = the twelve islands (the Dodecanese) |
|---|---|---|---|
| | ten | two | islands |

The number is placed in the plural when it represents personalities in history known by their number. For instance, the Forty Dervishes, or the Seven or Three Saints, well known in the Moslem religious history, are referred to simply by their number, with the plural sign attached thereto, the noun being omitted, as:

| | |
|---|---|
| kırklar | = the (known) forties [dervishes] |
| üçler | = the (known) threes [saints] |

| | | | |
|---|---|---|---|
| yarım | = (one half), | yarı | = (the half) |
| buçuk | = (half) | | |

(46a) **"Yarım"** and **"yarı"** are adjectives. Examples:

| Sizi | **yarım** | saatten | fazla | bekledim. |
|---|---|---|---|---|
| You | half | hour from | more | waited I. |

= I waited for you for more than half an hour.

| Zavallı | çocuk | **yarı** | aç | **yarı** | tok | **idi.** |
|---|---|---|---|---|---|---|
| Poor | child | half | hungry | half | full | was. |

= The poor child was half-starved.

(46b) The word **"nısıf"** also bears the same meaning as **"yarı"** or **"yarım"**, but is now very little used.

(46c) **"Buçuk"** is placed after a number only (cardinal and distributive). Examples:

| Bir | **buçuk** | saattir | bekliyorum. |
|---|---|---|---|
| One | half | hour is | I am waiting. |

= I have waited for an hour and a half.

| Üç | buçuk | kilo | olsun. |
|-----|-------|------|--------|
| Three | half | kilo | let it be. |

= Let it be three and a half kilos.

(4__c) **"Yarım"** is also a noun. It is placed in all the verbal cases It may be the *first word* in a "Definitive Combination" but not the *second one*. Examples:

| Bu | yarımı | ben | alırım, | | öteki | yarımı | o | alsın. |
|-----|--------|-----|---------|---|-------|--------|-----|--------|
| This | half | I | will take I | | the other | half | he | let him take. |
| | (obj. case) | | | | | (obj. case) | | |

= I will take this half let him take the other half.

| Bu | (yarımın | sahibi) | kimdir? |
|-----|----------|---------|---------|
| This | half of | the owner | who is. |
| | (gen. case) | (acc. case) | |

= Who is the owner of this half?

46ccc. **"Yarı"** and **"nîm"** are also used to convey the meaning of **"semi"**, the former being more generally used, as

yarı (or *nîm*) *resmî* = semi-official.

46d **"Yarı"** is also a noun. It is only used as the *second word* of a "Definitive Combination" and as such can be either the *subject of*, or a *verbal case* to, a verb. Examples:

| Dördün | yarısı (sub.) | ikidir. | | = half of four is two |
|--------|---------------|---------|---|----------------------|
| four of | the half | two is. | | |
| (gen. c.) | (acc. c.) | | | |

| Bunun | yarısını (obj.) | ben | alırım | = (I will take half of this). |
|-------|-----------------|-----|--------|------------------------------|
| This of | the half | I | will take I. | |
| (gen. c.) | (acc. c. and obj. c.) | | | |

(46e) **NOTE:** No conjunctions are used to join cardinal numbers *One hundred and twenty* (120), for instance is written *hundred twenty* (120).

(47) **Ordinal Numbers** are used to designate the order in which the objects ara placed. It is obtained by putting *ıncı, inci, uncu* or *üncü*, after the ordinal numbers (*bir, iki, üç,* etc.). They are placed before the *noun*, as:

| İngilterede | trenlerde | üçüncü mevki | vagonları | döşemelidirler. |
|---|---|---|---|---|
| England in | the trains in | third    class | carriages | upholstery with are. |

The noun can be omitted and the ordinal number only used, when the ordinal number, as the second word, is placed in a definitive combination form (see 24):

(a) It can be the subject of a verb (see 24m).
(b) It can be the object of a verb (see 24n).

Example:

| Piramitlerin | ikincisini | daha | görmedim. |
|---|---|---|---|
| The pyramids **of** | the second | yet | seen **not** have I. |
| | (acc. and obj. case) | | |

They can be, when used without the noun, subject to declension, as:

| (Abla.) | *üçüncüsünden* | = of the third |
|---|---|---|
| (Dat.) | *üçüncüsüne* | = to the third |

When they are placed in front of the noun, the noun only is subject to declension:

| (Obj.) | *üçüncü adamı* | = the third man |
|---|---|---|
| (Loc.) | *üçüncü sınıftan* | = of the third class |

(48) **DISTRIBUTIVE NUMBERS**

Distributive numbers are the numeral adjectives which are placed before the noun to establish the proportion of the division of the article.

The distributive adjective is obtained by adding *ar* and *er* to all numbers ending with a consonant and *şar* and *şer* to all numbers ending with a vowel, as:

| | | |
|---|---|---|
| *birer* = 1 each | *altışar* = 6 each | *yirmişer* = 20 each |
| *ikişer* = 2 each | *yedişer* = 7 each | *otuzar* = 30 each |
| *üçer* = 3 each | *sekizer* = 8 each | *kırkar* = 40 each |
| *dörder* = 4 each | *dokuzar* = 9 each | *altmışar* = 60 each |
| *beşer* = 5 each | *onar* = 10 each | *yüzer* = 100 eacb |
| | | *biner* = 1,000 each |

(48a) It is placed in a repetitive form when it means **"by"**. Examples:

| | | | |
|---|---|---|---|
| *Çocuklar* | *sınıftan* | *birer birer* | *çıkayorlardı.* |
| The children | the class **from** | one by one | coming out they were. |

= The children were coming out of the class one by one).

## (49)                    PROPORTIONAL NUMBERS

Two numbers are used together, the first one being in the locative, denoting division, and the second one being in the nominative case, showing the proportion, as:

| | |
|---|---|
| *üçte bir* | = one-third |
| *üçte iki* | = two-thirds |

It forms the second part of a definitive combination and is subject to declension as a definitive combination, not as an ordinary noun. Example:

| | |
|---|---|
| *bunun üçte biri* | = the third of this |
| *paranın üçte ikisi* | = two-thirds of the money |

(49a) It is placed in the "Nominative" case when it is the *subject* of a verb, the *Nominative case* being understood to be the Nominative case of a *Definitive Combination*, i.e. the second word being in the *Accusative* case. Example:

| *(Bu* | *paranın* | *üçte* | *ikisi) (24m)* | *benimdir.* |
|---|---|---|---|---|
| This | the money **of** | three **in** | the two (acc. case) | my is |

= Two-thirds of this money is mine.

(49aa) It is placed in the *"Objective"* case when it is the *object* of a verb. Examples:

111

| *(Bunun* | *üçte* | *biri* | *ni) (24n)* | *ben* | *isterim.* |
|---|---|---|---|---|---|
| this **of** | three | **in** the one | the | I | will want I |
| (gen. case) | | (acc. case) | (obj. case) | | |

= I want a third of this.

| *Bu* | *paranın* | *üçte* | *ikisini* | *aldım.* |
|---|---|---|---|---|
| This | the money **of** | three **in** | the two | I took |
| | (gen. case) | | (acc. case - obj. case) | |

= I took two-thirds of this money.

(49b) It is again placed in the *"Genitive" case* when another word or clause completes its meaning. Example

| *Bu* | *paranın* | *üçte* | *ikisinin* | *yarısı* | *Ahmet'e* | *aittir.* |
|---|---|---|---|---|---|---|
| This | the money **of** | three **in** | the two of | the half | Ahmet **to** | belongs |
| | | | (acc. case-gen. case) | | (dat. case) | |
| | | | | (acc. case) | | |

= Half of the two-thirds of this money belongs to Ahmet.

(49bb)  (49b) is now the **"objective"** case to a verb. Example:

| *Bu paranın* | *üçte* | *ikisi* | *nin* | *yarısı* | *nı Ahmet aldı.* |
|---|---|---|---|---|---|
| This the money of | three in | the two of | the | the half the Ahmet | took |
| (gen. case) | | (acc. case) | (gen. case) | | (obj. case) |
| | | | (acc. case) | | (subject) |

Ahmet took half of the two-thirds of this money).

# THE PERSONAL PRONOUN

(50) There are six PERSONAL pronouns.

| *ben* | = | I | *biz* | = | we |
|---|---|---|---|---|---|
| *sen* | = | thou | *siz* | = | you |
| *o* | = | he/she/it | *onlar* | = | they |

(50a) *Generally speaking the Personal pronoun in Turkish is not used as such, except for emphasis (see 58). In the verb conjugation it is replaced by its suffixal form (see 57ee, etc.). In the Verbal Cases (Declension of the Noun) it is used in its declined form.*

## (50b) THE DECLENSION OF THE PERSONAL PRONOUN

| nominative case | objective case | dative case |
|---|---|---|
| *ben* = I | *beni* = me | *bana* = to me |
| *sen* = you | *seni* = you | *sana* = to you |
| | | |
| *o* = he/she/it | *onu* = him/her/it | *ona* = to him/her/it |
| *biz* = we | *bizi* = us | *bize* = to us |
| *siz* = you | *sizi* = you | *size* = to you |
| *onlar* = they | *ondan* = them | *onlara* = to them |

| locative case | ablative case | possessive case |
|---|---|---|
| *bende* = in/at me | *benden* = from me | *benim* = my |
| *sende* = in/at you | *senden* = from you | *senin* = your |
| | | |
| *onda* = in/at him/her/it | *ondan* = from him/her/it | *onun* = his/her/its |
| *bizde* = in/at us | *bizden* = from us | *bizim* = our |
| *sizde* = in/at you | *sizden* = from you | *sizin* = your |
| *onlarda* = in/at them | *ondan* = from them | *onların* = their |

It is interesting to note that:

(50c) The *OBJECTIVE, DATIVE, LOCATIVE,* and the *ABLATIVE* cases are formed from the *NOMINATIVE CASE.*

(50d) The words *ben, sen* become *ban, san* in the *DATIVE* case. An "*n*" is inserted when forming the various cases, and the plural of the 3rd person.

113

(50e) **IMPORTANT RULE:** The *INSTRUMENTATIVE* and the *CAUSATIVE* cases are formed from the *POSSESSIVE* case, i.e. by placing *"için"* for the Causative, and *"ile"* for the Instrumentative case after all six persons of the Possessive case.

(50f) The *POSSESSIVE* case of the 1ST PERSON SINGULAR and PLURAL is made with *im*, instead of *in*. (see 23)


# THE DEFINITIVE COMBINATION OF A PRONOUN AND A NOUN OR A GERUND

(50h) The *personal pronouns* in the Possessive case (benim, my etc.), have their equivalents in suffixal form; these being called Definitive Personal Pronoun suffixes:


## CHART SHOWING DEFINITIVE PERSONAL PRONOUN SUPFIXES.

| PERS. PRON. IN POSS. C. (invariably omitted) | | ADD. TO VOW. END. WORDS. | | |
|---|---|---|---|---|
| | | Acc. C. Suf. | Def. Per. Pr. Suf. | |
| My | = *(Benim)* | omitted | **M** | = my |
| Your | = *(Senin)* | omitted | **N** | = your |
| His/her/its | = *(Onun)* | s *(ı, i, u, ü)* | - | = His/her/its |
| Our | = *(Bizim)* | omitted | **M** *(ı, i, u, ü)* **Z** | = our |
| Your | = *(Sizin)* | omitted | **N** *(ı, i, u, ü)* **Z** | = your |
| Their | = *(Onların)* | ı *(i)* (after the pl. sign *lar, ler*) | - | = their |

| PERS. PRON. IN POSS. C. (invariably omitted) | | ADD. TO CONS. END. WORDS. | | |
|---|---|---|---|---|
| | | Acc. C. Suf. | Def. Per. Pr. Suf. | |
| My | = *(Benim)* | ı *(i, u, ü)* | **M** | = My |
| Your | = *(Senin)* | ı *(i, u, ü)* | **N** | = Your |
| His/her/its | = *(Onun)* | ı *(i, u, ü)* | – | = His/her/its |

| Our | = (Bizim) | ı (i, u, ü) | M (ı, i, u, ü)Z | = Our |
|-----|-----------|-------------|-----------------|-------|
| Your | = (Sizin) | ı (i, u, ü) | N (ı, i, u, ü)Z | = Your |
| Their | = (Onların) | ı (i) (after the pl. | – | = Their |
| | | sign *lar, ler*) | | |

(50i) These *suffixes* are added to the *word* (denoting the object possessed), placed after the Personal pronoun, the two together forming a "definitive combination" (see 24c, d, and 24g(b)), there now being a definitive relationship.

(50j) When this word is placed after the *1st* and *2nd pers.* (sing. or plural) *Possessive Personal pronoun* it is subject to two rules:

(a) When it ends with a *consonant* the Accusative case suffix ı (i, u, ü) is inserted between the word and the pers. pronoun suffix (see 24e and chart 50h).

(b) When it ends with a *vowel* the Accusative case suffix sı (si, su, sü) is *omitted* and the *pers. pronoun suffix only* affixed.

(50k) *The 3rd person does not require a suffix to denote 3rd person*, and *is* placed in the *Accusative case* (see 24e). Examples:

Words End. with CONS.

| (benim) kitabım | = my book |
|-----------------|-----------|
| (senin) kitabın | = thy book |
| (onun) kitabı | = his/her book |

Words End. with VOWELS

| (bizim) odamız | = our room |
|----------------|------------|
| (sizin) komşunuz | = your neighbour |
| (onların) kapıları | = their doors |

(Pers. pronoun shown in brackets invariably omitted, see 50ll)

(50l) The 2nd word can be singular or plural (see 24j), as:

| (benim) kitaplarım | = my books |
|--------------------|------------|
| (onların) kitabı | = their book |

**(50ll) IMPORTANT RULE:** *With these Def. Combinations, there is one most important point to note, and that is, that although optional, the declined personal pronoun (Gen. case) is invariably dropped, but whether it is dropped or not, the Def Pers. suffix must always be used. This also applies to the Personal Verbal Pronoun suffixes (57e, 58). It is not superfluous to put the 1st word in the Gen. case, and then drop it, for unless this procedure is adhered to it will be difficult to appreciate, when studying phrase formation, the reason for the special structure of the word in the Acc. case (2nd word of the Def Com) (see 24b and bb), and although dropped, the meaning of the 1st word has to be understood to be still there.*

(50lll) When this Def. Combination, as such, is placed in any of the verbal cases (see 16-21), the 1st and 2nd pers. singular and plural, will be placed in the required case without interfering with their structure, (i.e. not removing the pers. suffix). When forming the 3rd pers. sing. and plural, an "N" will be inserted before the suffix of the required case, owing to the fact that, *there being no personal suffix for the 3rd person,* the word ends with the Acc. suffix, which is a vowel (see 24bb and 24p).

## THE COMPOUND PERSONAL PRONOUN

(50m) The word **kendi** = *self, own,* is used with the *personal pronoun* in a *"definitive combination"*, where it forms the second noun. In the *definitive formation* the word **kendi** is subject to rules.

| | | |
|---|---|---|
| *1st p. sing.* | : *kendim* | = myself |
| *2nd p. sing.* | : *kendin* | = yourself |
| *3rd p. sing.* | : *kendi(si)* | = himself, herself, itself |
| *1st p. pl.* | : *kendimiz* | = ourselves |
| *2nd p. pl.* | : *kendiniz* | = yoursel(f)ves |
| *3rd p. pl.* | : *kendileri* | = themselves |

(50n) *kendi* is usually used for *EMPHASIS* and is either used singly or together with the *Personal* pronoun. Example:

*Kendin öyle istedin.*      = yourself like that you wished
                                (You yourself wished it.)

(50p) The word *kendim* (in the accusative case) *kendin*, etc., is also used with the respective *Personal Pronoun* in the Nominative case. Example:

*Onu ben kendim bulurum.*      = I myself will find it.

(50q) *kendi* is also placed in front of *kendim* (in the Accus. Case, see 50h), *kendin*, etc., the latter one being put in the *DATIVE* case. Examples:

*Onu kendi kendime buldum.*      = I found it by myself.
*Kendi kendine düşün.*      = Think (it over) by yourself.

## The Declension of Kendi = Self, Own

(50r) *All the six persons of kendi are declinable.*

**1st Pers. Sing.**
(CASE)

| Nom. | : *kendim* | = myself |
|---|---|---|
| Obj. | : *kendimi* | = myself |
| Dat. | : *kendime* | = to at myself |
| Loc. | : *kendimde* | = in, on myself |
| Abl. | : *kendimden* | = from myself |
| Poss. | : *kendimin* | = of myself |
| Caus. | : *kendim için* | = for myself |
| Instr. | : *kendimle* | = with myself |

**2nd Pers. Sing.**

| *kendin* | = yourself |
|---|---|
| *kendini* | = yourself |
| *kendine* | = yourself |
| *kendinde* | = in, on yourself |
| *kendinden* | = from yourself |
| *kendinin* | = of yourself |
| *kendiniçin* | = for yourself |
| *kendinle* | = with yourself |

**3rd Pers. Sing.**

| Nom. | : *kendi* or *kendisi* | = himself, herself, itself |
|---|---|---|
| Obj. | : *kendini* or *kendisini* | = himself, herself, itself |
| Dat. | : *kendine* or *kendisine* | = to/for himself, herself, itself |
| Loc. | : *kendinde* or *kendisinde* | = in/on himself, herself, itself |
| Abl. | : *kendinden* or *kendisinden* | = from himself, herself, itself |
| Poss. | : *kendinin* or *kendisinin* | = of himself, herself, itself |
| Caus. | : *kendi için* or *kendisi için* | = for himself, herself, itself |
| Instr. | : *kendiyle* or *kendisiyle* | = with himself, herself, itself |

**1st Pers. pl.**

| Nom. | : *kendimiz* | = ourselves |
|---|---|---|
| Obj. | : *kendimizi* | = ourselves |
| Dat. | : *kendimize* | = to/for ourselves |
| Loc. | : *kendimizde* | = in/on ourselves |
| Abl. | : *kendimizden* | = from ourselves |

**2nd Pers. pl.**

| *kendiniz* | = yourselves |
|---|---|
| *kendinizi* | = yourselves |
| *kendinize* | = to/for yourselves |
| *kendinizde* | = in/on yourselves |
| *kendinizden* | = from yourselves |

| Poss. | : *kendimizin* | = of ourselves | *kendinizin* | = of yourselves |
|-------|---------------|----------------|--------------|-----------------|
| Caus. | : *kendimiz için* | = for ourselves | *kendiniz için* | = for yourselves |
| Instr. | : *kendimizle* | = with ourselves | *kendinizle* | = with yourselves |

**(CASE) 3rd Pers. pl.**

| Nom. | : *kendileri* | = themselves |
|------|---------------|--------------|
| Obj. | : *kendilerini* | = themselves |
| Dat. | : *kendilerine* | = to/for themselves |
| Loc. | : *kendilerinde* | = in/on themselves |
| Abl. | : *kendilerinden* | = from themselves |
| Poss. | : *kendilerinin* | = of themselves |
| Caus. | : *kendileri için* | = for themselves |
| Instr. | : *kendileriyle* | = with themselves |

# THE PERSONAL PRONOUN WITH OTHER WORDS

(50s) Any word placed after these Personal Pronouns such as an adverb, a conjunction, or any other modifying word is placed first in the "Definitive Combination", then in the *Locative, Causative* or *Instrumentative* case, thereby forming a Compound Adverb. Examples:

| *benim hakkımda* | = about me | *bizim hakkımızda* | = about us |
|------------------|------------|---------------------|-----------|
| *benim aleyhimde* | = against me | *bizim aleyhimizde* | = against us |
| *benim vasıtamla* | = through me | *bizim vasıtamızla* | = through us |
| *benim hatırım için* | = for my sake | *bizim hatırımız için* | = for our sake |

| *senin hakkında* | = about you | *sizin hakkınızda* | = about you |
|------------------|------------|---------------------|-----------|
| *senin aleyhinde* | = against you | *sixin aleyhinizde* | = against you |
| *senin vasıtanla* | = through you | *sizin vasıtanızla* | = through you |
| *senin hatırın için* | = for your | *sizin hatırınız için* | = for your sake |

| *onun hakkında* | = about him | *onların hakkında* | = about them |
|-----------------|-------------|---------------------|-------------|
| *onun aleyhinde* | = against him | *onların aleyhinde* | = against them |
| *onun vasıtasıyla* | = through him | *onların vasıtasıyla* | = through them |
| *onun hatırı için* | = for his sake | *onların hatırı için* | = for their sake |
| | | *(onların hatırları için* | = for their sake) |

(50t) When both words of the *"Definitive Combination"* are stated the 3rd *person plural* usually has the second word in the singular. If however, the 1st word is left out (see 24q) the 2nd word must be in the plural. (Examples in parentheses above.) Example:

*aleyhlerinde bir şey söyleyemem* = I cannot say anything against them

## SPECIAL FEATURES WITH EXAMPLES

(50u) The personal pronoun is usually dropped (see 50ll). Example:

*Hakkınızda iyi şeyler işittim.* = I heard good things about you.

(50v) The personal pronoun plays a special part in phrase formation: *ben* and *sen* denote sincerity and familiarity. Example:

*Ben seni dün gördüm.* = I saw thee yesterday.

(50x) *biz* and *siz* replacing *ben* and *sen* are used as signs of courtesy and modesty. Example:

*Biz sizi severiz.* = We like you.

(50y) This is carried a degree further by adding *"ler"* to *biz* and *siz (bizler, sizler)*. Example:

*Bizleri neden gelip görmüyorsunuz?* = Why don't you come and see us?
(us can refer to one person)

(50z) This latter form may also be used to denote *sarcasm*, this also being understood by the tone in which it is used. Example:

*Bizleri artık aramıyorsunuz.* = You are not looking us up any more.

(50z(i)) In a sentence where the 1st and 2nd, or 1st and 3rd person singular form the subject of the verb, the verb is put in the 1st person plural. Example:

*Ben ve sen gideriz.*                    = I and you (we will go).

(50z(ii)) When the 2nd and 3rd person singular form the subject of the verb, the verb is placed in the 2nd person plural. Example:

*Sen ve o gidersiniz.*                   = You and he (you) will go.

# POSSESSIVE PRONOUN
## (ki = that which is ...)

(51) The *Possessive Personal Pronoun* is obtained by adding *ki* to the personal pronoun in the possessive case. *Ki* will not be subject to harmony changes.

| | |
|---|---|
| **benimki** | = mine |
| **seninki** | = yours |
| **onunki** | = his, hers |
| **bizimki** | = ours |
| **sizinki** | = yours |
| **onlarınki** | = theirs |

(51a) "*ki*" can also be added to a noun, common or proper, an adverb or a pronoun, after first placing the word in the *possessive case* (see 23).

*Londra'nınki* = of London          *Ahmet'inki* = Ahmet's

(51b) The "*POSSESSIVE PRONOUN*" may be "*declined*" in all the cases. An "*n*" is inserted between the pronoun and suffixes in the objective, dative, locative, ablative, and possessive cases only.

| | | |
|---|---|---|
| *Nom.* | : *benimki* | = mine |
| *Obj.* | : *benimkini* | = mine |
| *Dat.* | : *benimkine* | = to mine |
| *Loc.* | : *benimkinde* | = in mine |
| *Abl.* | : *benimkinden* | = from mine |
| *Poss.* | : *benimkinin* | = of mine |
| *Instr.* | : *benimkiyle* | = with mine |
| *Caus.* | : *benimki için* | = for mine |

(51c) The "*Possessive Pronoun*" is made plural, if the word of which it is taking the place is plural, by adding "*ler*" after "*ki*". Examples:

*Ayşe'nin kitapları bulundu ama Osman'ınkiler* bulunmadı.
Ayşe's books have been found but those of Osman's haven't (been found).

(51d) *ki* forms a pronoun when put after any word in the Possessive case. Example:

*Ahmet'inki*      = that (thing) of Ahmet

(51e) *ki* forms an *adjective* when added to a noun in the *LOCATIVE* case. *This form is generadly used instead of* 51a *and* 51d.

*evdeki*          = that which is at home
*Londra'daki*     = that which is in London

(51f) It can form the first part of a *DEFINITIVE COMBINATION*, when another word is placed with it to modify or limit its meaning. Example:

*(Benimkinin) yarısını buldular.*
= They have found half (of that which is mine).

(51g) It may be a verbal case to a verb as :

*(Bizimkini) gördün mü?*
= Have you seen (ours)? (implying a relative or child belonging to the questioner)

| (Benimkinin | öbür | yarısını) | daha | bulmadılar. |
|---|---|---|---|---|
| of that which is mine | the other | the half | yet | have not found they |
| (gen. c.) | | (acc. c., obj. case) | | |

= They have not yet found (the other half of that which is mine).

# THE DEMONSTRATIVE PRONOUN

(52) The demonstrative pronouns are:

| | | | | |
|---|---|---|---|---|
| *bu* | = this (here) (close) | *bunlar* | = these (here) (close) | |
| *şu* | = that (here) (intermediate) | *şunlar* | = those (here) (intermediate) | |
| | or this (there) (intermediate) | | or these (there) (intermediate) | |
| *o* | = that (there) (far away) | *onlar* | = those (there) (far away) | |

(52a) *bu* is used for immediate present, as:

*Bunu bilirim.*     = I know this.

*o* is used for something distant in time or locality, as:

*Ona gelince daha neler var.*
   = When it comes to that there are many other things

*şu* is used for "distance brought into the present", as :

*Şu işten haberin var mı?*
   = Have you any knowledge of this affair?

(52b) The difference between a *Demonstrative Adjective* and a *Demonstrative Pronoun* is that an adjective always precedes a noun, and has no plural, even if put in front of a plural noun, whereas a *Demonstrative Pronoun* takes the place of a noun, is therefore by itself, and can be in the plural, according to the noun it replaces. Examples:

| | |
|---|---|
| *bu adam* | = this man (Demon. Adj.) |
| *bu adamlar* | = these men (Demon. Adj.) |
| *bunu tanırım* | = I know him or it. (Demon. Pro.) |
| *onları tanımam* | = I do not know them (Demon. Pro.) |

(52c) The *Demonstrative Pronoun* may be placed in any of the verbal cases.

(52cc) An "*n*" is inserted between the pronoun and the suffixes.

122

| Nom. Case | : bu, şu, o | = this, etc. |
|-----------|------------|--------------|
| Obj. Case | : bunu, şunu, onu | = this, etc. |
| Dat. Case | : buna, şuna, ona | = to this, etc. |
| Poss. Case | : bunun, şunun, onun | = of this, etc. |

| Nom. Case | : bunlar, şunlar, onlar | = these, etc. |
|-----------|------------|--------------|
| Obj. Case | : bunları, şunları, onları | = these, etc. |
| Dat. Case | : bunlara, şunlara, onlara | = to these, etc. |
| Poss. Case | : bunların, şunların, onların | = of these, etc. |

The Instru. and Caus. cases are obtained by placing *için* and *ile* after the pronoun in the possess. case.

(52d) The *Demonstrative Pronoun* may be part of a *"Definitive Combination"* Example:

*(Bunun sebebi)* (24) *nedir?*      = What is the reason of this (affair implied)?

(52e) It can be a verbal case. Example:

*(bunun sebebi)ni öğrenmek isterim.*
= I wish to learn the reason of this (affair implied).

(52f) The *Demonstrative Pronoun* may be placed in the *"Possessive Form"* by the addition of *ki* (when it is in the Possessive Pronoun form). It then has a *dual* function. Example:

*(Benim evim) buradadır.*      = My house is here, and
*Onunki de oradadır*      = his is there (his house is implied)

(52g) When a *Demonstrative Pronoun* in the plural is to be placed in the *"Possessive Form"*, first the *"ki"* is added, and then the plural suffix affixed. Examples:

*Bizim sorular güç idi, fakat onlarınkiler daha güç idi.*
= Our questions were difficult, but theirs were more difficult.

## THE PERSONAL VERBAL PRONOUN

*(53) The personal verbal pronouns are the personal pronoun suffixes which are used in the verb conjugation. They represent individually each person of the action, and are*

*used instead of the actual pronouns, these latter only being used when emphasis on the person is needed. For full details read 57e to l.*

## THE INDEFINITE PRONOUN

(54) The *Indefinite Pronoun* is an *Indefinite Adjective* which modifies and makes indefinite a person or object.

(54a) It is formed by placing the two words in a Def. Combination the noun in the Genitive case, and the indefinite adjective in the Accusative case, and then dropping the former. The *indefinite Pronoun* thus obtained *takes the place of that person or object* (noun). Example:

| *Her* | *adam* | *bir* | *değildir,* | *bazısı* | *iyidir,* | *bazısı* | *da* | *kötüdür.* |
|-------|--------|-------|-------------|----------|-----------|----------|------|-----------|
| every | man | one | not is, | some | good is | some | also | bad is |

= Every man is not the same, some are good some (also) are bad.

(54aa)

**indefinite indefinite
adjective pronoun**

| *bir* | = a | *biri* | = that one, someone |
|-------|-----|--------|---------------------|
| *bazı* | = some | *bazısı* | = those who, those which |
| *diğer* | = the other | *diğeri* | = the other (one) |
| *bir kısım* | = some | *bir kısmı* | = some (of it/them) |

(54b) All *Indefinite adjectives* (see 37) can be made *Indefinite Pronouns.*

## THE INTERROGATIVE PRONOUN

(55) The *interrogative pronoun* serves to modify the meaning of the verb and gives to it the interrogative sense without altering its form.

(55a) It is placed in front of the verb which is expressed in the *affirmative* form.

(55b) The interrogative pronouns (peculiar to the T. language) are:

| | |
|---|---|
| *kim* | = who? |
| *nasıl* | = how? |
| *kaç* | = how many? |
| *hangisi* | = which? |

Examples:

| | |
|---|---|
| *Kim geldi?* | = Who came? |
| *Nasıl geldiniz?* | = How did you come? |
| *Kaç kişisiniz?* | = How many are you? |
| *Hangisi sizindir?* | = Which is yours? |

# *KİMSE* = NOBODY, ANYBODY

(55c) *kim* is used when an interrogative remark is made about a person. It is also used to express *astonishment*, and *uncertainty*. Examples:

| | |
|---|---|
| *Orada kim var?* | = Who is there? |
| *Bakayım, kimdir* | = I will see who it is. |

(55cc) *kimse* (*nobody*) is used with the verb in the Negative, in the Interronegative, or (*anybody*) in the Interrogative. Examples:

| | |
|---|---|
| *Orada kimse yok.* | = There is nobody there. |
| *Evde kimse yok mu?* | = Is there nobody at home? |
| *Bahçede kimse var mı?* | = Is there anybody in the garden? |

(55ccc) *kim* can be placed in some verbal cases. Examples:

| | |
|---|---|
| *kim* | = who |
| *Onu kim gördü?* | = Who saw him? |
| | |
| *kimi* (obj.) | = whom |
| *Kimi* (obj.) *istiyorsun?* | = Whom do you want? |

| | |
|---|---|
| *kime* (dat.) | = to whom |
| *Kime söyledin?* | = Whom did you tell? |
| | |
| *kimden* | = from whom |
| *Kimden izin aldınız?* | = From whom did you get permission? |
| | |
| *kimde* | = in whom |
| *Kimde idi?* | = Who had it? |
| | |
| *kimin* | = of whom, whose |
| *Kimin kardeşidir?* | = Whose brother is he? |

(55d) **In certain cases *kim* is replaced by *kimin*.**

| | |
|---|---|
| *kiminle* | = with whom |
| *Kiminle geldin?* | = With whom did come? |
| | |
| *kimin için* | = for whom |
| *Kimin için istiyorsun?* | = For whom do you want (it)? |

(55dd) *kimin* may also be placed in the verbal cases. Examples:

| | |
|---|---|
| *kiminde var, kiminde yok* | = some have it, some have it not |

(55e) *kim* can be conjugated with the verb *imek*, and *olmak*: Examples:

| | |
|---|---|
| *kimsiniz?* | = who are you? |
| *kimdi?* | = who was it? |
| *kimmiş o?* | = who was he? (slight and sarcasm) |
| *kim oluyorsunuz?* | = who are you? (in defiance) |

## NE = WHAT

(55e) "*Ne*" is used when an *interrogative* remark is made about anything with the *exception of the human being*.

(55ee) It is subject to the same *variations as "kim."* Examples:

*ne dir?* = what is it?

| *Bu* | *(nenin* | *nesi)* | *dir?* | = (What does it belong to?) |
|------|----------|---------|--------|------------------------------|
| this | what of | what | is | |
| | (gen. case) | (acc. case) | | |

| *Onu* | *neden* | *böyle* | *yapıyorsunuz?* | = (Why are you doing it like this?) |
|-------|---------|---------|------------------|--------------------------------------|
| that | what from | like this | are doing you | |
| (obj. case) | | | | |

# HANGİ = WHICH

(55f) *HANGİ* is used in the same variations as *NE*, and *KİM*. The declension of *HANGİ* can only be carried out after it has been placed in the "Definitive Combination" form it being the second word and the first word being *BU* = THIS, or *BUNLAR* = THESE.

(55ff) *BU* or *BUNLAR* is afterwards generally dropped. Examples:

| *Bunların* | *hangisi* | *sizindir?* | = (Which of these is yours?) |
|------------|-----------|-------------|-------------------------------|
| of these | which | yours is | |
| gen. case | acc. case | gen. case | |

| *(Hangisi)ni* | *alacaksınız?* | = (Which one are you going to take?) |
|---------------|-----------------|--------------------------------------|
| which | you will take | |
| acc. case, | obj. case | |

| *Hangisinden* | *istiyorsunuz?* | = (Which do you want?) |
|---------------|------------------|-------------------------|
| of which | you want | |
| acc. case, | abl. case | |

# ADVERBS, CONJUNCTIONS, INTERJECTIONS
## THE ADVERB

(56) *Adverbs* in Turkish are words which limit or complete the meaning of the *verb* or the *adjective*. They are actually *nouns* or *adjectives* and it is only when they have a direct relationship to the verb that they become and are called *adverbs*.

(56a) It is very easy to detect this function of the adverb. It is either a plain adjective or an adjective modified by a suffix, or a noun modified by another noun or an adjective. Some of the adverbs are given here below:

| | | | |
|---|---|---|---|
| *bugün* | = today | *hep* | = all |
| *yarın* | = tomorrow | *o kadar* | = that much |
| *dün* | = yesterday | *bu kadar* | = this much |
| *dün akşam* | = yesterday evening | *birçok* | = much |
| *daima* | = always | *bir miktar* | = a quantity, a little |
| *daha* | = more | *öte* | = there |
| *erken* | = early | *beri* | = here |
| *geç* | = late | *aşağı* | = under |
| *sabahleyin* | = in the morning | *yukarı* | = above |
| *akşam* | = night, evening | *içeri* | = inside |
| *az* | = little | *dışarı* | = outside |
| *çok* | = much | *elbette* | = most certainly |
| *pek* | = very | *ihtimal* | = probably |
| *gayet* | = very much | *çokça* | = in a large quantity |
| *azca* | = in a small quantity | *iyi* | = well |
| *güzelce* | = in a nice manner | *fena* | = badly |
| *akıllıca* | = intelligently | *dahi* | = furthermore, also (the |
| *asla* | = never | | abbrev. is da (hard) and de (soft) |
| *yok* | = not | | according to word it follows. |
| *nasıl* | = how | | It is always written separately) |
| *ne için* | = what for | *yavaş* | = slowly |
| *böyle* | = like this | *yavaşça* | = slowly |
| *şöyle* | = like that | *o derece* | = at such a degree |
| *birdenbire* | = suddenly | *beraber* | = in company, with |
| *derhal* | = immediately | *bunun için* | = for this, for that |
| *de* | = also | *nasıl* | = how |
| *hatta* | = so much so, to such a degree | | |

(566) It is essential to remember that these words have the dual function of performing the duties of both an adjective and an adverb. This depends on whether they qualify a noun or modify the meaning of a verb. Study these two examples:

| Yemeği (güzel pişiriyor). | = He/she cooks the food (well) |
| (Güzel yemek) pişiriyor. | = He/she does (good cooking) |

(56c) An *adjective* in a repetitive form also forms an adverb. Example:

*Bebek*  **tatlı**  **tatlı**  *uyuyor.*
(baby  sweet  sweet  sleeps)
= Baby sleeps sweetly. (Baby is in a sweet sleep).

*Güzel*  *güzel*  *oturuyorduk.*
(beautiful  beautiful  were sitting we)
= We were sitting beautifully (we were sitting peacefully).

(56d) An adjective or a *noun* is made an *adverb* when the suffix *ca, ce, (ça, çe; see Ph.* 31b) is added to it. Examples:

| Akıllıca hareket ediniz. | = Behave intelligently. |
| Yavaşça yürüyünüz. | = Walk slowl.y |
| İnsanca hareket ediniz. | = Behave like a man. |

(56dd) *sına* or *sine* can also be added in some cases to (56d) where *comparison* is made with a certain amount of emphasis. Example:

*İnsafsızcasına*  *hareket*  *etti.*
pitilessly  behaviour  did he
= He behaved without mercy.

(56ddd) *âne* and *en* are added to certain nouns and adjectives of Persian and Arabic origin to form *adverbs*. Examples:

| mükerrer | = repeated | anud | = obstinate |
| mükerreren | = repeatedly | anudâne | = obstinately |

129

# THE CONJUNCTION

(56e) The *conjunction* is a word which joins two or more sentences together.

(56f) It is very much used in the Turkish formation of phrases though every effort is made to avoid its repetition.

(56g) There are also special gerundial verbal expressions, whereby the conjunction is eliminated (see 116, etc.)

(56h) There are two kinds of *conjunctions*. Both kinds will join the two sentences but the first one will also join them in their meanings whereas the second one will mark disjunction in their meanings.

(56i) Some of the *copulative conjunctions* are given below:

| | | | |
|---|---|---|---|
| *hem* | = and (equality) | *demek ki* | = it is called, that means that |
| *ve* | = and | *zira* | = because, for |
| *bari* | = at least | *ne zaman ki* | = at the time when, directly |
| *gibi* | = as | *sanki* | = as if, as though |
| *eğer* | = if, whether | *beraber* | = together, though |
| *ile* | = with | *ile beraber* | = although |
| *güya* | = as if, just as though | *bundan dolayı* | = therefore |
| *ona göre* | = accordingly | *çünkü* | = because |

*ise, sa,* or *se* = if (when followed by *da, de,* or *dahi* means "although" (see 56j).

Some examples are given here below:

| *Her gün* | *gelir* | *ve* | *gider.* | = every day he comes and goes. |
|---|---|---|---|---|
| every day | comes he | and | goes he | |

| *Eğer* | *gelirse* | *gideriz.* | | = we shall go if he comes. |
|---|---|---|---|---|
| if | comes he if | will go we | | |

| *Ona göre* | *hareket* | *ediniz.* | | = act accordingly. |
|---|---|---|---|---|
| accordingly | act | do you | | |

| *Güya* | *adam* | *olmuş.* | = just as though he were a man. |
|--------|--------|----------|--------------------------------|
| as if  | man    | became   |                                |

| *Ne zaman ki* | *mektubunuzu aldım* | *hemen* | *hareket ettim.* |
|---------------|---------------------|---------|------------------|
| at the time when | letter your took I | at once | depaxted I |

= Directly I received your letter I departed.

| *Söylemekle beraber* | *yapmaz.* | =Although he is saying it he will not do it |
|----------------------|-----------|---------------------------------------------|
| saying although | will not do he. | |

| *Doğru* | *ise* | *gidelim.* | = If it is right let us go |
|---------|-------|------------|----------------------------|
| correct | it is if | let us go. | |

## DISJUNCTIVE CONJUNCTIONS

(56j) Some of the disjunctive conjunctions are

| *ama* | = but | *ya* | = either, or |
|-------|-------|------|--------------|
| *ancak* | = but, however | *halbuki* | = whereas |
| *yahut* | = or | *gerçi* | = notwithstanding |
| *fakat* | = but | *ise de* | = although, though |
| *şayet* | = if (by chance) | *her neyse* | = anyhow, anyway |
| *ne* | = neither, nor | *ister* | = whether |

Some examples are given below:

| *Geldim* | *fakat* | *sizi* | *bulamadım.* = I came but I did not find you. |
|----------|---------|--------|-----------------------------------------------|
| came I | but | you | did not find I |

| *İyi(dir)* | *ama* | *çok* | *güçtür.* = It is good, but it is very difficult. |
|------------|-------|-------|--------------------------------------------------|
| good is | but | very | difficult is. |

| *Şayet* | *gelemezsem* | *beni* | *affediniz.* |
|---------|--------------|--------|--------------|
| lest | could not come if I | me | forgive you |

= Please excuse me if I am not able to come.

| Siz | söylediniz | **ama** | **ben inanmadım.** |
|-----|-----------|---------|--------------------|
| you | mentioned | but | believe did not I |

= You had mentioned it but I did not believe it.

| Dün gelmediniz, | | **her neyse,** | şimdi | ne yapacaksınız? |
|-----------------|---|----------------|------|------------------|
| yesterday did not come you | | however | now | what will you do |

= You did not come yesterday, however, what will you do now?

| İster | gelsin | **ister** | gelmesin | **biz gideriz.** |
|-------|--------|-----------|----------|------------------|
| if he wishes | let come him | if wishes he | let him not come | will go we |

= Whether he comes or not we will go.

## THE INTERJECTION

(56k) The *interjection* in Turkish is formed of natural expressions, or words exclaiming the respective emotions. Some of the *interjections* are given below:

| | | | |
|---|---|---|---|
| *a* | = I say | *acayip* | = wonderful |
| *be* | = I say, hey | *aferin* | = bravo, well done |
| *be adam* | = hey (man) | *yazık* | = what a pity |
| *hay* | = hey, here | *ne güzel* | = how nice |
| *ha* | = Eh?; Oh yeah!; Wow! | *de bakalım* | = now then |
| *hay Allah* | = good gracious | *aman* | = alas, mercy, pity |
| *vay* | = oh, indeed | *haydi bakalım* | = come on then |
| *vah* | = what a pity | *adam sen de* | = Take it easy!, Never mind! |
| *vah vah* | = ah, alas | *vay canına* | = wow, gosh, Christ |
| *ya* | = is that so! | *vay başıma* | = woe is me |
| *uf* | = pooh | | |

(56l) Some interjections are placed at the beginning and some at the end of the sentence. Some examples:

| | |
|---|---|
| *baksana a! be adam!* | = hey! I say! look here man |
| *adam sende! benim neme gerek!* | = what does it matter, of what interest is it to me? |
| *ya! öyle mi imiş ?* | = is that so! was it so? |
| *oyunu kazandılar ha!* | = so they have won the game! |

# THE VERB

(57) *The Turkish Verb* in its *primary* form is composed of the *root* word and the *verbal infinitive* suffix *mak* (Hard) and *mek* (Soft).

(57a) There are eight conjugative Moods, and several GERUNDIAL MOODS.

(57b) In a sentence the VERB comes *right at the end*.

(57c) One special feature to note with the Turkish verb is that by taking various suffixes it can express itself in all forms and tenses without the help of any other word. Here, for instance, are a few of the tenses which can be formed from the verb *sevmek* = to love:

| | |
|---|---|
| *seviyorum* | = I love, I am loving (Present tense, Indicative Mood) |
| *seviyordum* | = I was loving (Present tense, Narrative Mood) |
| *seviyormuşum* | = It is said that I was loving (Present tense, Reportative Mood) |
| *seviyorsam* | = if I am loving (Present tense, Conditional Mood) |
| *severim* | = I love (Indefinite tense, Indicative Mood) |
| *severdim* | = I did love (Indefinite tense, Narrative Mood) |
| *severmişim* | = It is said that I used to love (Indefinite tense, Reportative Mood) |
| *sevsem* | = if I be loving (Present tense, Subjunctive Mood), etc. |

## VERB CONJUGATION

(57d) The conjugation is carried out as follows:

First the *tense* suffix is added to the verb root (which in many cases will already have had a "voice" suffix attached), then the *mood* suffix and finally the *personal verbal pronoun* suffix (see 58a).

### PERSONAL VERBAL PRONOUN SUFFIXES

*(57e) The personal verbal pronoun suffixes are endings taking the place of the personal pronoun in the conjugation of all principal and auxiliary verbs. They are equivalent to the*

133

*English Pers. Pronoun, and the verb is never conjugated without them. The ordinary Pers Pronouns "Ben", etc., are only used for emphasis (see 50 and 58). It is neceseary to draw attention to the fact that, in some tenses, suffixes of the same person and number differ from each other. There is also some difference between these and the POSSESSIVE PERSONAL PRONOUN suffixes.*

### The Personal Verbal Pronoun Suffixes are:

## INDICATIVE MOOD

## OPT. MOOD

### (57ee) Present, Past Repeatative, Future, Indefinite

### (57eeee), Present

| | | |
|---|---|---|
| 1st pers. sing. | : *ım, im, um, üm* | *yım, yim* |
| 1st pers. plu. | : *ız, iz, uz, üz* | *lım, lim* |
| 2nd pers. sing. | : *sın, sin, sun, sün* | *sın, sin* |
| 2nd pers. plu. | : *sınız, siniz, sunuz, sünüz* | *sınız, siniz* |
| 3rd pers. sing. | : (no suffix, see 57l) | |
| 3rd pers. plu. | : *lar, ler* (being pl. suf.) | *lar, ler* |

NOTE: In the Indefinite tense only of the primitive verb *İmek*, it is essential to use *d(ı, i, u, ü)r* for the 3rd pers. (see 62t and 67i and j.)

### (57eee) PAST ATTESTATIVE

### SUBJ. AND COND. MOOD

| Added to *dı, di, du, dü,* or *tı, ti, tu,* tü, *when joined as tense suffix, the* vowels of the *tense* and pers. *pronoun suffixes merging into one another* (see 57f) | | Added to *idi* (Mood suff. when separate) | (57eeeee) Present | |
|---|---|---|---|---|
| | | | Cond. suf. *(sa)* | Cond. suf. *(se)* |
| 1st pers. sing. | : *ım, im, um, üm* | ...*m,* | ... *m* | ... *m* |
| 1st pers. plu. | : *ık, ik, uk, ük* | ...*k,* | ... *k* | ... *k* |
| 2nd pers. sing. | : *ın, in, un, ün* | ...*n,* | ... *n* | ... *n* |
| 2nd pers. plu. | : *ınız, iniz, unuz, ünüz* | ...*niz,* | ... *nız* | ... *niz* |
| 3rd pers. sing. | : – – – – | ... – | ... . | ... . |
| 3rd pers. plu. | : *lar, ler, lar, ler* | ...*ler,* | ... *lar* | ... *ler* |
| | (Being plural suffix.) | | | |

(57eeeeee)

*Imperative Mood ADD. To* **Cons.** END. VERB ROOT

| | | |
|---|---|---|
| **PRESENT** | SING. | verb root only, no suffix added (1) |
| 2nd PERS. | PLUR. | *ın, ınız; in, iniz; un, unuz; ün, ünüz* (3) |
| **ABSENT** | SING. | *sın, sin, sun, sün* |
| 2nd PERS. | PLUR. | *sınlar, sinler sunlar, sünler* |

*Imperative Mood*   ADD. To **Vow.** END. VERB ROOT

| | | |
|---|---|---|
| **PRESENT** | SING. | verb root only, no suffix added (1) |
| 2nd PERS. | PLUR | *yın, yınız; yin, yiniz; yun, yunuz; yün, yünüz* (2) |
| **ABSENT** | SING. | *sın, sin, sun, sün* |
| 2nd PERS. | PLUR. | *sınlar sinler sunlar, sünler* |

For explanation of (1), (2) and (3) see 101a.

*GELMEK* = to come 1 st Per. Sin.

| | 1 st Per. Sin. | 1 st Per. Pl. | 2nd Per. Sin. | 2nd Per. Pl. |
|---|---|---|---|---|
| Present Tense | : *geliyorum* | *geliyoruz* | *geliyorsun* | *geliyorsunuz* |
| Past Repeat. Tense | : *gelmişim* | *gelmişiz* | *gelmişsin* | *gelmişiniz* |
| Future Tense | : *geleceğim* | *geleceğiz* | *geleceksin* | *geleceksiniz* |
| Indefinite Tense | : *gelirim* | *geliriz* | *gelirsin* | *gelirsiniz* |
| Past Attest. Tense | : *geldim* | *geldik* | *geldin* | *geldiniz* |
| Cond. : Indef. Tense | : *gelir isem* | *gelir isek* | *gelir isen* | *gelir iseniz* |
| Subj. Indef. Tense | : *gelsem* | *gelsek* | *gelsen* | *gelseniz* |
| Opt. : Indef. Tense | : *geleyim* | *gelelim* | *gelesin* | *gelesiniz* |
| Imp. Mood PRESENT | : --- | --- | *gel* | *gelin, geliniz* |
| Imp. Mood ABSENT | : --- | --- | *gelsin* | *gelsinler* |

(57f) The *1 st person singular* suffix is either *ım, im, um* or *üm*, throughout the verb conjugation, according to the last vowel in the word to which it is being added. As the suffix for the *Past tense Attestative ends* with one of these *four vowels*, the *two vowels* will merge into one.

There is no other change except in the INTERROGATIVE and INTERRONEGATIVE forms of all the tenses where a "y" is inserted before the

PERSONAL VERBAL *suffix (yım, yim, yum, yüm)*, as the word ends with a vowel. This also takes place in the *Affirmative* form of the *Indefinite tense* of the *Optative* and *Potential (oblig.)* *Moods* of the primitive Verb, and in the *Indefinite tense* of the auxiliary verb *İmek*, if in the latter case the word *(noun, adjective, pronoun)* ends with a vowel. This also applies to 57ff.

(57ff) **NOTE:** The *1st person plural* suffix *is ız, iz, uz, üz* for the PRESENT, PAST REPE-ATATIVE, FUTURE and INDEFINITE *tenses*. There is no change except in the INTERROGATIVE and INTERRONEGATIVE forms, and in the *affirmative* of the *Indefinite tense, Opt.* and *Pot. oblig. moods,* where the same rules as shown in 57f apply.

(57fff) The *1st person plural* suffix is *ık, ik, uk* or *ük, for the Past Attest. tense,* but as this tense *ends* with one of these four vowels, the two vowels will merge into one. In the Subjunctive, and the Condit. Mood suffixes, the vowel sounds *ı, i, u, ü,* are changed to *a* and *e* only.

(57g) The *2nd person singular* suffix is *ın, in, un,* or *ün,* and the *2nd person plural* is *ınız, iniz, unuz* or *ünüz,* for the *Past Attest. tense,* the vowels *ı, i, u, ü,* merging into the tense suffix (see similar remark in 57fff).

(57h) The *2nd Person SINGULAR* suffix is *"s.n"* (*sın, sin, sun, sün*) in the other four tenses. (57ee, 57eeee).

(57i) The *2nd Person PLURAL* is *"s.n.z"* (*sınız, siniz, sunuz, sünüz*).

(57ii) In Turkish the 2nd person singular and the 2nd person plural, have each their special functions. The 2nd person singular, which is in the most general use is used for *general address among the common class, and in endearing conversation between friends and equals.* The 2nd person plural is used for *regular address in polite circles, and for business purposes.*

(57j) The vowels between (*n* and *z*) or *s, n,* and *z* are sound letters and are subject to alteration. In all cases the suffixes are subject to Graduation of Sound (Ph. 19-23c).

(57k) **NOTE:** As explained in (70ccc) when sound letters have to be inserted they have to be in harmony with the last vowel in the *verb root,* and this governing of the sound also affects the vowels in the suffixes *nız, sın,* and *sınız,* changing them in some instances to *niz, nuz, nüz,* etc., to be in harmony with the rest of the word.

**(57kk)** *NOTE: The PERS VERBAL PRONOUN SUFFIXES in 57ee and 57eee are also added to nouns and adjectives, when the latter are conjugated with the verb TO BE (İMEK).*

**(57l)** *There is no specific suffix added to form the 3rd person singular.*

*When a verb root has had a tense and a mood suffix affixed it automatically becomes the 3rd person singular. If it is meant to be any other person than the 3rd, the appropriate suffix must be affixed.* Example:

> *yazacak* represents the future tense of the Indicative Mood
> *okuyor* represents the present tense of the Indicative Mood.

In the meantime *yazacak* also represents the 3rd person singular of that tense and mood and similarly *okuyor* represents the 3rd person singular of that tense and mood.

**(57dd)** When conjugating the primitive verb *İmek* with a noun pronoun, or adjective in the *Indef. tense* (only) it is necessary to add to the word *dır* and *dırlar* to form the 3rd pers. sing. and plural (see 62t).

**(57m)** By adding the signs of plurality *lar* or *ler* the 3rd person plural is obtained. Examples:

| | | | |
|---|---|---|---|
| *yazacak* | = he will write | *yazacaklar* | = they will write |
| *okuyor* | = he reads | *okuyorlar* | = they read |

Therefore apart from any gerundial moods, the student will detect when reading, that if the verb does not carry the endings of the first or second person, singular or plural, or the suffix *lar or ler it is in the 3rd person singular.*

**(57n)** NOTE: It is easy to distinguish a verb in the 3rd person singular, as it is a word generally ending with the verbal suffixes *yor, .r (ır), d. (dı), m.ş (mış), cek, se* or their mutated equivalent, without the first or second personal pronoun in the singular or plural, or the suffix *lar* for the 3rd person plural.

**(57p)** NOTE: When the verb is in the 3rd person plural ending with *lar* or *ler* it is easy to distinguish it from a noun in the plural (see 3) for it will contain one of the verbal suffixes followed by *lar* or *ler* whereas the noun will have the *lar* or *ler* added only.

(57q) All verb changes (tense and mood formation) are carried out in the 3rd person singular and *verb formation* is carried out with the *verb root.*

(58) The personal pronouns (*ben* (I), *sen* (thou), *o* (he, she, or it), *biz* (we), *siz* (you), *onlar* (they)), when used, are placed in front of the verb, but, as already mentioned, the person and number being represented by suffixes added to the root word, they are unnecessary except when the "doer" wishes to emphasize his personality. For instance, when one wishes to give an answer to a question such as: *"kim geliyor?"* (*"who* is coming?") it is necessary to use the personal pronoun: *ben geliyorum* (*I* am coming), whereas to the question, "geliyor *musunuz?"* ("are you coming?") it will be correct to leave out the personal pronoun and say simply, *"geliyorum"* ("coming am") (see also 50ll).

(58a) In the construction of the verb (*conjugation*), first the Negative (if any) then the Tense, then the Mood, then the Interrogative (if any) and finally the Person and Number, all being represented by suffixes, are affixed to the root word (*verb root*) (57 and 57d). Examples:

### Pres. Tense, Indic. Mood.

*geliyorum*　= (I) am coming (from *gelmek* "to come")

| | |
|---|---|
| *gel* | = root word |
| *i* | = sound letter (70ccc) |
| *yor* | = present tense |
| *u* | = euphony vowel of the pers. pronoun |
| *m* | = 1st. p. sing. pers. v. pro. suff. |

### Future Tense, Indic. Mood.

*geleceğiz*　= (we) will come (from *gelmek* "to come")

| | |
|---|---|
| *gel* | = root word |
| *e* | = opt. mood letter |
| *ceğ* | = future tense (ceğ * cek) |
| *i* | = euphony vowel of the pers. pronoun |
| *z* | = 1st p. pl. pers. v. pro. suff. |

(58b) The VERB also in all its aspects (verb conjugation, verb formation) and its governing of words, clauses, or sentences (verbal cases) is subject to the rules detailed in the chapters on *Phonetics (i.e. respective endings for HARD or SOFT verb roots, meaning the same, but changing their vowel sound to be euphonious with the last vowel sound of the word to which they are being added.*

## PRESENT TENSE

| | *görmek* = to see | *kazmak* = to dig |
|---|---|---|
| (Affirm.) | *görüyorum* = I see | *kazıyorum - I dig* |
| (Neg.) | *görm(ü)yorum* = I do not see | *kazm(ı) yorum* = I do not dig |
| (Interr.) | *görüyor muyum* = do I see | *kazıyor muyum* = do I dig |
| (Interr. Neg.) | *görm(ü)yor muyum* = do I not see | *kazm(ı)yor muyum* = do I not dig |

## INDEFINITE TENSE

| | *görürüm* | *gelirim* | *bakarım* | *uydururum* |
|---|---|---|---|---|
| | I will see | I will come | I will look | I will concoct |
| (root) | *gör* | *gel* | *bak* | *uydur* |
| (sound letter) | *ü* | *i* | *a* | *u* |
| (tense) | *r* | *r* | *r* | *r* |
| (euph. vow.) | *ü* | *i* | *ı* | *u* |
| (for "ben") | *m* | *m* | *m* | *m* |

*Examples:*

## PAST TENSE

| | *gördüm* | *geldim* | *baktım* | *uydurdum* |
|---|---|---|---|---|
| | I saw | I came | I looked | I concocted |
| (root) | *gör* | *gel* | *bak* | *uydur* |
| (tense) | *d* | *d* | *t* | *d* |
| (euph. vow.) | *ü* | *i* | *ı* | *u* |
| (for "ben") | *m* | *m* | *m* | *m* |

# FORMS OF THE VERB

Three of the four forms of the verb, the *Negative*, the *Interrogative*, and the *Interronegative* are represented by words (suffixes) which are interposed between the verb root and the personal suffix.

## THE NEGATIVE FORM

(59) For the *PRESENT PAST ATTESTATIVE*, and *PAST REPEATATIVE* Tenses the *NEGATIVE FORM* is obtained by placing *ma* (Hard) or *me* (Soft) next to the verb root before the *tense, mood,* and *personal* suffixes. Examples:

| | | | |
|---|---|---|---|
| *kalmak* | = to remain | | |

Present:

| | | | |
|---|---|---|---|
| *kalıyor* | = he/she remains | *kalm(ı)yor* | = he/she does not remain |

Past Attestative:

| | | | |
|---|---|---|---|
| *kaldı* | = he/she remained | *kalmadı* | = he/she did not remain |

Past Repeatative:

| | | | |
|---|---|---|---|
| *kalmış* | = it is said that he/she remained | *kalmamış* | = it is said that he/she did not remain |

(59a) **NOTE:** This form represents the tense in the negative and as such the 3rd person of that tense. *To obtain the other five persons of the tense the respective personal verbal suffixes are added to this form. This form is a general rule.*

(59b) For the *INDEFINITE TENSE* the *NEGATIVE FORM* is obtained by placing next to the verb root, before the mood and personal suffixes: *ma* (Hard) *me* (Soft) (not subject to graduation) for the 1st person singular. The tense letter "*r*" is dropped. Examples:

Indefinite Tense:

| | | | |
|---|---|---|---|
| *kalırım* | = I will stay | *kalmam* | = I will not stay |
| *yıkarım* | = I will demolish | *yıkmam* | = I will not demolish |
| *gelirim* | = I will come | *gelmem* | = I will not come |
| *gülerim* | = I will laugh | *gülmem* | = I will not laugh |

(59c) *ma* (Hard) *me* (Soft) (not subject to graduation), followed by *ız, iz* (personal suffix) preceded by servile letter "*y*" for the 1 st person plural. (See 57ee) Examples:

| | | | |
|---|---|---|---|
| *kalırız* | = we will stay | *kalmayız* | = we will not stay |
| *yıkarız* | = we will demolish | *yıkmayız* | = we will not demolish |
| *geliriz* | = we will come | *gelmeyiz* | = we will not come |
| *güleriz* | = we will laugh | *gülmeyiz* | = we will not laugh |

(59d) *ma* (Hard), *me* (Soft) (not subject to graduation) followed by "*z*" (the tense suffix) replacing the tense letter "*r*", followed by personal suffix for the 2nd and 3rd person singular, and plural. Examples:

## INDEFINITE TENSE

| | | | |
|---|---|---|---|
| *kalırsın* | = you will stay | *kalmazsın* | = you will not stay |
| *kalırsınız* | = you will stay | *kalmazsınız* | = you will not stay |
| *gelirsin* | = you will come | *gelmezsin* | = you will not come |
| *gelirsiniz* | = you will come | *gelmezsiniz* | = you will not come |
| *kalır* | = he will stay | *kalmaz* | = he will not stay |
| *kalırlar* | = they will stay | *kalmazlar* | = they will not stay |
| *gelir* | = he will come | *gelmez* | = he will not come |
| *gelirler* | = they will come | *gelmezler* | = they will not come |

(59e) For the *FUTURE TENSE* the *NEGATIVE FORM* is obtained by placing next to the verb root before the tense, mood, and personal suffixes: *ma* (Hard), *me* (Soft) followed by *ya* and *ye* respectively, to all persons.

(59ee) The "*ya*" and "*ye*" has no connection with the negative suffix *ma, me*. It is the (*a, e, ya, ye* (opt. 104aa)) which has been removed and placed in a fresh position owing to the fact that the particle for NEGATION has to be placed next to the verb root. Example:

| | | |
|---|---|---|
| *gelecek* = he/she will come | *gelmeyecek* | = he/she will not come |
| *kalacak* = he/she will stay | *kalmayacak* | = he/she will not stay |
| *yıkayacak* = he/she will wash | *yıkamayacak* | = he/she will not wash |
| *yürüyecek* = he/she will walk | *yürümeyecek* | = he/she will not walk |

(59f) I cannot emphasize too much how important it is in verb conjugation to take notice of the ending letter of the *Verb Root*, when suffixes are to be affixed. Let us take for instance, two verbs similar in construction, where one has an extra letter at the end, a vowel. Examples:

| Infinitive | : *yıkmak* | = to demolish | *yıkamak* | = to wash |
| Infinitive | : *kurmak* | = to establish | *kurumak* | = to get dry |

*Indefinite Tense:*

| Aff. | : *yıkarım* | = I will demolish | *yıkarım* | = I will wash |
| Interr. | : *yıkar mıyım* | = will I demolish | *yıkar mıyım* | = will I wash |
| Neg. | : *yıkmam* | = I will not demolish | *yıkamam* | = I will not wash |
| Int. neg. | : *yıkmaz mıyım* | = will I not demolish | *yıkamaz mıyım* | = will I not wash |

*Future Tense :*

| Aff. | : *kuracağım* | = I shall establish | *kuruyacağım* = | I shall get dried |
| Inter. | : *kuracak mıyım* | = shall I establish | *kuruyacak mıyım* | = shall I get dry |
| Neg. | : *kurmayacağım* | = I shall not establish | *kurumayacağım* | = I shall not get dry |
| Int.Neg. | : *kurmayacak mıyım* | | *kurumayacak mıyım* | =shall I not get dry |
| | | = shall I not establish | | |

(59g) Special features of the *Negative Form:*

(59h) When the 3rd person singular of the Indefinite tense in the *Negative* form immediately follows after the 3rd person singular in the *Affirmative* form it denotes **sudden occurrence** (see 73k). This is very much used.

(59i) When the 2nd person **absent** singular or plural of the Imperative mood is placed in the *Negative* form it also denotes *fear*, or contempt. Examples:

(fear)       *Aman beni görmesin!*
         = pity ! me let him not see (I hope he will not see me!)

(contempt)       *İstemem, gelmesin.*
         = I do not desire, let him not come. (I don't want him to come.)

(59j) The *Negative* form may also be used to denote the opposite of the statement. Examples:

| | |
|---|---|
| *Tembel değilim.* | = I am not lazy (actual meaning). |
| (See 68p) | I am laborious (implied meaning) |
| *Yalan söyle(mi)yorum.* | = I am not lying (actual meaning). |
| (See 59l) | I am telling the truth (implied meaning) |
| *Hızlı konuş(mu)yor.* | = He/she does not speak loudly (actual meaning). |
| (See 59l) | he/she speaks softly (implied meaning) |

(59k) The *negative* sense is *emphasized* or made *more definite* by the addition of certain adjectives (adverbs). Examples:

| | |
|---|---|
| **Gerçekten gelmedi.** | = Really he/she did not come |
| **Şüphesiz hata değildi.** | = Undoubtedly it was not a fault |

(59l) **NOTE:** *Though I have throughoat the book given the Particle for NEGATION as ma, me for Hard and Soft words, not subject to mutation, I must make mention that in the PRESENT and FUTURE tenses INDICATIVE MOOD and the INDEFINITE TENSE OPTATIVE MOOD the ma and me should actually be replaced by mı, mi, mu, or mü, according to the sound letter of the verb root to which it is being added.*

*It is again a question of harmony and to make a distinction between the interrogative and the negative I have kept to ma and me. I feel this would avoid confusion and once the student is master of fhe language he will acquire that special ease with which these subtleties are carried out (see 70d).*

## THE INTERROGATIVE FORM

(60) For the *present, past repeatative, indefinite* and *future* tenses the *interrogative form* is obtained by placing *mı (mi, mu, mü) after* the mood or tense and *in front* of the personal suffix. This does not apply to the 3rd Person Plural.

Examples:

## Affirmative

| Pres. tense | : *geliyorum* | = I come |
|---|---|---|
| Past rep. tense | : *gelmişim* | = it is said that I have come (or I came) |
| Indef. tense | : *gelirim* | = I will come |
| Future tense | : *geleceğim* | = I will come |

## Interrogative

| Present tense | : *geliyor muyum* | = do I come? |
|---|---|---|
| Past rep. tense | : *gelmiş miyim* | = is it said that I have come? (or I came) |
| Indef. tense | : *gelir miyim* | = will I come? |
| Future tense | : *gelecek miyim* | = will I come? |

(60a) The *Interrogative particle mı (mi, mu, mü) is not joined to the word it follows. It stands by itself, its vowel changing to be in harmony with the last vowel in the preceding word*, and personal suffixes, when following, are joined to it, preceded by the letter "y" in the 1st and 2nd pers. sing. and plural, as two vowels cannot come together. Examples:

*Geliyor mu?*　　　　　 = Is he/she coming?
comes he/she?

*O mu geldi?*　　　　　 = Is it he/she who came?
he/she? came

*Geliyor musunuz?*　　 = Are you coming?
coming? are you

*Gelir miyim?*　　　　　 = Will I come?
will come ? am I

(60b) *In the past attestative tense, the Indefinite tense of the optative mood and the 3rd person plural of all the tenses mı, (mi) is placed AFTER the personal suffixes.*

Examples:

## Affirmative

| | | |
|---|---|---|
| Past attest. tense (Ind.) | : *geldim* | = I have come (or I came) |
| Indef. tense (optative) | : *geleyim* | = let me come |
| 3rd pers. pl. pres. tense (Ind.) | : *geliyorlar* | = they are coming |
| 3rd pers. pl. past rept. tense (Ind.) | : *gelmişler* | = it is said they have come |
| 3rd pers. pl. indef. tense (Ind.) | : *gelirler* | = they will come |
| 3rd pers. pl. future tense (Ind.) | : *gelecekler* | = they will come |

## Interrogative

| | | |
|---|---|---|
| Past attest. tense | : *geldim mi* | = have I come? |
| Indef. tense (optative) | : *geleyim mi* | = may I come? |
| 3rd pers. pl. pres. tense | : *geliyorlar mı* | = are they coming? |
| 3rd pers. pl. past rept. tense | : *gelmişler mi* | = is it said that they have come? |
| 3rd pers. pl. indef. tense | : *gelirler mi* | = will they come? |
| 3rd pers. pl. future tense | : *gelecekler mi* | = will they come? |

(60c) The *interrogative* form in the *NARRATIVE* and *REPORTATIVE MOODS* is obtained by placing the interrogative particle before "*idi*", "*imiş*" or their mutated equivalents plus the RESPECTIVE PERSONAL VERBAL PRONOUN Suffixes. This is best learnt from the illustration of the conjugation of the verbs *imek* and *olmak* (see 62 and 63). Example:

| NARRATIVE MOOD INDEFINITE TENSE | REPORTATIVE MOOD FUTURE TENSE |
|---|---|
| *kalır mı idim* | *gelecek mi imişim* |
| *kalır mı idin* | *gelecek mi imişsin* |
| *kalır mı idi* | *gelecek mi imiş* |
| *kalır mı idik* | *gelecek mi imişiz* |
| *kalır mı idiniz* | *gelecek mi imişsiniz* |
| *kalır mı idiler* | *gelecek mi imişler* |

(60d) **NOTE:** It must be borne in mind that there is no suffix for the 3rd person (see 57l). When reference is made to the 3rd person singular I mean the form obtained by adding the tense and mood suffix or suffixes to the verb root. To carry out any of the three forms the verb must first be reduced to the 3rd person singular and then the required suffixes affixed (see 58a).

## SPECIAL FEATURES OF THE INTERROGATIVE FORM

(60e) When the *Past Attestative* is placed in the *interrogative* form and is followed by another verb in the *affirmative* form it denotes the *definite occurrence* of the second action on the *immediate completion* of the first one. This is very much used (see 71c). Example:

| Orhan | uyandı | mı | sokağa | çıkarız |
|-------|--------|-----|--------|---------|
| Orhan | woke up | ? | street to | go we |

(We will go out as soon as Orhan wakes up)

NOTE: *It is interesting to note that the first verb is placed in the past to denote its completion.*

When the *Indefinite tense* is put in the *interrogative form* it also denotes supplication (see 73j).

(60f) For the purpose of drawing attention to itself the *OBJECT* of the Verb may be placed in the interrogative form, instead of the verb. Examples:

| Kalemi | mi | istiyorsunuz? | (Is it the pen you wish to have?) |
|--------|-----|---------------|-----------------------------------|
| the pen | ? | want you | |
| (obj. case) | | | |

*Bugün mü geldin?*    = Is it to day that you hast come?

| Beni | mi | görmek | ist(i)yorsunuz? | = is it me (whom) you wish to see? |
|------|-----|--------|-----------------|-----------------------------------|
| me | ? | to see | desire you (70ccc) | |

(60g) The personal pronoun may be used in the interrogative and the verb left in the affirmative, when attention is to be drawn to the "doer". Example:

| Siz | mi | gidiyorsunuz? | = Is it you (who) are going? |
|-----|-----|---------------|------------------------------|

In both cases the *Interrogative* particle *(mı, mi, mu, mü)* instead of being placed after the tense suffix of the verb, is placed after the object (in the objective case), or after the personal pronoun, the subject (in the nominative case).

(60h) The interrogative particle is also used to denote amazement:

| *Birdenbire* | *bana* | *bağırmasın mı?* | = Did he not shout at me (suddenly)! |
|---|---|---|---|
| suddenly | me to | did he not shout | |

(The mood is the *imperative* 2nd person *singular absent,* which is the only mood employed to express this type of sentence.)

## INTERROGATIVE PRONOUNS

(60k) The following words also may be used to denote the interrogative, the verb then being placed in the affirmative. They are called the Interrogative Pronouns (see 55):

| *kaç* | = how many | *nereye* | = where to (Dat. Case) |
|---|---|---|---|
| *nasıl* | = how | *ne vakit* | = what time (when) |
| *hangi* | = which | *neyi* | = what (Obj. Case) |
| *nereyi* | = where (Obj. Case) | | |

Examples:

| *Hangi* | *eve* | *girdi?* | = Into which house did he go? |
|---|---|---|---|
| which | house *to* | he went in | |

| *Nereye* | *gidiyorsun?* | = Where are you going to? |
|---|---|---|
| where *to* | art thou going | |

| *Ne zaman* | *gelecek?* | = When will he come? |
|---|---|---|
| when | he/she will come | |

## THE INTERRONEGATIVE FORM

(61) For the *"present"*, *"past repeatative"* and *"indefinite"* tenses the *interronegative form* is obtained by placing *mı, mi* (only) after the tense and mood suffix and in front of the personal suffix of the Verb in the *negative form.*

(61a) *"mu"* is inserted (instead of any of the mutated forms of *mı* in the *present tense only.* Examples:

147

### Negative

| | | |
|---|---|---|
| Present tense | *: gelm(i)yorum (591)* | = I am not coming |
| Past repeat. tense | *: gelmemişim* | = it is said I have not come |
| Indefinite tense | *: gelmem* | = I will not come |
| Future tense | *: gelmeyeceğim (591)* | = I will not come |

### Interronegative

| | | |
|---|---|---|
| Present tense | *: gelm(i)yor muyum (591)* | = am I not coming |
| Past repeat. tense | *: gelmemiş miyim* | = is it said that I have not |
| Indefinite tense | *: gelmez miyim* | = will I not come (see 59d) |
| Future tense | *: gelmeyecek miyim* | = will I not come(see 591,59e and ee) |

(61b) In the *past attestative, the present* tense of the *Optative Mood* and the *3rd person plural* of all the tenses *(mı, mi)* is placed *after* the *personal* suffixes. Examples:

### Negative

| | | |
|---|---|---|
| 1st p. sg. past attest. tense | *: gelmedim* | = I have not come |
| 1st p. sg. indef. tense (opt.) | *: gelmeyeyim (591)* | = let me not come |
| 3rd pers. pl. pres. tense | *: gelmiyorlar (591)* | = they are not coming |
| 3rd pers. pl. past rept. tense | *: gelmemişler* | = it is said that they have not come |
| 3rd pers. pl. indef. tense | *: gelmezler* | = they will not come |
| 3rd pers. pl. future tense | *: gelmeyecekler* | = they will not come |

### Interronegative

| | | |
|---|---|---|
| 1st p. sg. past attest. tense | *: gelmedim mi* | = have I not come |
| 1st p. sg. indef. tense (opt.) | *: gelmeyeyim mi (591)* | = may I not come |
| 3rd pers. pl. pres.tense | *: gelmiyorlar mı (591)* | = are they not coming |
| 3rd pers. pl. past rept. tense | *: gelmemişler mi* | = is it said that they have not come |
| 3rd pers. pl. indef. tense | *: gelmezler mi* | = will they not come |
| 3rd pers. pl. future tense | *: gelmeyecekler mi (591)* | = will they not come |

(61c) The formation of the *Interronegative* form of the *Narrative, Reportative* and *Conditional* Moods *(idi, imiş, ise)* is best learnt from the illustration of the conjugation of the verbs *imek* and *olmak* (see 62, etc.).

(61cc) **NOTE:** Great care must be taken not to form the *Interronegative* from the *Interrogative* form, as in the latter some of the suffixes may have had their vowel sounds changed for reason of euphony, in the process of building up the word.

(61d) For exercise in the adaptation of the rules shown throughout the chapter of Verbs it is essential to begin by using words or Verbs (Verb roots) composed of the Vowels *a, ı,* and *e, i.* It is easier to carry out the Verb conjugation, in all tenses, moods and forms when such words or Verbs have been selected. The harmony of sounds of *ır, dı, mış, sa, cak* (tense terminations), *ma, me* (negative) and *mı, mi* (interrogative) is simple and regular. Examples:

Infinitive

| | | | |
|---|---|---|---|
| *kalmak* | = to remain | *yılmak* | = to fear |
| *gelmek* | = to come | *bilmek* | = to know |

# INDICATIVE MOOD

## INDEFINITE TENSE

| | | | | |
|---|---|---|---|---|
| Aff. | : *kalır* | *yılar* | *gelir* | *bilir* |
| Inter. | : *kalır mı* | *yılar mı* | *gelir mi* | *bilir mi* |
| Neg. | : *kalmaz* | *yılmaz* | *gelmez* | *bilmez* |
| Int. Neg. | : *kalmaz mı* | *yılmaz mı* | *gelmez mi* | *bilmez mi* |

## PAST TENSE ATTESTATIVE

| | | | | |
|---|---|---|---|---|
| Aff. | : *kaldı* | *yıldı* | *geldi* | *bildi* |
| Inter. | : *kaldı mı* | *yıldı mı* | *geldi mi* | *bildi mi* |
| Neg. | : *kalmadı* | *yılmadı* | *gelmedi* | *bilmedi* |
| Int. Neg. | : *kalmadı mı* | *yılmadı mı* | *gelmedi mi* | *bilmedi mi* |

## PAST TENSE REPEATATIVE

| | | | | |
|---|---|---|---|---|
| Aff. | : *kalmış* | *yılmış* | *gelmiş* | *bilmiş* |
| Inter. | : *kalmış mı* | *yılmış mı* | *gelmiş mi* | *bilmiş mi* |
| Neg. | : *kalmamış* | *yılmamış* | *gelmemiş* | *bilmemiş* |
| Int. Neg. | : *kalmamış mı* | *yılmamış mı* | *gelmemiş mi* | *bilmemiş mi* |

## FUTURE TENSE

| | | | | |
|---|---|---|---|---|
| Aff. | : *kalacak* | *yılacak* | *gelecek* | *bilecek* |
| Inter. | : *kalacak mı* | *yılacak mı* | *gelecek mi* | *bilecek mi* |
| Neg. | : *kalmayacak* | *yılmayacak* | *gelmeyecek* | *bilmeyecek* |
| Int. Neg. | : *kalmayacak mı* | *yılmayacak mı* | *gelmeyecek mi* | *bilmeyecek mi* |

## SUBJUNCTIVE MOOD
### INDEFINITE TENSE

| | | | | |
|---|---|---|---|---|
| Aff. | : *kalsa* | *yılsa* | *gelse* | *bilse* |
| Neg. | : *kalmasa* | *yılmasa* | *gelmese* | *bilmese* |

(61e) Whereas if words or verbs composed of *o, u* and *ö, ü* are taken the verb terminations and personal suffixes are subject to graduation and variation. The harmony is still regular and simple though graduated, but rather irregular in sound when all the four forms are put together.

INFINITIVE

*koymak* = to put      *kurumak* = to dry      *görmek* = to see      *yürümek* to walk

## INDICATIVE MOOD
### INDEFINITE TENSE

| | | | | |
|---|---|---|---|---|
| Aff. | : *koyar* | *kurur* | *görür* | *yürür* |
| Inter. | : *koyar mı* | *kurur mu* | *görür mü* | *yürür mü* |
| Neg. | : *koymaz* | *kurumaz* | *görmez* | *yürümez* |
| Int. Neg. | : *koymaz mı* | *kurumaz mı* | *görmez mi* | *yürümez mi* |

### PAST TENSE ATTESTATIVE

| | | | | |
|---|---|---|---|---|
| Aff. | : *koydu* | *kurudu* | *gördü* | *yürüdü* |
| Int. | : *koydu mu* | *kurudu mu* | *gördü mü* | *yürüdü mü* |
| Neg. | : *koymadı* | *kurumadı* | *görmedi* | *yürümedi* |
| Int. Neg. | : *koymadı mı* | *kurumadı mı* | *görmedi mi* | *yürümedi mi* |

### PAST TENSE REPEATATIVE

| | | | | |
|---|---|---|---|---|
| Aff. | : *koymuş* | *kurumuş* | *görmüş* | *yürümüş* |
| Int. | : *koymuş mu* | *kurumuş mu* | *görmüş mü* | *yürümüş mü* |
| Neg. | : *koymamış* | *kurumamış* | *görmemiş* | *yürümemiş* |
| Int. Neg. | : *koymamış mı* | *kurumamış mı* | *görmemiş mi* | *yürümemiş mi* |

### FUTURE TENSE

| | | | | |
|---|---|---|---|---|
| Aff. | : *koyacak* | *kuruyacak* | *görecek* | *yürüyecek* |
| Inter. | : *koyacak mı* | *kuruyacak mı* | *görecek mi* | *yürüyecek mi* |
| Neg. | : *koymayacak* | *kurumayacak* | *görmeyecek* | *yürümeyecek* |
| Int. Neg. | : *koymayacak mı* | *kurumayacak mı görmeyecek mi* | *yürümeyecek mi* |

## SUBJUNCTIVE MOOD
### PRESENT TENSE

| | | | | |
|---|---|---|---|---|
| Aff. | : *koysa* | *kurusa* | *görse* | *yürüse* |
| Neg. | : *koymasa* | *kurumasa* | *görmese* | *yürümese* |

# THE VERB *İMEK*

*imek* = to be

(62) Owing to the importance of the verb *imek* = *to be* as a *primitive* and also as an *auxiliary* verb it is essential to study the following with careful attention.

The verb *imek* = *to be, as a primitive verb,* is conjugated with a noun, a pers. pronoun, or an adjective, but out of the five usual tenses of the Indicative Mood it only provides the *Indefinite, Past Attestative,* and *Past Repeatative.* The remaining two, i.e. the *Present* and the *Future are provided by the verb olmak* = to be, become get.

The verb *imek* **as an auxiliary verb,** also provides the *Narrative, Reportative,* and *Conditional* Moods of the verb in general.

The suffixes *dı (di, du, dü), mış, (miş, muş, müş),* are primarily the *tense suffixes* for the *past attestative* and *past repeatative tense* respectively, for verbs in general including the *verb İMEK* as a *primitive verb.* Similarly *sa* and *se* are *tense suffixes* forming the *indefinite tense of the subjunctive mood* of verbs in general, and the *indefinite tense of the conditional mood* of the *verb İMEK* as a *primitive verb.*

uThey can also be the abbreviated forms of *idi, imiş,* and *ise,* which are used to obtain the *Narrative, Reportative,* and *Conditional moods* of the primitive verb in general, and the *Past Attestative* and *Past Repeatative tenses* of the *Optative, Potential,* and *Subjunctive Moods.*

(62a) When the verb *imek,* as a primitive verb, is conjugated in the above tenses with a **noun, a pers. pronoun,** or an **adjective,** it is actually correct to write it and use it as a separate word in the forms of *idi, imiş* and *ise,* for both hard and soft words, the "*i*" being the verb root of *imek.* Owing, however, to the fact that the accent of a word has to be on the *last* syllable (see Ph. 4), and as in the course of utterance the two words are inclined to merge into one another, the accent is transferred to the last syllable of *idi, imiş,* and *ise,* and this forces the initial "*i*" of these suffixes to be dropped and the abbreviated form joined to the noun, pronoun or adjective.

(62aa) When they are joined on to the word, *idi* and *imiş* become subject to the rules of graduation of sounds (see Ph. 28bb) and become *dı, di, du, dü,* and *mış, miş, muş, müş,* and *ise* becomes *sa, se* (see Ph. 8, 9) when added to consonant-ending words.

(62b) When the word ends with a vowel the "*i*" instead of being dropped is changed to a "*y*" (*ydi,* etc., and *ymiş,* etc.). Examples:

| | |
|---|---|
| *dana idi* or *danaydı* | = it was a calf |
| *sürü idi* or *sürüydü* | = it was a herd |
| *dana imiş* or *danaymış* | = it is said that it was a calf |
| *kuru imiş* or *kuruymuş* | = it is said that it was dry |
| *dana ise* or *danaysa* | = if it is a calf |
| *sürü ise* or *sürüyse* | = if it is a herd |

NOTE: When the word ends with *ı* or *i* it is preferable to use *ise* separately.

(62c) Rules (62 a, b, and d) also apply when *idi, imiş,* and *ise* are used to form the NARRATIVE, REPORTATIVE, and CONDITIONAL moods of Verbs.

(62d) *dı (di, du, dü)* as a tense suffix (see 71 a and b) and as an abbrev. form of *idi,* is subject to a further consonant change from *d* to *t* when the verb root noun, pronoun, or adjective ends with one of the sharp consonants (*ç, f, h, k, p, s, ş, t*) (Ph. 29 and 30). Examples:

## PAST (ATTESTATIVE) TENSE OF VERBS

(*dı,* etc.) and (*tı* etc.) as a past tense suffix (see 71)

| | | |
|---|---|---|
| *bırakmak* | *bıraktı* | = he/she left |
| *kaçmak* | *kaçtı* | = he/she ran away |
| *atmak* | *attı* | = he/she threw |
| *susmak* | *sustu* | = he/she kept silent |
| *görüşmek* | *görüştü* | = he/she interviewed |

# THE VERB İMEK CONJUGATED IN THE PAST TENSE WITH A NOUN, PRONOUN OR ADJECTIVE

(*dı*, etc.) and (*tı*, etc.) as the abbreviated form of "*idi*" (62a-62d)

| | | |
|---|---|---|
| *kabak idi* | or *kabaktı* | = it was a marrow |
| *vakit idi* | or *vakitti* | = it was time |
| *genç idi* | or *gençti* | = he/she was young |
| *Rus idi* | or *Rustu* | = he/she was Russian |
| *gümüş idi* | or *gümüştü* | = it was silver |

(62e) The *Affirmative* is obtained by placing *idi*, followed by the respective personal suffix, *after* the noun or adjective or:

(62f) Joined on, in which case the initial "*i*" is dropped when joined to a consonant-ending word, and changed to "*y*" when joined to a vowel-ending word.

(62g) (*di*, etc.) when joined on to the word is subject to graduation changes in harmony with the word (Ph. 28-28b). Examples:

| | | |
|---|---|---|
| *şişman idim* | or | *şişmandım* |
| *akıllı idim* | or | *akıllıydım* |

(62h) *The Interrogative is obtained by placing mı (mi, mu, mü) after the noun, pronoun, or adjective, followed by "idi" (plus the respective personal suffix) separately, or:*

(62i) Joined on, in which case the initial *i* is changed to *y* and the SECOND "*i*" graduated according to the vowel in *mı (mi, mu, mü)*.

(62j) (*mı*, etc.) is also subject to graduation to be in harmony with the last syllable of the word which it follows. Examples:

| (62k), (62j) | | (62i) | |
|---|---|---|---|
| *şişman mı idim* | or | *şişman mıydım* | = was I fat |
| *iyi mi idim* | or | *iyi miydim* | = was I good |
| *doğru mu idim* | or | *doğru muydum* | = was I right |
| *küçük mü idim* | or | *küçük müydüm* | = was I small |

153

(62k) The *Negative* is obtained by placing *after* the *noun, pronoun* or *adjective*, both soft or hard, the soft word "*değil*" followed by *idi* separately, or:

(62l) Joined on (in which case the initial "*i*" is dropped) plus the respective personal suffix.

(62m) Here *di* is in harmony with the last syllable of *değil* (Ph. 28-28b). Example:

| şişman | değil | idim | or | şişman değildim = I was not fat |
|--------|-------|------|-----|------------------------------|
| fat | not | was I | | |

(62n) The *Interronegative* is obtained by placing after the *noun, pronoun* or *adjective*, both soft and hard, the soft word *değil* followed by *mi* after which "*idi*" is placed separately, or:

(62p) Joined on, in which case the initial "*i*" is changed to "*y*" plus the respective personal suffix.

(62q) *Mi* and *idi*, in this form, will not be subject to mutation, as they follow and have to harmonize with *değil*, which does not change. The word is now neutral as far as the verb is concerned. Example:

| şişman | değil | mi | idim | or | şişman değil miydim = was I not fat? |
|--------|-------|-----|------|-----|-------------------------------------|
| fat | not | ? | was (I) | | |

(62r) *These rules of harmony are also applied throughout the verb conjugation, the word (noun, pronoun or adjective) being replaced by the verb root.*

### THE VERB İMEK CONJUGATED IN THE INDEFINITE TENSE WITH A NOUN, PRONOUN, OR ADJECTIVE

(62s) The Pers. Verbal Pronoun suffix (*um*, etc., *sın*, etc.), used in the present tense of the primitive verb in general (see 57ee) also forms the Indefinite tense of the verb *imek*.

The Indefinite tense of the verb İmek = to be (and in some cases "to do"), in Turkish is identical to the Present tense in English.

To form the Indefinite tense the *Pers. Verbal Pronoun* suffixes are added to the *noun, pronoun,* or *adjective* (see Chart 62t).

*In the pronunciation of the noun, pronoun, and adjective when conjugated in the Indefinite tense, a slight pause is effected between the word and the personal verbal pronoun suffix, though the latter is not written separately.*

When the word to be conjugated is a pers. pronoun, instead of a noun or adjective, it is no more a mere pers. pronoun, but a pronoun of a qualifying or complementary nature in relation to the verb.

It is here where one has to remember and differentiate between the pers. verbal pronouns, *ben, sen, o,* which are dropped (see 58) and *ben, sen, o,* the personal pronouns *which are now not the subject but the attribute of the subject.*

To illustrate this point in the examples hereunder, I have shown the subject, the pers. verbal pronouns, which are usually dropped, in brackets.

| *(Ben)* | *benim* | : (I) I am | = It is I |
| *(Ben)* | *adamım* | : (I) man am | = I am a man |
| *(Ben)* | *gencim* | : (I) young am | = I am young |
| *(Ben)* | *ben idim* | : (I) I was | = It was I |
| *(Ben)* | *adam idim* | : (I) man was | = I was a man |
| *(Ben)* | *genç idim* | : (I) young was | = I was young |

As we have seen in the above examples *benim* does not mean "I am" (see 62t), but "it is I" where "*ben*" is dropped, and it must on no account be confused with "*benim*" = my (see 50b).

(62ss) The **INDEFINITE** tense is used for both the **PRESENT**, and for the **FUTURE** when it is accompanied by a word denoting the future. (see 70e-j, 73c-i, 74b-c). Examples:

| *Saat* | *üçe* | kadar | evdeyim. | = I am at home till three o'clock. |
| hour | three *to* | till | home at am | |
| | (dat. case) | | | |

| *Yarın* | *öğleden* | *sonra* | *evdeyim.* |
| (tomorrow | noon from | after | home at am) |
| | (ablat. case) | | |

= Tomorrow I am at home after lunch (Tomorrow afternoon I shall be at home.)

## INDICATIVE MOOD OF THE VERB "imek = TO BE"
### INDEFINITE TENSE
### Conjugated with noun, adjective or personal pronoun

**\* for 1st person singular = I**

For consonant-ending words      = *um, im, um, üm* = I am
For vowel-ending words      = *yım, yim, yum, yüm* = I am

| **+** | **?** | **—** |
|---|---|---|
| *şişmanım* | *şişman mıyım* | *şişman değilim* |
| (I am fat) | (am I fat) | (I am not fat) |
| *benim* | *ben miyim* | *ben değilim* |
| It is I | Is it I | It is not I |
| *iyiyim* | *iyi miyim* | *iyi değilim* |
| I am good | am I good? | I am not good |

**\* for 2nd person singular = You**

For consonant- and vowel- ending words    = *sın, sin, sun, sün* = you are

| | | |
|---|---|---|
| *şişmansın* | *şişman mısın?* | *şişman değilsin* |
| you art fat | art you fat? | you art not fat |
| *iyisin* | *iyi misin* | *iyi değilsin* |
| you art good | art you good? | you art not good |

**\* for 3rd person singular = he/she/it**

For consonant- and vowel- ending words      = *dır, dir, dur, dür*
For sharp consonant-ending words      = *tır, tir, tur, tür*

| | | |
|---|---|---|
| *şişmandır* | *şişman mıdır* | *şişman değildir* |
| (he/she is fat) | (is he/she fat?) | (he/she is not fat) |
| *(o) o dur* | *(o) o mudur* | *(o) o değildir* |
| (It is he) | (Is it he?) | (It is not he) |
| *küçüktür* | *küçük müdür* | *küçük değildir* |
| (he/she is small) | (is he/she small?) | (he/she is not small) |

**\* for 1st person plural = we**

For consonant-ending words        = *ız, iz, uz, üz*       = we are
For vowel-ending words            = *yız, yiz, yuz, yüz* = we are

| + | ? | – |
|---|---|---|
| *biziz* | *biz miyiz* | *biz değiliz* |
| (It is us) | (Is it us?) | (It is not us) |
| *küçüğüz* | *küçük müyüz* | *küçük değiliz* |
| (we are small) | (are we small?) | (we are not small) |

**\* for 2nd person plural = you**

For consonant and vowel ending words = *sınız, siniz, sunuz, sünüz* = you are

| | | |
|---|---|---|
| *güzelsiniz* | *güzel misiniz* | *güzel değilsiniz* |
| (you are beautiful) | (are you beautiful?) | (you are not beautiful) |
| *boylusunuz* | *boylu musunuz* | *boylu değilsiniz* |
| (you are tall) | (are you tall?) | (you are not tall) |

**\* for 3nd person plural = they**

For consonant and vowel ending words = *dırlar, dirler, durlar, dürler* = they are
For sharp consonant and vowel ending words = *tırlar, tirler, turlar, türler* = they are

| | | |
|---|---|---|
| *güzeldirler* | *güzel midirler* | *güzel değildirler* |
| (they are beautiful) | (are they beautiful?) | (they are not beautiful) |
| *Türktürler* | *Türk müdürler* | *Türk değildirler* |
| (they are Turks) | (are they Turks?) | (they are not Turks?) |

**Note:** When the words (noun, pronoun or adjective) end with one of the sharp consonants (*ç, k, p, t*) and when the personal suffix begins with a vowel the (*ç, k, p, t*) change to (*b, c, d, ğ*) (see Ph. 31 ).

In the following chart I have given a variety of examples to familiarize the student with the appearance and the sound of the words.

# 62u PAST TENSE (ATTESTATIVE)
## Conjugated with noun, adjective or personal pronoun (see 62)

**\* BEN / I**

| Separate: | *ben idim* | = I was (+); | *mı/mi/mu/mü idim* | = was I (?) |
|---|---|---|---|---|
| | *değil idim* | = I was not (-); | *değil mi idim* | = Was I not (-/?) |
| Contraction: | *bendim* | = I was (+); | *mıydım/miydim/muydum/müydüm* | |
| | | | | = was I (?) |
| | *değildim* | = I wasn't (-); | *değil miydim* | = Wasn't I (-/?) |

| | | | |
|---|---|---|---|
| *şişmandım* | *şişman mıydım* | *şişman değildim* | *şişman değil miydim* |
| I was fat | was I fat | I was not fat | was I not fat |
| | | | |
| *kızgındım* | *kızgın mıydım* | *kızgın değildim* | *kızgın değil miydim* |
| I was angry | was I angry | I was not angry | was I not angry |
| | | | |
| *yorgundum* | *yorgun muydum* | *yorgun değildim* | *yorgun değil miydim* |
| I was tired | was I tired | I was not tired | was I not tired |

**\* SEN / YOU (singular)**

| Separate : | *sen idin* | = you were (+); | *mı/mi/mu/mü idin* | = were you (?) |
|---|---|---|---|---|
| | *değil idin* | = you were not (-); | *değil mi idin* | = were you not (-/?) |
| Contraction: | *sendin* | = you were (+); | *mıydın/miydin/muydun/müydün* | |
| | | | | = were you (?) |
| | *değildin* | = you weren't (-); | *değil miydin* | = weren't you (-/?) |

| | | | |
|---|---|---|---|
| *yatalaktın* | *yatalak mıydın* | *yatalak değildin* | *yatalak değil miydin* |
| you were bedridden | were you bedridden | you were not bedridden | were you not bedridden |
| | | | |
| *kılıbıktın* | *kılıbık mıydın* | *kılıbık değildin* | *kılıbık değil miydin* |
| you were henpecked | were you henpecked | you weren't henpecked | weren't you henpecked |
| | | | |
| *soğuktun* | *soğuk muydun* | *soğuk değildin* | *soğuk değil miydin* |
| you were cold | were you cold | you weren't cold | weren't you cold |

158

**\* O / HE (SHE/IT)**

Note: In the example below only he is used.

| Separate : | o idi | = he was (+); | mı/mi/mu/mü idi | = was he (?) |
| | değil idi | = he was not (-); | değil mi idi | = was he not (-/?) |
| Contraction: | oydu | = he was ( ); | mıydı/miydi/muydu/müydü | = was he (?) |
| | değildi | = he wasn't (-); | değil miydi | = wasn't he (-/?) |

| akıllıydı | akıllı mıydı | akıllı değildi | akıllı değil miydi |
| he was clever | was he clever | he was not clever | was he not clever |

| kuruydu | kuru muydu | kuru değildi | kuru değil miydi |
| he was dry | was he dry | he was not dry | was he not dry |

| boyluydu | boylu muydu | boylu değildi | boylu değil miydi |
| he was tall | was he tall | he was not tall | was he not tall |

**\* BİZ / WE**

| Separate : | biz idik | = we were (+); | mı/mi/mu/mü idik | = were we (?) |
| | değil idik | = we were not (-); | değil mi idik | = were we not (-/?) |
| Contraction: | bizdik | = we were (+); | mıydık/miydik/muyduk/müydük | =were we(?) |
| | değildik | = we weren't (-); | değil miydik | = weren't we (-/?) |

| güzeldik | güzel miydik | güzel değildik | güzel değil miydik |
| we were beautiful | were we beautiful | we were not beautiful | were we not beautiful |

| girgindik | girgin miydik | girgin değildik | girgin değil miydik |
| we were pushful | were we pushful | we were not pushful | were we not pushful |

| sürgündük | sürgün müydük | sürgün değildik | sürgün değil miydik |
| we were exiled | were we exiled | we were not exiled | were we not exiled |

**\* SİZ / YOU (plural)**

| Separate : | siz idiniz | = you were (+); | mı/mi/mu/mü idiniz | = were you (?) |
| | değil idiniz | = you were not (-); | değil mi idiniz | = were you not (-/?) |
| Contraction: | sizdiniz | = you were (+); | mıydınız/miydiniz/muydunuz/müydünüz | |
| | | | | = were you (?) |
| | değildiniz | = you weren't (-); | değil miydiniz | = weren't you ( /?) |

159

| | | | |
|---|---|---|---|
| *bitkindiniz* | *bitkin miydiniz* | *bitkin değildiniz* | *bitkin değil miydiniz* |
| you were exhausted | were you exhausted | you were not exhausted | were you not exhausted |

| | | | |
|---|---|---|---|
| *tetiktiniz* | *tetik miydiniz* | *tetik değildiniz* | *tetik değil miydiniz* |
| you were vigilant | were you vigilant | you were not vigilant | were you not vigilant |

| | | | |
|---|---|---|---|
| *küçüktünüz** | *küçük müydünüz* | *küçük değildiniz* | *küçük değil miydiniz* |
| you were small | were you small | you were not small | were you not small |

## * ONLAR / THEY

**Separate** : *onlar idiler* = they were (+); *mı/mi/mu/mü idiler*
= were they (?)

*değil idiler* = they were not (-); *değil mi idiler*
= were they not(-/?)

**Contraction** : *idiler* = they were (+); *mıydılar/miydiler/muydular/müydüler*
= were they (?)

*değildiler* = they weren't (-); *değil miydiler*
= weren't you (-/?)

| | | | |
|---|---|---|---|
| *neşeliydiler* | *neşeli miydiler* | *neşeli değildiler* | *neşeli değil miydiler* |
| they were cheerful | were they cheerful | they were not cheerful | were they not cheerful |

| | | | |
|---|---|---|---|
| *iyiydiler* | *iyi miydiler* | *iyi değildiler* | *iyi değil miydiler* |
| they were good | were they good | they were not good | were they not good |

| | | | |
|---|---|---|---|
| *köylüydüler* | *köylü müydüler* | *köylü değildiler/değillerdi* | *köylü değil miydiler / değiller miydi* |
| they were villagers | were they villagers | they were not villagers | were they not villagers |

* *Note change of vowel sound of tense and pers. suffix from ü in the interrog. to i in the negative, due to its having to be in harmony with the last vowel in the negative word değil which has been placed in front.*

## 62u PAST TENSE (REPEATATIVE)
### (It is said; in the interronegative the meaning is "Is it said I am not?")

**\* BEN / I**

**Separate** : *ben imişim* = It is said I was
**Contraction for closed syllables** : *mışım, mişim, muşum, müşüm*
**Contraction for open syllables** : *ymışım, ymişim, ymuşum, ymüşüm*

*zayıf imişim*
it said I was weak

*zayıf mı imişim*
is it said I was weak

*zayıf değil imişim*
it is said I was not weak

*zayıf değil mi imişim*
is it said I was not weak

*zayıfmışım*
it is said I was weak

*zayıf mıymışım*
is it said I was weak

*zayıf değilmişim*
it is said I wasn't weak

*zayıf değil miymişim*
is it said I wasn't weak

**\* SEN / YOU (singular)**

**Separate** : *sen imişsin* = It is said you were
**Contraction for closed syllables** : *mışsın, mişsin, muşsun, müşsün*
**Contraction for open syllables** : *ymışsın, ymişsin, ymuşsun, ymüşsün*

*zayıf imişsin*
it said you were weak

*zayıf mı imişsin*
is it said you were weak

*zayıf değil imişsin*
it is said you were not weak

*zayıf değil mi imişsin*
is it said you were not weak

*zayıfmışsın*
it is said you were weak

*zayıf mıymışsın*
is it said you were weak

*zayıf değilmişsin*
it is said you were not weak

*zayıf değil miymişsin*
is it said you were not weak

**\* O / HE/SHE/IT**

Note: In the example below only he is used.

| Separate | : *o imiş* = It is said he was |
| Contraction for closed sylables | : *mış, miş, muş, müş* |
| Contraction for open sylables | : *ymış, ymiş, ymuş, ymüş* |

*zayıf imiş*
it said he was weak

*zayıf mı imiş*
is it said he was weak

*zayıf değil imiş*
it is said he was not weak

*zayıf değil mi imiş*
is it said he was not weak

*zayıfmış*
it is said he was weak

*zayıf mıymış*
is it said he was weak

*zayıf değilmiş*
it is said he wasn't weak

*zayıf değil miymiş*
is it said he wasn't weak

**\* BİZ / WE**

| Separate | : *biz imişiz* = It is said we were |
| Contraction for closed sylables | : *mışız, mişiz, muşuz, müşüz* |
| Contraction for open sylables | : *ymışız, ymişiz, ymuşuz, ymüşüz* |

*zayıf imişiz*
it said we were weak

*zayıf mı imişiz*
is it said we were weak

*zayıf değil imişiz*
it is said we were not weak

*zayıf değil mi imişiz*
is it said we were not weak

*zayıfmışız*
it is said we were weak

*zayıf mıymışız*
is it said we were weak

*zayıf değilmişiz*
it is said we weren't weak

*zayıf değil miymişiz*
is it said we weren't weak

**\* SİZ / YOU (plural)**

| | |
|---|---|
| **Separate** | : *siz imişsiniz*    = It is said you were |
| **Contraction for closed sylables** | : *mışsınız, mişsiniz, muşsunuz, müşsünüz* |
| **Contraction for open sylables** | : *ymışsınız, ymişsiniz, ymuşsunuz, ymüşsünüz* |

*güzel imişsiniz*
it said you were beautiful

*güzel mi imişsiniz*
is it said you were beautiful

*güzel değil imişsiniz*
it is said you were not beautiful

*güzel değil mi imişsiniz*
is it said you were not beautiful

*güzelmişsiniz*
it is said you were beautiful

*güzel miymişsiniz*
is it said you were beautiful

*güzel değilmişsiniz*
it is said you were not beautiful

*güzel değil miymişsiniz*
is it said you were not beautiful

**\* ONLAR / THEY**

| | |
|---|---|
| **Separate** | : *onlar imişler*    = It is said they were |
| **Contraction for closed sylables** | : *mışlar, mişler, muşlar, müşler* |
| **Contraction for open sylables** | : *ymışlar, ymişler, ymuşlar, ymüşler* |

*zengin imişler*
it said they were rich

*zengin mi imişler*
is it said they were rich

*zengin değil imişler*
it is said they were not rich

*zengin değil mi imişler*
is it said they were not rich

*zenginmişler*
it is said they were rich

*zengin miymişler*
is it said they were rich

*zengin değilmişler*
it is said they weren't rich

*zengin değil miymişler*
is it said they weren't rich

163

# CONDITIONAL MOOD

## PRESENT TENSE

### * BEN / I

| | |
|---|---|
| Separate | : *isem* |
| Contraction for closed sylables | : *sam, sem* |
| Contraction for open sylables | : *ysam, ysem* |

*zayıf isem*  
*zayıfsam*  
if I am weak

*zayıf değil isem*  
*zayıf değilsem*  
if I am not weak

*iyi isem*  
*iyiysem*  
if I am good

*iyi değil isem*  
*iyi değilsem*  
if I'm not good

### * SEN / YOU (singular)

| | |
|---|---|
| Separate | : *isen* |
| Contraction for closed sylables | : *san, sen* |
| Contraction for open sylables | : *ysan, ysen* |

*zayıf isen*  
*zayıfsan*  
if you are weak

*zayıf değil isen*  
*zayıf değilsen*  
if you aren't weak

*iyi isen*  
*iyiysen*  
if you are good

*iyi değil isen*  
*iyi değilsen*  
if you aren't good

### * O / HE/SHE/IT

**Note:** In the examples below only he is used.

| | |
|---|---|
| Separate | : *ise* |
| Contraction for closed sylables | : *sa, se* |
| Contraction for open sylables | : *ysa, yse* |

*zayıf ise*  
*zayıfsa*  
if he is weak

*zayıf değil ise*  
*zayıf değilse*  
if he isn't weak

| *iyi ise* | *iyi değil ise* |
| *iyiyse* | *iyi değilse* |
| if he is good | if he isn't good |

## * BİZ / WE

**Separate** : *isek*
**Contraction for closed sylables** : *sak, sek*
**Contraction for open sylables** : *ysak, ysek*

| *zayıf isek* | *zayıf değil isek* |
| *zayıfsak* | *zayıf değilsek* |
| if we are weak | if we aren't weak |

| *iyi isek* | *iyi değil isek* |
| *iyiysek* | *iyi değilsek* |
| if we are good | if we aren't good |

## * SİZ / YOU (plural)

**Separate** : *iseniz*
**Contraction for closed sylables** : *sanız, seniz*
**Contraction for open sylables** : *ysanız, yseniz*

| *zayıf iseniz* | *zayıf değil iseniz* |
| *zayıfsanız* | *zayıf değilseniz* |
| if you are weak | if you aren't weak |

| *iyi iseniz* | *iyi değil iseniz* |
| *iyiyseniz* | *iyi değilseniz* |
| if you are good | if you aren't good |

## * ONLAR / THEY

**Separate** : *iseler*
**Contraction for closed sylables** : *salar, seler*
**Contraction for open sylables** : *ysalar, yseler*

| *zayıf iseler* | *zayıf değil iseler* |
| *zayıfsalar* | *zayıf değilseler* |
| if they are weak | if they aren't weak |

| *iyi iseler* | *iyi değil iseler* |
| *iyiyseler* | *iyi değilseler* |
| if they are good | if they aren't good |

# THE VERB *OLMAK* AS A PRIMITIVE VERB

(63) The verb *Olmak* (to get, to become, to be) is a primitive verb when it is conjugated with a **noun, adjective,** or a **verbal adjective** (see 32b), these latter being placed in front of the verb (see also **imek** = to be).

(63a) **NOTE:** In general conversation between friends the 2nd person singular "you" is invariably used (see 57ii).

For full details of TENSES and MOODS.

## INDICATIVE MOOD
### OF THE VERB *OLMAK* = TO GET, TO BECOME, TO BE

### PRESENT TENSE

| affirmative | | negative | interrogative |
|---|---|---|---|
| *oluyorum* | = I get (I'm getting) | *olmuyorum* | *oluyor muyum* |
| *oluyorsun* | = you get (you're getting) | *olmuyorsun* | *oluyor musun* |
| *oluyor* | = he/she/it gets (he/she/it is getting) | *olmuyor* | *oluyor mu* |
| *oluyoruz* | = we get we're getting | *olmuyoruz* | *oluyor muyuz* |
| *oluyorsunuz* | = you get (you're getting) | *olmuyorsunuz* | *oluyor musunuz* |
| *oluyorlar* | = they get (they're getting) | *olmuyorlar* | *oluyorlar mı* |

**NOTE:** But not "*I am*". *I am* is derived from "**imek**" to be shown in (62)

### PAST TENSE (ATTESTATIVE)

| affirmative | | negative | interrogative |
|---|---|---|---|
| *oldum* | = I got, or became | *olmadım* | *oldum mu* |
| *oldun* | = you got, or became | *olmadın* | *oldun mu* |
| *oldu* | = he/she/it got, or became | *olmadı* | *oldu mu* |
| *olduk* | = we got, or became | *olmadık* | *olduk mu* |
| *oldunuz* | = you got, or became | *olmadınız* | *oldunuz mu* |
| *oldular* | = they got, or became | *olmadılar* | *oldular mı* |

**NOTE:** But not "*I was*". *I was* is obtained from "**imek**" = to be, shown in (62)

## PAST TENSE (REPEATATIVE)

NOTE: *It is said that I got,* etc., repeat for all other persons and only got is used.

| affirmative | | negative | interrogative |
|---|---|---|---|
| *olmuşum* | = I got | *olmamışım* | *olmuş muyum* |
| *olmuşsun* | = you got | *olmamışsın* | *olmuş musun* |
| *olmuş* | = he/she/it got | *olmamış* | *olmuş mu* |
| *olmuşuz* | = we got | *olmamışız* | *olmuş muyuz* |
| *olmuşsunuz* | = you got | *olmamışsınız* | *olmuş musunuz* |
| *olmuşlar* | = they got | *olmamışlar* | *olmuşlar mı* |

## INDEFINITE TENSE

| affirmative | | negative | interrogative |
|---|---|---|---|
| *olurum* | = I will get become, or be | *olmam* | *olur muyum* |
| *olursun* | = you get, become, be | *olmazsın* | *olur musun olur* |
| | = he/she get, become, be | *olmaz* | *olur mu* |
| *oluruz* | = we will get, become, be | *olmayız* | *olur muyuz* |
| *olursunuz* | = you get, become, be | *olmazsınız* | *olur musunuz* |
| *olurlar* | = they get, become, be | *olmazlar* | *olurlar mı* |

## FUTURE TENSE

| affirmative | | negative | interrogative |
|---|---|---|---|
| *olacağım* (k = ğ Ph. 31) | = I will get, become, be | *olmayacağım* or ol*muyacağım, (etc see 59l)* | *olacak mıyım* |
| *olacaksın* | = you will get, become, be | *olmayacaksın* | *olacak mısın* |
| *olacak* | = he will get, become, be | *olmayacak* | *olacak mı* |
| *olacağız* (k = ğ Ph. 31) | = we will get, become, be | *olmayacağız* | *olacak mıyız* |
| *olacaksınız* | = you will get, become, be | *olmayacaksınız* | *olacak mısınız* |
| *olacaklar* | = they will get, become, be | *olmayacaklar* | *olacaklar mı* |

NOTE: To form the interronegative see (61) to (61b) and (61cc).

# NARRATIVE MOOD

## PRESENT TENSE

NOTE: The first form (where *idi* is separate) may be conjugated, if so desired. This applies to all such compound forms.

|  | **affirmative** | **negative** | **interrogative** |
|---|---|---|---|
| *oluyor idim* or *oluyordum* | =I was becoming, getting | *olmuyor idim* *olmuyordum* | *oluyor mu idim* *oluyor muydum* |
| *oluyor idin* | =you were becoming, getting | *olmuyordun* | *oluyor muydun* |
| *oluyor idi* | =he/she/it was becoming, getting | *olmuyordu* | *oluyor muydu* |
| *oluyor idik* | =we were becoming, getting | *olmuyorduk* | *oluyor muyduk* |
| *oluyor idiniz* | =you were becoming, getting | *olmuyordunuz* | *oluyor muydunuz* |
| *oluyor idiler* | =they were becoming, getting | *olmuyorlardı* | *oluyor muydular* |

## PAST TENSE (ATTESTATIVE)

| **affirmative** |  | **negative** | **interrogative** |
|---|---|---|---|
| *oldu idim* or *olduydum* | =I had become or got | *olmadı idim* *olmadıydım* | *oldu mu idim* *oldu muydum* |
| *oldu idin* | =you had become, or got | *olmadıydın* | *oldu muydun* |
| *oldu idi* | =he/she/it had become, got | *olmadıydı* | *oldu muydu* |
| *oldu idik* | =we had become, got | *olmadıydık* | *oldu muyduk* |
| *oldu idiniz* | =you had become, got | *olmadıydınız* | *oldu muydunuz* |
| *oldu idiler* or *olduydular,* or *oldulardı* | =they had become, got | *olmadıydılar* | *oldu muydular* |

## PAST TENSE (REPEATATIVE)
### (It is said ...)

|  | **affirmative** | **negative** | **interrogative** |
|---|---|---|---|
| *olmuş idim* or *olmuşdum* | =I had got, become | *olmamış idim* *olmamıştım* | *olmuş mu idim* *olmuş muydum* |
| *olmuş idin* | =you hadst got, become | *olmamıştın* | *olmuş muydun* |
| *olmuş idi* | =he/she/it had got, become | *olmamıştı* | *olmuş muydu* |
| *olmuş idik* | =we had got, become | *olmamıştık* | *olmuş muyduk* |
| *olmuş idiniz* | =you had got, become | *olmamıştınız* | *olmuş muydunuz* |
| *olmuş idiler* or *olmuşdular* or *olmuşlardı* | =they had got, become | *olmamışlardı* | *olmuş muydular* |

# INDEFINITE TENSE

| affirmative | | negative | interrogative |
|---|---|---|---|
| *olur idim*<br>or *olurdum* | = I used to, or would become, got | *olmaz idim*<br>*olmazdım* | *olur mu idim*<br>*olur muydum* |
| *olur idin* | = you used to, or would become, got | *olmazdın* | *olur muydun* |
| *olur idi* | = he used to, or would become, got | *olmazdı* | *olur muydu* |
| *olur idik* | =we used to, or would become, got | *olmazdık* | *olur muyduk* |
| *olur idiniz* | = you used to, or would become, got | *olmazdınız* | *olur muydunuz* |
| *olur idiler*<br>or *olurlardı* | =they used to, or would become, got | *olmazlardı* | *olur muydular* |

# FUTURE TENSE

| affirmative | | negative | interrogative |
|---|---|---|---|
| *olacak idim*<br>or *olacaktım* | = I will have been, become, got | *olmayacaktım* | *olacak mıydım* |
| *olacaktın* | = you will have been, become, got | *olmayacaktın* | *olacak mıydın* |
| *olacaktı* | = he/she/it shall have been, become, got | *olmayacaktı* | *olacak mıydı* |
| *olacaktık* | = we will have been, become, got | *olmayacaktık* | *olacak mıydık* |
| *olacaktınız* | = you will have been, become, got | *olmayacaktınız* | *olacak mıydınız* |
| *olacaklardı* | = they will have been, become, got | *olmayacaklardı* | *olacak mıydılar* |

# REPORTATIVE MOOD
## (It is said that ...)

### PRESENT TENSE

| affirmative | | negative | interrogative |
|---|---|---|---|
| *oluyor imişim*<br>or *oluyormuşum* | = I am getting, becoming | *olmuyor imişim*<br>*olmuyormuşum* | *oluyor mu imişim*<br>*oluyor muymuşum* |

### PAST TENSE (REPEATATIVE)

| affirmative | | negative | interrogative |
|---|---|---|---|
| *olmuş imişim*<br>or *olmuşmuşum* | = I had become, got | *olmamış imişim*<br>*olmamışmuşum* | *olmuş mu imişim*<br>*olmuş muymuşum* |

### INDEFINITE TENSE

| affirmative | | negative | interrogative |
|---|---|---|---|
| *olur imişim*<br>or *olurmuşum* | = I would become, get, be | *olmaz imişim*<br>*olmazmışım* | *olur mu imişim*<br>*olur muymuşum* |

## FUTURE TENSE

| affirmative | | negative | interrogative |
|---|---|---|---|
| *olacak imişim* | = I will get, become, be | *olmayacak imişim* | *olacak mı imişim* |
| or *olacakmışım* | | *olmayacakmışım* | *olacak mıymışım* |

## POTENTIAL MOOD (85)
### (Obligation)

### INDEFINITE TENSE

| affirmative | | negative | interrogative |
|---|---|---|---|
| *olmalıyım* | = I must become, get, be | *olmamalıyım* | *olmalı mıyım* |

### PAST TENSE (ATTESTATIVE)

| affirmative | | negative | interrogative |
|---|---|---|---|
| *olmalı idim* | =I ought to have become, got, been | *olmamalı idim* | *olmalı mı idim* |
| or *olmalıydım* | | *olmamalıydım* | *olmalı mıydım* |

### PAST TENSE (REPEATATIVE)
#### (It is said that ...)

| affirmative | | negative | interrogative |
|---|---|---|---|
| *olmalı imişim* | = I should have become, got, been | *olmamalı imişim* | *olmalı mı imişim* |
| or *olmalıymışım* | | *olmamalıymışım* | *olmalı mıymışım* |

NOTE: The 3rd pers. is usually used to denote "probability" as:

*Ahmet evde olmalı*                        = Ahmet should be at home.

*By the addition of "dır" the statement is made certain (see also 67n).*

## SUBJUNCTIVE MOOD

### INDEFINITE TENSE

| affirmative | | negative |
|---|---|---|
| *olsam* | = if I be, become, or get | *olmasam* |
| *olsan* | = if you be, become, get | *olmasan* |
| *olsa* | = if he/she be, becomes, gets | *olmasa* |
| *olsak* | = if we be, become, get | *olmasak* |
| *olsanız* | = if you be, become, get | *olmasanız* |
| *olsalar* | = if they be, become, get | *olmasalar* |

## PAST TENSE (ATTESTATIVE)

**affirmative**

| | |
|---|---|
| *olsa idim* | = if I were, became, got |
| or *olsaydım,* etc. | |
| *olsa idin* | = if you were, became, got |
| *olsa idi* | = if he/she were, became, got |
| *olsa idik* | = if we were, became, got |
| *olsa idiniz* | = if you were, became, got |
| *olsa idiler* | = if they were, became, got |
| or *olsaydılar* | |
| or *olsalardı* | |

**negative**

*olmasa idim*
or *olmasaydım*
*olmasaydın*
*olmasaydı*
*olmasaydık*
*olmasaydınız*
*olmasaydılar*
or *olmasalardı*

## PAST TENSE (REPEATATIVE)
### (It is said that ...)

**affirmative**

| | |
|---|---|
| *olsa imişim* | = if I had been, become, got |
| or *olsaymışım,* etc. or | |
| *olsa imişsin* | = if you had been, become, got |
| *olsa imiş* | = if he/she had been, become, got |
| *olsa imişiz* | = if we had been, become, got |
| *olsa imişsiniz* | = if you had been, become, got |
| *olsa imişler* | = if they had been, become, got |
| or *olsalarmış* | |

**negative**

*olmasa imişim*
or *olmasaymışım*
*olmasaymışsın*
*olmasaymış*
*olmasaymışız*
*olmasaymışsınız*
*olmasaymışlar*

# CONDITIONAL MOOD

The formation and conjugation of this mood is exactly the same as that of the Indicative Mood with the addition of the conditional suffix and some more tenses.

## PRESENT TENSE

**affirmative**

| | |
|---|---|
| *oluyor isem* | = if I am becoming/getting |
| or *oluyorsam* | |

**negative**

*olmuyor isem*
or *olmuyorsam*

## PAST TENSE (ATTESTATIVE)

**affirmative**
*oldu isem*  = if I have become/got/been

**negative**
ol*madı isem* or *olduysam*
*olmadıysam*

## PAST TENSE (REPEATATIVE)
### (It is said that ...)

**affirmative**
*olmuş isem*  = if I have become/got/been
or *olmuşsam*

**negative**
ol*mamış isem*
*olmamışsam*

## INDEFINITE TENSE

**affirmative**
*olur isem*  = if I become/get/be
or *olursam*

**negative**
*olmaz isem*
*olmazsam*

## CONDITIONAL OBLIGATION

**affirmative**
*olmalı isem*  = if I must become/get/b
or *olmalıysam*

**negative**
ol*mamalı isem*
*olmamalıysam*

## IMPERATIVE MOOD

### PRESENT TENSE

| **affirmative** | | **negative** | |
|---|---|---|---|
| *ol* | = be you, become you, get you | *olma* | = be you not |
| *olunuz* | = be ye, become ye, get ye | *olmayınız* | = be you not |
| *olsun* | = let him be, become, get | *olmasın* | = be he not |
| *olsunlar* | = let them be, become, get | *olmasınlar* | = be they not |

## INTERROGATIVE AND INTERRONEGATIVE

There is no interrogativenor interronegative to 2nd person singular and plural "Present", but there is to the 2nd person singular and plural "Absent" (see 103).

| olsun *mu* | = must he be? | olmasın *mı* | = must he not be? |
| olsunlar *mı* | = must they be? | olmasınlar *mı* | = must they not be? |

## OPTATIVE MOOD

### INDEFINITE TENSE (also used for Present Tense)

| **affirmative** | | **negative** |
|---|---|---|
| olayım | = let me be, become, get | olmayayım |
| olasın | = be you (free will) | olmayasın |
| ola | = let her/him be, become, get | olmaya |
| olalım | = let us be, become, get | olmayalım |
| olasınız | = be you (free will) | olmayasınız |
| olalar | = let them be, become, get | olmayalar |

### PAST TENSE (ATTESTATIVE)

| **affirmative** | | **negative** |
|---|---|---|
| olaidim | = I wish I had been, become, got | olmaya idim |
| or olaydım | | or olmayaydım |
| ola idin | = I wish you had been, become, got | olmayaydın |
| ola idi | = I wish he/she had been, become, got | olmayaydı |
| ola idik | = I wish we had been, become, got | olmayaydık |
| ola idiniz | = I wish you had been, become, got | olmayaydınız |
| ola idiler | = I wish they had been, become, got | olmayaydılar |
| or olaydılar | | |

### PAST TENSE (REPEATATIVE) (It is said that ...)

| **affirmative** | | **negative** |
|---|---|---|
| ola imişim | = I wished I had been/become/got | olmaya imişim |
| or olaymışım | | or olmayaymışım |
| ola imişsin | = I wished you had been/become/got | olmayaymışsın |
| ola imiş | = I wished he had been/become/got | olmayaymış |
| ola imişiz | = I wished we had been/become/got | olmayaymışız |
| ola imişsiniz | = I wished you had been/become/got | olmayaymışınız |
| ola imişler | = I wished they had been/become/got | olmayaymışlar |
| or olaymışlar | | or olmayalarmış |

# THE VERB *BULUNMAK*
## [to be (in a state of), to be confronted with]

(64) This verb is used to describe the state of a person placed in the presence of a fact, or a completed action. It is a reflexive verb.

(64a) As a primitive verb it is conjugated with the *verbal noun* (12) or an ordinary noun, both being first placed in the locative case.

(64b) As an auxiliary verb it is conjugated with the past participle of a primitive verb. The conjugation is similar to 66e.

The difference between the verbs *bulunmak* and *olmak* (see 66) is that the *latter* one is *carrying out* the completion, and the former one is faced with the completed action. Examples:

| | |
|---|---|
| *bitirmiş oldum* | = I had finished |
| *bitirmiş bulundum* | = I had been in a state of having finished |

I am placed with the result of the completed action.

It is conjugated in exactly the same way as olmak or any other primitive verb.


## PRESENT PARTICIPLE OF *OLMAK* AND *BULUNMAK*

(65) The *present participle* is *obtained* by adding *AN* to the verb roots *ol* and *bulun*.

| | |
|---|---|
| *olan* | = who or which is |
| *bulunan* | = who or which is in a state of |

(65a) It may be followed by or preceded by a noun. Example:

*İstanbul'da olan* = that which is in Istanbul

(65b) It may be used by itself. Example:

*olan oldu* = what has happened has happened

(65c) It is preceded by an adjectiveor a past participle. Example:

**görmüş**    *olan*    *var* = there are people who have seen (the incident is implied)
(seen    who is    there is)

## PAST PARTICIPLE OF *OLMAK* AND *BULUNMAK*

The past participle is obtained by adding muş to the verb root. Example:

*olmuş*        = got, become, been
*bulunmuş*    = been in a state of

**NOTE:** *The past participle must not be confused with the third person of the past tense repeatative or with the reportative mood.*

(65e) The conjugation of the *Past Participle* of the verbs *olmak, bulunmak*, and of any other primitive verb is carried out with the help of the three auxiliary verbs *olmak, imek,* and *bulunmak*. This form is used when the action is *definitely* completed, giving us all the "perfect" tenses of the English verb conjugation. Examples:

*olmuş*        = been
*bulunmuş*    = been in a state of
*görmüş*     = seen
*bitirmiş*    = finished

Let us take the future tense of the verbs olmak and bulunmak, for instance:

*olacağım*                 = I will be
*iyi olmuş olacağım*     = I will have recovered
*bitirmiş olacağım*       = I will have finished
*bulunmuş olacağım*    = I will be in a state of having been
*iyi olmuş bulunacağım*  = I will be in a state of having become well
*görmüş bulunacağım*   = I will be in a state of having seen

(65f) This participle asserts the *definite, absolute completion* of the action.

(65g) It is generally used together with the *Present Participle* and denotes that the ***action***
is *already completed.*

    *olmuş olan*      = which has been completely finished

## THE VERB OLMAK AS AN AUXILIARY VERB

(conjugated with a past participle of a primitive verb)

(66) The verb ***olmak*** is an *AUXILIARY* verb as well as a *PRIMITIVE* verb.

It is an auxiliary verb when it is conjugated with the *past participle* of any other *primitive
or modified* verb, and as such this form of conjugation gives us the definite state of
completion or realization of the action of the verb. For instance when ***bitiririm*** is used, a
simple statement that the ACTION WILL BE TAKING PLACE, is made in the
*indefinite* tense, whereas, when ***bitirmiş olurum*** is used an assertion is made, in the
Indefinite tense, that the ACTION WILL BE COMPLETED. Examples:

    *siz hazırlanınız,*    ben de    o zamana kadar    işimi ***bitirmiş olurum***.
    (you get ready,    I too    to that time till    my work completed I would be)
    = you get ready, I also will have completed my work by that time

If we used ***bitiririm*** = "I will finish", it would be a mere statement, whereas ***bitirmiş
olurum*** = "I will have finished", is a definite statement that the work will be finished by a
stated time.

(66a) The verb ***olmak*** is also conjugated, in the *Past tense attest. only, with the 3rd pers.
of the Indefinite* and *Future tenses* (see 32b and c), where the sense of *actuality* (Indef.)
and *anticipation* (Future) is entertained.

The Negative sense is obtained:

(66b) Either by placing the Verb *olmak* in the *negative form*; thus *denying* the
*completion* of the action in a simple manner.

(66bb) Or by placing the "*past participle*" in the *negative form* and *keeping* the Verb
**olmak** in the *affirmative* form; thus asserting that the action is *not completed* or *still
incomplete (drawing attention to this fact).*

(66c) A question is usually put in the *INTERROGATIVE* form of this form of verb when anxiety is felt as to the completion of the action.

| Yarın | saat | beşte | işini | **bitirmiş** | olur musun? |
|-------|------|-------|-------|------|------|
| (tomorrow | hour | at five | your work | completed | will you be?) |

Will you have your work completed by 5 o'clock tomorrow?

(66d) But it would be proper and perhaps is of more common usage to express the same question as hereunder, using the verb in the *"facultative"* sense of the *PAST PARTICIPLE* in question, in this case of *bitirmiş* = completed.

The *POTENTIAL MOOD* (facultative) being *bitirebilmek* = to know to finish (to be able to finish), (see 107). Examples:

| Yarın saat | beşte | işini | bitirebilir misin |
|-----------|-------|-------|-------|
| | | | (or bitirebilecek misin)? |
| tomorrow hour | five at | work thy wilt | you be able to finish? |
| ( | | | or *will you be able to finish*)? |

*(Will you be able to finish your work by 5 o'clock to-morrow?*

(66e) *The Following are some of the most used Tenses of the Verb Olmak conjugated as an Auxiliary Verb with a Past Participle of a Primitive Verb:*

### INDEFINITE TENSE (INDICATIVE MOOD)

| Aff. | : işimi bitirmiş olurum | = I will have my work finished |
|------|-------------------------|-------------------------------|
| Neg. | : işimi bitirmemiş olurum | = I will have my work unfinished |
| | or | not finished |

### PAST TENSE (ATTESTATIVE) (INDICATIVE MOOD)

| Aff. | : işimi bitirmiş oldum | = I had my work finished |
|------|------------------------|--------------------------|
| Neg. | : işimi bitirmemiş oldum | = I had my work unfinished |

### FUTURE TENSE (INDICATIVE MOOD)

| Aff. | : işimi bitirmiş olacağım | = I shall have my work finished |
|------|---------------------------|----------------------------------|
| Neg. | : işimi bitirmemiş olacağım | = I shall have my work unfinished |

177

### INDEFINITE TENSE (NARRATIVE MOOD)

**Aff.**  : *işimi bitirmiş olurdum*   = I would have had my work finished
**Neg.**  : *işimi bitirmemiş olurdum*   = I would have had my work unfinished

### FUTURE TENSE (NARRATIVE MOOD)

**Aff.**  : *işimi bitirmiş olacaktım*   = I should have my work finished
**Neg.**  : *işimi bitirmemiş olacaktım*   = I should have my work unfinished

### INDEFINITE TENSE (CONDITIONAL MOOD)

**Aff.**  : *işimi bitirmiş olursam*   = If I would have my work finished
**Neg.**  : *işimi bitirmemiş olursam*   = If I would have my work unfinished

### PAST TENSE (ATTESTATIVE) (Conditional Mood)

**Aff.**  : *işimi bitirmiş olsa idim*   = if I had finished my work
**Neg.**  : *işimi bitirmemiş olsa idim*   = if I had my work unfinished

### PAST TENSE (ATTESTATIVE) (OPT. MOOD, BİTİRMİŞ OLMAK)

**Aff.**  : *işimi bitirmiş olaydım*   = I wish I had my work finished
**Neg.**  : *işimi bitirmemiş olaydım*   = I wish I had my work unfinished

The *negative* of the simple form (66a) is easily obtained by using the negative of the respective tense of the Primitive Verb. For instance the last example will be expressed as:

### PAST TENSE (ATTESTATIVE) (OPT. MOOD, BİTİRMEK)

*(k    )* *işimi bitirmeyeydim* = I wish I had not finished my work. (see 105d)

# EMPHATIC FORM OF THE VERB

(67) In the Turkish language EMPHASIS is obtained by using:

*Brief* and *pointed statements,*
*Interrogative,* or *exclamatory* forms,
The *potential* (obligatory) and *imperative* moods, and

(67a) *DIR (tır, dur, dür)* meaning "IS" after the tense and person suffixes with certain tenses.

(67b) When speaking of an action the emphasis is placed either on the action, or, to draw attention, on the "Doer" of the action.

(67c) The emphasis is placed on the "Doer" by using the respective *PERSONAL PRONOUN* in front of the verb, or in any appropriate place in the sentence, and the verb is left in the affirmative form.

(67d) In the INTERROGATIVE and INTERRONEGATIVE forms the EMPHASIS is placed on the subject, the object of the verb, or on any one of the other verbal cases of the verb by placing the word of INTERROGATION *mı, (mi, mu, mü)* after the subject, or the direct. object (objective case) of the verb or the verbal case in question, the verbs being kept in the AFFIRMATIVE or NEGATIVE respectively. Examples:

simple form emphatic form

| | | | |
|---|---|---|---|
| *geliyorum* | = (I) am coming | *ben geliyorum* | = **I** am coming (I do come) |
| *gördün* | = (you) have seen | *sen gördün* | = **you** you have seen |
| *gidecek* | = (he) will go | *o gidecek* | = **he** will go |
| *gidecek miyim?* | = will I be going? | *ben mi gideceğim* | = Is it **I** who will be going? |
| *geldi mi?* | = has he come? | *o mu geldi?* | = is it **he** who came? |

In the following examples the emphasis, in the interrogative form, is on the subject, or on the various verbal cases of the verb:

*GELEN*      *O*      *MU İDİ?*                      = was it he who came?
(who came    he?    was he)

*ANKARA'DAN* (Dat. Case)   MI *GELİYORSUNUZ?*      = Are you coming from Ankara?
(Ankara from?           coming are you)

| | | | |
|---|---|---|---|
| *BANA* (Dat. Case) | *MI* | *HİTAP EDİYORSUNUZ?* = Are you addressing me? | |
| (I to | ? | address you are doing) | |

*ANKARA'DAN BURCU MU*    *GELDİ?* = Is it Burcu who came from Ankara?
(Ankara from    *Burcu*   ?    *came she*)

*BENİ* (Obj. Case)    *Mİ*    *İSTİYORSUNUZ?* = Is it me who you want?
(me        ?    wanting are you)

*BENIM İÇİN* (Caus. Case)   *Mİ*    *İSTEDİ?* = Is it for me that he asked (it)?
(I of    for (for me)      ?    wanted he)

*Sinan*   *BENİMLE* (Inst. Case)   *Mİ*     *GELECEK?*
(Sinan I of with (with me)    ? she    will come)
= Is it with me Sinan will be coming?

(67e) Emphasis is also obtained by placing an adjective or a noun in front of the verb.

(67 f) *EMPHASIS* is also obtained by adding the *EMPHATIC* word *KENDİ* = *(self)* to which is affixed the respective personal pronoun suffix, preceded by the personal pronoun, this latter, however, not being essential. Examples:

*ben*     *kendim*     *bitiririm* = I will finish (it) myself
(I       myself     finish will I)

*KENDİNİZ*     *Mİ*     *BİTİRECEKSİNİZ* = will you yourself finish (it)?
(yourself       ?       finish will you)

*(ONLAR)*   *KENDİLERİ*    *Mİ*   *yapacaklar* = will they themselves do (it)?
(they      themselves     ?    do will they)

NOTE: In the last example onlar could be omitted.

(67g) The verb is also placed in the *Emphatic* form by *stressing* the *fact* of the action having been *completed*, the verb being placed in the *past participle* form, and conjugated with the verbs *olmak* or *bulunmak* (see 64b).

Examples:

| OLAYI | GÖRMÜŞ | BULUNUYORUM = I myself actually saw the incident |
|---|---|---|
| the incident | seen | in the state of am I |

| OLAYI | GÖRMÜŞ | OLDUM = I happened to have seen the incident |
|---|---|---|
| the incident | seen | been have I |

(67h) Emphasis is also obtained by:

1. Using the *present participle* of any verb in a repetitive form, the first one being in the *nominative* case and the second one in the *dative* case. This form is used to convey the idea that the action of the verb is being shared by many persons or things at one time. Examples:

*askere giden gidene* = people were enrolling one after the other

| *çocuklardan* | bağıran | bağıra*na* |
|---|---|---|
| (the children **from** | who was shouting | who was shouting **to**) |
| = the children were continually shouting | | |

2. Using the *present participle* followed by the *past participle*, thus emphasising the fact of the action having been commenced and completed.

| *vaktiyle* | *yapan yapmış* = the one who started the job completed it |
|---|---|
| in previous time | making has made |

## THE POSITION AND FUNCTION OF *DIR* (*TIR*, ETC.)

(67i) *dır (dir, dur, dür) -tır (tir, tur, tür)* is believed to be the suffix of the 3rd person of a now extinct verb.

It forms the *3rd person singular* and *plural* of the *Indefinite (present) tense* of the verb *imek*, when the conjugation is carried out with a *noun, pronoun,* or *objective*. It is translated as "is".

(67j) *d* changes to *t* when the *verb root, noun,* or *adjective* ends with a *sharp* consonant (see Ph. 29 to 30b). Example:

*iyidir* = he/she is well          *küçüktür* = he/she is small

The negative "*değil*" may be followed by "*dir*", but this latter is not essential, being used, usually, only for emphasis (see 67a). Examples:

| | |
|---|---|
| *İbrahim evde değildir.* | = İbrahim is not at home. |
| *İbrahim evde değil.* | = İbrahim is not at home. |

It is not used in the regular verb conjugation, but when *supposition, certainty,* or *definiteness* is to be expressed it is added to the *Present, Future,* and *Past Tense Repeatative.*

(67k) It is added to the *present tense* when reference is made to a *supposition* about people, as:

*Şu an uyuyorlardır.* = At this moment they are sleeping.

(67l) It is added to the *future tense* to denote *certainty*, as:

*Bundan böyle çalışacaktır.*
= From now onwards he will definitely work.

(67m) It is added to the *past repeatative* to denote *certainty* uor *strong belief* of the occurrence, though it is not being witnessed or ascertained by the "speaker". **This form is in every day use in Turkish.** Example:

*Tarık şimdiye kadar Londra'ya varmıştır.*
= Tarık has arrived in London by now.

(67n) It is added to the present tense, past tense repeatative, and future tense of the impersonal and unipersonal verbs, and the 3rd pers. of the Indef. tense, Pot. (oblig.) mood of Olmak-to be, for the purpose of emphasis. Example:

| *Bu işi* | *çabuk* | *yapmanız* | *lazımdır.* |
|---|---|---|---|
| this work | quick | doing your | necessary is |

= Your doing this work quickly is necessary.
(it is necessary for you to do this work quickly.)

# VAR, YOK, GEREK, DEĞİL

**VAR** = there is (claiming possession, asserting existence or presence)
**YOK** = there is not (denying possession, existence or presence)
**GEREK** = it is necessary (stating the necessity of)
**DEĞİL** = it is not (denying the state of being)

(68) These four words may be used in a sentence in their primitive meaning, both in the *affirmative* or *interrogative* forms, as shown hereunder. Examples:

## INDICATIVE MOOD
## PRESENT TENSE

| | |
|---|---|
| *sokakta bir adam var* | = *there is* a man in the street |
| *orada kimse var mı?* | = *is there* anybody there? |
| *kimse yok* | = there is nobody |
| *kimse yok mu?* | = isn't there anybody? |
| *öyle gerek* | = it is necessarily so |
| *öyle mi gerek?* | = is it necessary (to be) like that? |
| *burada değil* | = he/she/it is not here |
| *burada değil mi?* | = is he/she/it not here? |

(68a) *dir (dır, dur, dür) tır (tir, tur, tür)* = "is" may be added for emphasis, to the present tense in all the forms of the four words *var, yok, gerek,* and *değil*. Each word has a particular part to play and will be treated separately.

### VAR = TO HAVE          YOK = NOT TO HAVE

(68b) These two words with the help of the *auxiliary* verb *imek*, form the verb *"to have"* and *"not to have"* (possession). They are conjugated in the three tenses of the *Indicative* Mood: *Indefinite, past attestative, past repeatative,* and the *present tense* of the *Conditional Mood.*

(68c) The *"negative"* form of *var* is obtained by replacing it by *yok* instead of adding *ma* or *me*, the usual negation suffixes. Examples:

| (Simple form) | | (Simple form) | |
|---|---|---|---|
| *benim var* | = I have | *benim yok* | = I have not |

| benim var idi | = I had | benim yok idi = I had not |
|---|---|---|
| benim var imiş | = it is said I had | benim yok imiş = it is said that I had not |
| benim var ise | = if I had | benim yok ise = if I had not |
| | (Emphasis, 67a) | (Emphasis, 67a) |
| benim vardır | = I have | benim yoktur = I have not |

(68d) The *"Interrogative"* form is obtained by placing *"mı"* after *"var"*. Example:
*benim var mı? = have I?*

(68e) The *"Interronegative"* form is obtained by placing "ma" after yok. Example:
*benim yok mu? = have I not?*

(68f) The *mı, mi, mu, mü* can also be placed after the noun, whether the noun is the object or the subject of the verb (see 10).
To form the conjugation:

(68g) No. 1. The *"object possessed"* is placed next to the *personal pronoun*, both making a *DEFINITIVE COMBINATION "*, i.e. the *personal pronoun* is placed in the *genitive case*, the noun, singular or plural, definite or indefinite is placed in the *accusative case* plus the def. pers. pronoun suffixes (see 50h, i, j, k), and both are placed in front of *var*.

(68h) *var* does not change for any person, the person being shown firstly by the personal pronoun and secondly by the definitive personal pronoun suffixes of the noun (50h).
(68i) The personal pronouns may be omitted (see 50l)

## INDICATIVE MOOD
### PRESENT TENSE

(68h) *I (etc.) have a book*                (68i) *I (etc.) have books*
(my) (book pers. suffix)              books (with pers suffix)
(there is)                           (there is)

Usually omitted

| | | | | | | |
|---|---|---|---|---|---|---|
| 1st Pers. Sing. | : | *ben* | im | *kitabım var* | *kitaplarım* | *var* |
| 2nd Pers. Sing. | : | *sen* | in | *kitabın var* | *kitapların* | *var* |
| 3rd Pers. Sing. | : | *on* | un | *kitabı var* | *kitapları* | *var* |
| 1st Pers. Plu. | : | *biz* | im | *kitabımız var* | *kitaplarımız* | *var* |
| 2nd Pers. Plu. | : | *siz* | in | *kitabınız var* | *kitaplarınız* | *var* |
| 3rd Pers. Plu. | : | *onlar* | ın | *kitabı var* | *kitapları* | *var* |

(68i) *I (etc.) have three books*
(*three*) (*see 46*) (*book, pers. suffix*) (*there is*)

*Usually omitted*

| | | | | | |
|---|---|---|---|---|---|
| 1st Pers. Sing. | : | *ben* | *im* *üç* | *kitabım* | *var* |
| 2nd Pers. Sing. | : | *sen* | *in* *üç* | *kitabın* | *var* |
| 3rd Pers. Sing. | : | *on* | *un* *üç* | *kitabı* | *var* |
| 1st Pers. Plu. | : | *siz* | *im* *üç* | *kitabımız* | *var* |
| 2nd Pers. Plu. | : | *siz* | *in* *üç* | *kitabınız* | *var* |
| 3rd Pers. Plu. | : | *onlar* | *ın* *üç* | *kitabı* | *var* |

(68j) The conjugation can also be made in a different way. No. 2. The *Personal Pronoun* is placed in the *Locative* case (see 18), the noun left in the *Nominative* case (definite or indefinite, singular or plural), followed by "*var*" which does not change throughout the conjugation. The Pers. Pronoun in the Loc. case is never omitted.

## INDICATIVE MOOD
### PRESENT TENSE

*I* (etc.) *have a book* (indefinite)

| | | | |
|---|---|---|---|
| 1st Pers. Sing. | : | *bende* | *kitap var* |
| 2nd Pers. Sing. | : | *sende* | *kitap var* |
| 3rd Pers. Sing. | : | *onda* | *kitap var* |
| 1st Pers. Plu. | : | *bizde* | *kitap var* |
| 2nd Pers. Plu. | : | *sizde* | *kitap var* |
| 3rd Pers. Plu. | : | *onlarda* | *kitap var* |
| | | *in me* | *book there is* |

*I* (etc.) *have one book* or *three books* (definite)

| | | | | | | |
|---|---|---|---|---|---|---|
| 1st Pers. Sing. | : | *bende* | *bir* | or | *üç* | *kitap var* |
| 2nd Pers. Sing. | : | *sinde* | *bir* | or | *üç* | *kitap var* |
| 3rd Pers. Sing. | : | *onda* | *bir* | or | *üç* | *kitap var* |
| 1st Pers. Plu. | : | *bizde* | *bir* | or | *üç* | *kitap var* |
| 2nd Pers. Plu. | : | *sizde* | *bir* | or | *üç* | *kitap var* |
| 3rd Pers. Plu. | : | *onlarda* | *bir* | or | *üç* | *kitap var* |
| | | *in me* | *one* | or | *three* | *book there is* |

(68k) The *PAST tense ATTESTATIVE* is obtained by placing *separately "idi"* or *jointly "dı"* after "*var*" in both forms

## INDICATIVE MOOD
### PAST TENSE ATTESTATIVE

|              | *Form (g) No. 1*           | *Form (j) No. 2*          |
|--------------|----------------------------|---------------------------|
| I had a book | = *benim kitabım var **idi*** | *bende bir kitap var **idi*** |
|              | = *benim kitabım **vardı*** | *bende bir kitap **vardı*** |

(68kk) The *PAST tense REPEATATIVE* is obtained by placing *separately "imiş"* or *jointly "mış"* after "*var*" in both forms.

## INDICATIVE MOOD
### PAST TENSE REPEATATIVE (It is said that ...)

|              | *Form (g) No. 1*              | *Form (j) No. 2*             |
|--------------|-------------------------------|------------------------------|
| I had a book | = *benim kitabım var **imiş*** | *bende bir kitap var **imiş*** |
|              | = *benim kitabım **varmış*** | *bende bir kitap **varmış*** |

(68l) The *indeftnite* and the *future tense* is obtained with the help of the verbs *olmak* or *bulunmak.*

### INDEFINITE TENSE

|          | Form (g) No. 1                  | Form (j) No. 2            |
|----------|---------------------------------|--------------------------|
| I have   | = ben*im bir kıtabım bulunur*   | *bende bir kitap bulunur* |
| a book   | = ben*im bir kitabım olur*      | not with *olmak*          |

### FUTURE TENSE

|             | Form (g) No. 1                    | Form (j) No. 2              |
|-------------|-----------------------------------|----------------------------|
| I shall have | = ben*im bir kitabım bulunacak*  | *bende bir kitap bulunacak* |
| a book      | = ben*im bir kitabım olacak*      | *bende bir kitap olacak*    |

**NOTE:** There is that slight **nuance** which is to be borne in mind with reference to *olmak* and *bulanmak* (see 64 & 64b).

(68m) *olmak and bulunmak* (reflexive) will give many other moods.

(68mm) NOTE: Both verbs (*olmak, bulunmak*) are conjugated in the 3rd Person Singular.

## CONDITIONAL MOOD

(68n) *The present tense of the Conditional Mood is obtained by placing "ise" separately or "sa" jointly after "var".*

### PRESENT TENSE

|  | Form (g) No. 1 | Form (j) No. 2 |
|---|---|---|
| If I have a book | = *benim kitabım var ise* | *bende bir kitap var ise* |
|  | = *benim kitabım varsa* | *bende bir kitap varsa* |

### *DEĞİL* = NO, NOT

(68p) The word *değil* is used to denote *negation*. It serves to form the *negative* and *interronegative* forms of the verb *imek* when that verb is conjugated with a NOUN, PRONOUN, or ADJECTIVE. Examples:

| | |
|---|---|
| *yalan değil* = | it is not a lie |
| *doğru değil* = | it is not correct |
| *onlar değil* = | it is not they |

### *GEREK* = NECESSARY

The word *GEREK* is used in various ways:

Examples:

| *İnsanlar* | *için* | *çalışmak* | *gerektir.* | = It is necessary for man to work. |
|---|---|---|---|---|
| man | for | to work | necessary is | |

| *Senin* | *nene* | | *gerek.* | = What does it matter to you. |
|---|---|---|---|---|
| of yours | to your what | | necessary | |

187

*GEREK* is also used as a *Conjunction.*

a)
| *LÜZUM* | = necessity |
| *İMKÂN* | = possibility |
| *ZARURET* | = need |

(b)
| *LÂZIM* | = necessary |
| *MÜMKÜN* | = possible |
| *ZARURÎ* | = imperative |

(68r) Other *nouns* (a) or *adjectives* (b) such as the above are used with *var* and *yok* (a), and *dır* and *değil* (b) respectively. Examples:

| *buna* | *lüzum* | *var* | = there is need for this |
| (to this) | need | there is (dat. case) | |

| *bu* | *zarurî* | *dir* | = this is needed |
| (this) | needful | is (nom. case) | |

| *lâzım* | *değildir* | | = it is not wanted |
| (necessary) | is not (nom. case) | | |

## THE FUNCTION OF THE VERB *ETMEK*
### (to actuate, to perform, to do - not to emphasis)

(68s) The verb *etmek* is placed after an *abstract* or an ordinary *noun* to form a verb of that noun. Examples:

| *telefon* | = telephone | *telefon etmek* | = to telephone |
| *tembih* | = advise | *tembih etmek* | = to advise |
| *tecrit* | = insulation | *tecrit etmek* | = to insulate |
| *ikram* | = offer | *ikram etmek* | = to offer |
| *göç* | = migration | *göç etmek* | = to migrate |

(68t) It is usually written *separately* when the word is of more than *one syllable*. It is *added to the word* when it is a word of *one syllable*, and if there is only *one consonant* following the vowel in this syllable *this will be doubled*, so that the original sound of the word is not interfered with. *This rule, howeoer, is not always applied.* Examples:

| *zan* | = belief | *zannetmek* | = to believe |
| *af* | = forgiveness | *affetmek* | = to forgive |
| *sulh* | = peace | *sulhetmek* | = to make peace |
| *sarf* | = spending | *sarfetmek* | = to spend |

(68u) There are *certain words of two syllables* of *foreign origin* which *drop the last vowel* when added to the verb *etmek*. Example:

| | | | |
|---|---|---|---|
| *lütuf* | = grace, kindness | *lütfetmek* | = to be kind |
| *zikir* | = mentioning | *zikretmek* | = to mention |

(68uu) **Note:** These same words (68u) are subject to the *same structural change* when placed in the *objective, accusative* (in Def. Com.), *dative,* and *possessive cases.* (see 23f). Examples:

**nominative case**                **accusative/objective case**

| | | | |
|---|---|---|---|
| *zikir* | = mentioning | *zikri* | = the mentioning |
| *lütuf* | = kindness | *lütfu* | = the kindness |

**dative case**                **possessive case**

| | | | |
|---|---|---|---|
| *zikre* | = to the mentioning | *zikrin* | = of the mentioning |
| *lütfa* | = to the kindness | *lütfun* | = of the kindness |

**Note:** Such nouns are marked in the Dictionary. There are some words of Turkish origin following the same rule.

(68uuu) They retain their original form in the other cases. Examples:

**nominative case**        **locative case**        **ablative case**

| | | | | |
|---|---|---|---|---|
| *zikir* | = mentioning | *zikir*de = in mentioning | *zikir*den = from mentioning |
| *lütuf* | = kindness | *lütuf*ta = in kindness | *lütuf*tan = from kindness |

## UNIPERSONAL VERBS

I purposely use the expression unipersonal to distinguish these verbs from the impersonal ones.

(69) They are very few and always used. Some are given hereunder:

| | |
|---|---|
| *iktiza etmek* | = to require, to be required |
| *icapetmek* | = to be, or to become obligatory, unavoidable |
| *lâzım gelmek* | = to be, or become necessary |

(69a) They are conjugated in the 3rd person of all the tenses and in all moods except the imperative mood, bearing in mind that there is no 3rd person pronoun (*o* = it) in front of the verb. Examples:

*Bu*       (*işin böyle olması*)       *iktiza eder.*
this       (work *of* like this being)       required it is
(gen. c.) (acc c.)
 = It is required that this work should be like this.

*Böyle*       *yapmak*       *icap ediyor muydu?*   = Was it necessary to do it this way?
like this       to do       was it necessary?

*Bu*   (*işin terk edilmesi*)       *lâzım*       *gelmez.*
this (work of giving up)       necessary       come will not
                                 = It is not necessary to give up this work.

## IMPERSONAL VERBS

(69b) These verbs are conjugated in the 3rd person singular with the respective nouns in front of the verb, in all the moods except the "*Imperative*".

| | |
|---|---|
| *güneş batmak* | = to set (the sun) |
| *güneş çıkmak* | = to rise (the sun) |
| *gök gürlemek* | = to thunder |
| *şimşek çakmak* | = to flash (the lightning) |
| *rüzgâr esmek* | = to blow (the wind) |
| *yağmur yağmak* | = to rain |

## FIGURATIVE VERBS

(69c) These verbs are conjugated in the ordinary manner and form and in all persons.

| | |
|---|---|
| *kalmak* | = to remain *(actual meaning)* |
| *mecbur kalmak* | = to be obliged (compulsion) (figurative) |
| *zorunda kalmak* | = to be compelled (figurative) |

| | |
|---|---|
| *görmek* | = to see *(actual meaning)* |
| *gün görmek* | = to live comfortably (figurative) |
| *iş görmek* | = to work (figurative) |
| *memleket görmek* | = to travel (figurative) |

| | |
|---|---|
| *çekmek* | = to pull *(actual meaning)* |
| *aşk çekmek* | = to be love-sick (figurative) |
| *güçlük çekmek* | = to experience difficulty (figurative) |
| *elem çekmek* | = to suffer (figurative) |
| *beyaza çekmek* | = to make a fair copy of (figurative) |
| *kahır çekmek* | = to suffer (figurative) |

| | |
|---|---|
| *düşmek* | = to fall *(actual meaning)* |
| *zayıf düşmek* | = to get thin (figurative meaning) |
| *fakir düşmek* | = to become poor (figurative meaning) |

## THE MAIN TENSES OF THE VERB

(70) There are five tenses in the Turkish verb conjugation, i.e.: *present, past attestative, past repeatative, indefinite (geniş zaman), and the future.*

(70a) To understand this special division one must always bear in mind that the "*doer*" is either a mere agent in the enactment of the action (76) or is carrying out the action with his desire and free will (104), secondly that the action has either taken place in the presence or the absence of the "*speaker*" *(past attestative tense)* and *(past repeatative tense)* and finally that the action may be of an habitual or of a volitional character both in the *present* and in the *future (indefinite tense)*.

# THE PRESENT TENSE (ŞİMDİKİ ZAMAN)
## (yor)

(70b) THE PRESENT TENSE represents the time when the action of the verb is actually taking place. Example:

Yağmur yağıyor.                    = It rains or it is raining.

(70bb) This tense also represents the *progreseive form of the verb*. *Example:*

Çocuklar bahçede oynuyorlar.       = The children play in the garden,    or
                                     The children are playing in the garden

(70c) *It is formed by adding*
*yor* to the verb root, this in the meantime forming the *3rd person singular* (see 571). To obtain the other *5 persons* the *respective personal verbal pronoun suffixes* are added to the *3rd person singular* (see 57ee).

(70cc) When the verb root ends with the *vowels a* or *e* these latter are changed to *ı* and *i* respectively. The *other vowels do not change*. Examples:

| | | |
|---|---|---|
| yarala(mak) | yaralıyor | = he injures |
| lekele(mek) | lekeliyor | = he stains |
| koru(mak) | koruyor | = he protects |
| yürü(mek) | yürüyor | = he walks |

(70ccc) A sound letter *ı, i, u,* or *ü,* is inserted between the *verb root* and the *suffix* when the *verb root ends* with a *consonant,* the *one in harmony* with the *last vowel* in the *verb root* being chosen, i.e. *a* by *ı, e* by *i, o* and *u* by *u, ö* and *ü* by *ü*. Examples:

| | | | |
|---|---|---|---|
| salmak | = salıyor | görmek | = görüyor |
| sokmak | = sokuyor | girmek | = giriyor |

(70d) Though it may seem difficult at first to understand the working of the *sounds*, it is really very simple and is done automatically if the chapter on MUTATION and GRADUATION of SOUND (Ph. 19-32) is well studied and grasped. It will be found that, in the present tense, it is more generally in the form of a *drop* than a *repetition*.

In some cases this harmony also affects the negative suffix *ma, me* causing its vowel to change (see 591). Examples:

| | | | | | |
|---|---|---|---|---|---|
| *salmayor* | or | *salmıyor* | *görmeyor* | or | *görmüyor* |
| *kalmayor* | or | *kalmıyor* | *girmeyor* | or | *girmiyor* |
| *sokmayor* | or | *sokmuyor* | *bitirmeyor* | or | *bitirmiyor* |

**Note:** This is the only tense where the *personal verbal suffix* for both *hard* and *soft verb roots* does not change, due to the fact that the *present* tense suffix *"yor"* is added to both hard and soft words and the personal suffix has to be in accordance with that, irrespective of the fact that the rest of the word may be *"soft"*.

(70dd) **Note:** Throughout the verb chapter, in the conjugation, the English to all six persons of one verb in any tense is being given, only.

As an exercise the student can apply the same form to all other verbs, the English of the Infinitive being put at the head of each column.

### Present Tense
*kalmak* = to stay

| | |
|---|---|
| I stay, am staying | kal*ıyorum* |
| You stay, are staying | kal*ıyorsun* |
| He stays, is staying | kal*ıyor* |
| We stay, are staying | kal*ıyoruz* |
| You stay, are staying | kal*ıyorsunuz* |
| They stay, are staying | kal*ıyorlar* |

| *koymak* = | *gelmek* = | *görmek* = |
|---|---|---|
| to put | to come | to see |
| *koyuyorum* | *geliyorum* | *görüyorum* |
| *koyuyorsun* | *geliyorsun* | *görüyorsun* |
| *koyuyor* | *geliyor* | *görüyor* |
| *koyuyoruz* | *geliyoruz* | *görüyoruz* |
| *koyuyorsunuz* | *geliyorsunuz* | *görüyorsunuz* |
| *koyuyorlar* | *geliyorlar* | *görüyorlar* |

(70e) *This tense is also used in other senses, peculiar to the language. It is absolutely necessary to take note of these peculiarities as they form the key to thought expression in Turkish, and play a very important part.*

We shall give full details with reference to all tenses and moods separately, in their turn.

(70f) It is very common for a tense to have several ways of expressing the thought. It would not be incorrect for the student to say, for instance:

*Yarın Ankara'ya gideceğiz.* (future tense)
= Tomorrow we will go to Ankara.

But it will be more Turkish to say:

*Yarın Ankara'ya gidiyoruz.* (present tense)
= Tomorrow we are going to Ankara.

as explained hereunder.

This form of this tense corresponds to the English "future in the present" which is usually marked in Turkish by any word denoting the future, i.e. *yarın* (tomorrow), *gelecek hafta* (next week, etc.), etc.

(70g) Like the "indefinite" tense it also denotes that the work will be done in the future, the future being mentioned. Example:

Gelecek      hafta     sınava       *giriyor.*
(shall come   week     to exams    he enters)
= Next week he/she sits for his/her exam.

(70h) That the work is being *repeated*. Example:
*Daima        böyle                    yapıyorsunuz.*
(always       like this                doing are you)
= You are always behaving like this.

(70i) That the work is of an *habitual* nature. Example:
*Üç       senedir      paltosuz           geziyorum.*
(three    year is       coat without       walk I)
= For three years I am going without a coat (I have been going).

(70j) When reference is being made to a person or persons in the nature of a supposition "*dır*" is added to the 3rd person singular and plural. Example:

*Bu dakika       çocuklar      uyuyorlardır.*
(this minute     children      sleeping are they is)
= At this minute the children are sleeping.

## THE PAST TENSE (Attestative) (GÖRÜLEN GEÇMİŞ ZAMAN)
### (dı, di, du, dü; tı, ti, tu, tü)

(71) The PAST TENSE ATTESTATIVE is used when referring to an action which the speaker *actually carried out himself*, or which he *actually witnessed* carried out by a second party.

(71a) It is formed by adding *dı, di, du, dü* to all verb roots ending with a vowel or the consonants *ğ, l, m, n, r, y* (Ph. 15) and *v, g, j* (Ph. 15a), the vowel in the suffix to be in harmony with the last vowel in the word (see Ph. 28). This automatically forms the 3rd person singular. To form the other five persons the appropriate suffixes must be added. Examples:

| *kapadı* | = he/she closed | *söyledi* | = he/she said |
| *kaldı* | = he/she stayed | *gördü* | = he/she saw |

(71b) These endings are changed to *tı, ti, tu, tü* when the verb root ends with one of the consonants *ç, f, h, k, p, s, ş, t* (Ph. 31b). Examples:

| *kaçtı* | = he/she ran away | *kesti* | = he/she cut |
| *korktu* | = he/she got frightened | *küstü* | = he/she got angry |

### Past Tense (Attestative)

|  | kapamak = | = koymak | = gelmek | = öpmek |
|  | to close | to put | to come | to kiss |
|---|---|---|---|---|
| I closed | = *kapadım* | *koydum* | *geldim* | *öptüm* |
| You closed | = *kapadın* | *koydun* | *geldin* | *öptün* |
| He closed | = *kapadı* | *koydu* | *geldi* | *öptü* |
| We closed | = *kapadık* | *koyduk* | *geldik* | *öptük* |
| You closed | = *kapadınız* | *koydunuz* | *geidiniz* | *öptünüz* |
| They closed | = *kapadılar* | *koydular* | *geldiler* | *öptüler* |

**This tense is also used in another sense, peculiar to the language:**

(71c) When placed in the *interrogative form* and followed by another verb in the *indefinite tense* affirmative form, the first verb gives the meaning *"as soon as"* or *"no sooner than"*. Example:

| *Tren* | *yolcusu* | *nu* | *aldı* | *mı* | *haraket* | *eder.* |
|--------|-----------|------|--------|------|-----------|---------|
| (train | passenger | its | has taken | ? | depart | will) |

(has the train finished taking its passengers (?) the train goes.)
= As soon as the passengers have embarked, the train will start.

**Explanation:** The start of the second action is subject to the completion of the first one. The Interrogative form simply marks this dependency in a question form, the answer being "yes it has finished", and the second action thereupon takes place.

## THE PAST TENSE (Repeatative) (DUYULAN GEÇMİŞ ZAMAN)
### *(mış, miş, muş, müş)*

(72) The PAST TENSE REPEATATIVE is used when the speaker has come to know of the completion of the action, but *did not actually witness it.* When he makes mention *he only repeats what he has heard,* and he therefore uses the *past participle* of the verb, marking the completion of the action. Example:

*(Sınıfta) birinciliği (kazanmışım.)*
(in the class) being first (it is said that I have earned)
= (He says I have been promoted to the top of the class).

(72a) It is formed by adding:
*mış, miş, muş, müş,* to both consonant and vowel-ending verb roots, then adding the p. pr. suffixes (see 57ee). Example:

| | |
|---|---|
| *kaçmış* | = it is said he/she had run away |
| *kesmiş* | = it is said he/she had cut |
| *korkmuş* | = it is said he/she had got frightened |
| *küsmüş* | = it is said he/she had got angry |
| *korumuş* | = it is said he/she had protected |
| *yürümüş* | = it is said he/she had walked |

# Past Tense Repeatative
*kalmak* = to stay

| | |
|---|---|
| It is said that I had stayed | = *kalmışım* |
| It is said that you had stayed | = *kalmışsın* |
| It is said that he had stayed | = *kalmış* |
| It is said that we had stayed | = *kadmışız* |
| It is said that you had stayed | = *kalmışsınız* |
| It is said that they had stayed | = *kalmışlar* |

| *koymak* = to put | *gelmek* = to come | görmek = to see |
|---|---|---|
| *koymuşum* | *gelmişim* | *görmüşüm* |
| *koymuşsun* | *gelmişsin* | *görmüşsün* |
| *koymuş* | *gelmiş* | *görmüş* |
| *koymuşuz* | *gelmişiz* | *görmüşüz* |
| *koymuşsunuz* | *gelmişsiniz* | *görmüşsünüz* |
| *koymuşlar* | *gelmişler* | *görmüşler* |

**This tense is also used in other senses, peculiar to the language:**

(72b) To express *a rumour, self glorification* or *contempt.* Example:

| | | |
|---|---|---|
| (72c) | *İstanbul'da kar yağmış* | = it is said it snowed in Istanbul |
| (72d) | *ben çok büyük işler yapmışım* | = I have carried out many big deeds (boasting) |
| (72e) | *bu işi başaracakmış* | = he says that he is going to get the work through |

(72f) When the person repeating what he has heard is *convinced of the correctness* of the assertion, although he has not seen the completion of the action, he will mark his *conviction* by adding *dır, dir, dur, dür, (tır, tir, tur, tür)* to the *past tense repeatative.* Example:

*o bu işi yapmıştır*  = he/she has executed this work

**Note:** Care must be taken to sound the "s" following the "ş" in 2nd. pers. sing. and plural.

# THE INDEFINITE TENSE (GENİŞ ZAMAN)
*(r, ar, er, ır, ir, ur, ür)*

(73) The action is expressed in the INDEFINITE TENSE for both the *present* and the *future* when it is of an habitual (present) or volitional (future) character. Example:
*Banu bahçede uyur* = Banu would sleep in the garden (habit)

(73a) It is formed by adding *"r"* only to vowel-ending verb roots, then the personal pro. suffix (see 57ee). Example:

| | | | |
|---|---|---|---|
| *yaralar* | = he/she injures | *kekeler* | = he/she stutters |
| *korur* | = he/she protects | *yürür* | = he/she walks |

(73b)A sound letter, *a, e, ı, i, u* or *ü,* is inserted between the verb root and the suffix of all words ending with a consonant, and the laws of mutation and graduation of sound applied.

To get the right sound letter is a matter of careful adaptation of the said laws. The natural Turkish euphony is the strongest guide. Example:

| | |
|---|---|
| *salmak - salar* = he attacks | *dolmak - dolar* = it fills |
| *kalmak - kalır* = he remains | *bulmak - bulur* = he finds |
| *koymak - koyar* = he puts | *görmek - görür* = he sees |
| *sokmak - sokar* = he stings | *sürmek - sürer* = he drives |

(73bb) The INDEFINITE tense denoting in general CONSENT, DESIRE, HABIT, or DETERMINATION is being translated in the *English sense* of "WILL" for the first *person*, and "SHALL" for the second and third *person*.

## The Indefinite Tense

| | *kalmak* = to stay | *koymak* = to put | *gelmek* = to come | *yürümek* = to walk |
|---|---|---|---|---|
| I will stay | = kalırım | koyarım | gelirim | yürürüm |
| You will stay | = kalırsın | koyarsın | gelirsin | yürürsün |
| He will stay | = kalır | koyar | gelir | yürür |
| We will stay | = kalırız | koyarız | geliriz | yürürüz |
| You will stay | = kalırsınız | koyarsınız | gelirsiniz | yürürsünüz |
| They will stay | = kalırlar | koyarlar | gelirler | yürürler |

**This tense is also used in other senses, peculiar to the language:**

(73c) To denote permanent *facts, consent, delay,* the *future,* etc. Examples:

| (73d) | (fact) | bütün dünya gece uyur | =the whole world sleeps (in)the night |
|---|---|---|---|
| (73e) | (habit) | o çocuk daima bisiklete *biner* | = that child always rides a bicycle |
| (73f) | (desire) | bu mektubu *postaya atarsınız* | = you will post this letter |
| (73g) | (consent) | peki sofrayı *kurarım* | = very well, I will lay the table |
| (73h) | (delay) | yemeğimi sonra yerim | = I will have my dinner afterwards |
| (73i) | (future) | sizi yarın görürüm | = I will see you tomorrow |

(73j) It also denotes *Imploration* when put in the *Interrogative* form. Example:

*Bana bu lütfu yapar mısınız?* = Would you do me this favour?

(73k) It also denotes the sudden occurrence of another action when the 3rd person singular in the affirmative is followed by the same person in the negative form. Example:

| Sokağa | çıkar | çıkmaz | yağmur | başladı. |
|---|---|---|---|---|
| (to the street | goes | does not go | the rain | began) |

= I no sooner went out than the rain started.

(73l) **Note:** This latter must not be confused with the same tense when it is used in the same forms and order, but in the 1st person singular or any person and number of the doer, and in the ordinary meaning. Example:

| Çıkarım | çıkmam, | size | ne | oluyor? |
|---|---|---|---|---|
| (will go out | I will not go out I | you to | what | happens) |

= Whether I go out or not, what does it matter to you?

| İşine | gider, | gitmez | kendisinin | bileceği | bir şeydir. |
|---|---|---|---|---|---|
| (his work to | will go he, | will not go he | himself of | would know one thing is) |

= Whether he would go to his work or not he knows best.

These latter two forms should be noted and carefully digested as they are very much used.

# THE FUTURE TENSE (GELECEK ZAMAN)
## (cak, cek)

(74) The FUTURE TENSE formed from the *OPTATIVE MOOD* (denoting the free will and desire of the "*doer*") is the tense expressing in a simple manner the fact that the action will take place in a time to come. I will translate it with "WILL" as it is in English.

    *gelecekler*        = they will come

(74a) It is formed by adding *cak, cek* to the OPTATIVE MOOD (see Opt. M. 105), to which the pers. pron. suffixes are added.

| | | | |
|---|---|---|---|
| *kalmak* | = to stay | *kalacak* | = he/she/it will stay |
| *gelmek* | = to come | *gelecek* | = he/she/it will come |
| *okumak* | = to read | *okuyacak* | = he/she/it will read |
| *yürümek* | = to walk | *yürüyecek* | = he/she/it will walk |

Note: The *k* of *cak* and *cek* changes to *ğ* when adding a personal suffix beginning with a vowel (Ph. 31 and 36).

### Future Tense
*kalmak* = to stay

| | |
|---|---|
| I will stay | = *kalacağım* |
| Thou will stay | = *kalacaksın* |
| He will stay | = *kalacak* |
| We will stay | = *kalacağız* |
| You will stay | = *kalacaksınız* |
| They will stay | = *kalacaklar* |

*koymak* = to put    *gelmek* = to come    *görmek* = to see

| | | |
|---|---|---|
| *koyacağım* | *geleceğim* | *göreceğim* |
| *koyacaksın* | *geleceksin* | *göreceksin* |

| koyacak | gelecek | görecek |
|---------|---------|---------|
| koyacağız | geleceğiz | göreceğiz |
| koyacaksınız | geleceksiniz | göreceksiniz |
| koyacaklar | gelecekler | görecekler |

**This tense is also used in other senses, peculiar to the language. To express:**

(74b) The *possibiliły* of the occurrence. Example:

*Gelen tren Ankara postası olacak.* = The coming train will be the Ankara Mail.
(The coming train may be the Ankara Mail.)

(74c) *Concernment* in the action. Example:

*Bu işe siz bakacaksınız.* = You will attend to this work.

(74d) *Emphasis tır, tir* is added to the third person. Example:

*bu işi yarın yapacaktır* =  (this work to-morrow he will do)
he will do this work tomorrow without fail

(74e) **Note:** When the future tense is to be placed in the negative form the negation suffixes (*ma, me*) have to be placed next to the verb root (see 59e) (see also 59l). Therefore the optative suffixes (*a, e* or *ya, ye,* see 104aa) are removed and re-affixed after the negation suffix. As two vowels cannot come together it will be necessary to insert a "y" between the *negation* suffix and the *Opt.* suffix if this had not already been done when first affixing the Opt. suffix (see 104aa). If it *had* been done it will then be only a matter of shifting ("*ya*", "*ye*") from the first position to the second. Examples:

| *kalacağım* | = I will stay | *kalmayacağım* | = I will not stay *okuyacağım* |
|---|---|---|---|
| | = I will read | *okumayacağım* | = I will not read |

(74f) **Note:** There is a noticeable difference between the negative of the *future* tense, *indicative* mood (*göreceğim, görmeyeceğim*) and the negative of the future tense, *potential* mood (facultative) (*görebileceğim, göremeyeceğim*), owing to the fact that *meyeceğim* is the negative form of *bileceğim* in the second example, where *göre* is kept intact and *bile* is dropped (see *potential* mood (facultative)).

# MOODS (KİPLER)

(75) The *Moods* or *MANNER OF EXPRESSION* in the verb conjugation play a very strong part in expressing what is known in English as the *simple*, progressive, and emphatic forms.

The verbal expression of the action taking place and finishing in the present time (*present perfect tense*) or having taken place and been finished in the past (*pluperfect tense*) is in Turkish obtained not by the sense of *tense*, but by the sense of *mood*.

(76) In Turkish the verb is brought into motion under the effect of two motives:

    **(a)** The mere agency of the doer.
    **(b)** The free desire and anxiety of the doer.

These two aspects must be borne in mind when we think of the verb.

The Moods as already mentioned serve as the fundamental basis for the expression of thoughts or action. This is better understood by the study of the examples:

| | | |
|---|---|---|
| Imperative Mood: | *yarın buraya gel* | = come here tomorrow |
| (Injunction) | | (you must come without fail) |
| | | |
| Potential obligation: | *yarın buraya gelmelisin* | = tomorrow you must come here |
| (Compulsion) | | |
| | | |
| Optative: | *yarın buraya gelesin* | = make effort to come tomorrow |
| (Free will-desire) | | |

By a more thorough study of all the moods together with the tenses the student will find all the various forms of the English verb. He will be able to see how comprehensively self-sufficient and ingeniously devised the Turkish verb is.

This division (76a, b) creates the two main MOODS:

| | | | | |
|---|---|---|---|---|
| *(a)* The *IMPERATIVE MOOD* | : *gel* = come | | *kal* = stay | |
| *(b)* The *OPTATIVE MOOD* | : *gele* = coming | | *kala* = staying | |
| | | (free will) | | (free will) |

202

FROM the *IMPERATIVE MOOD*, with the help of auxiliaries, the following Moods and tenses are derived:

The *INDICATIVE MOOD* (In the 3rd person):

| | | | |
|---|---|---|---|
| *(a)* | The Present Tense | : *geliyor* | = he/she comes |
| *(b)* | The Past Tense (Attestative) | : *geldi* | = he/she came, or has come |
| *(c)* | The Past Tense (Repeatative) | : *gelmiş* | = it is said he/she came, or has come |
| *(d)* | The Indefinite Tense (geniş) | : *gelir* | = he/she comes, or will come |

| | | |
|---|---|---|
| The NARRATIVE MOOD | : *geliyor idi* | = he/she was coming |
| The REPORTATIVE MOOD | : *geliyor imiş* | = it is said he/she was coming |
| The CONDITIONAL MOOD | : *geliyor ise* | = if he/she comes or is coming |
| The SUBJUNCTIVE MOOD | : *gelse* | = if he/she come |
| The POTENTIAL MOOD (Obligation) | : *gelmeli* | = he/she must come |

The *GERUNDIAL MOODS* (see 124, 128, 129, 130, 131, 132, 134, 135, 136, 137, 138.)

FROM the *OPTATIVE MOOD*, with the help of auxiliaries, we derive:

The Future Tense of the *INDICATIVE MOOD*.

The POTENTIAL MOOD (Facultative).

The various GERUNDIAL MOODS (see 127 and 133).

## THE INDICATIVE MOOD (BİLDİRME KİPİ)

(77) The *Indicative* Mood expresses the simple or ordinary manner of action of the verb and includes all the five tenses, giving out also the sense of completion or perfection of the action.

(78) The grouping of the fundamental five tenses in their primitive forms make the *Indicative Mood*.

(78a) There is therefore no Mood suffix for the Indicative Mood.

Indicative Mood of *gitmek* = to go
## PRESENT TENSE

| Affirmative | Interrogative | Negative | Interronegative |
|---|---|---|---|
| I (etc.) go, | am I (etc.), | I (etc.) am | am I (etc.) not |
| am going | going | not going, do | going |
| | | not go | |
| | | | |
| *gidiyorum* | *gidiyor muyum* | *gitmiyorum* | *gitmiyor muyum* |
| *gidiyorsun* | *gidiyor musun* | *gitmiyorsun* | *gitmiyor musun* |
| *gidiyor* | *gidiyor mu* | *gitmiyor* | *gitmiyor mu* |
| *gidiyoruz* | *gidiyor muyuz* | *gitmiyoruz* | *gitmiyor muyuz* |
| *gidiyorsunuz* | *gidiyor musunuz* | *gitmiyorsunuz* | *gitmiyor musunuz* |
| *gidiyorlar* | *gidiyorlar mı* | *gitmiyorlar* | *gitmiyorlar mı* |

## PAST TENSE (ATTESTATIVE)

| Affirmative | Interrogative | Negative | Interronegative |
|---|---|---|---|
| I (etc.) went | did I (etc.) | I (etc.) did | did I (etc.) not |
| | go | not go | go |
| | | | |
| *gittim* | *gittim mi* | *gitmedim* | *gitmedim mi* |
| *gittin* | *gittin mi* | *gitmedin* | *gitmedin mi* |
| *gitti* | *gitti mi* | *gitmedi* | *gitmedi mi* |
| *gittik* | *gittik mi* | *gitmedik* | *gitmedik mi* |
| *gittiniz* | *gittiniz mi* | *gitmediniz* | *gitmediniz mi* |
| *gittiler* | *gittiler mi* | *gitmediler* | *gitmediler mi* |

## PAST TENSE (REPEATATIVE)

| Affirmative | Interrogative | Negative | Interronegatioe |
|---|---|---|---|
| It is said | Is it said that | It is said that | Is it said that |
| that I (etc.) went | I (etc.) went go | I (etc.) did not go | I (etc.) did not |
| | | | |
| *gitmişim* | *gitmiş miyim* | *gitmemişim* | *gitmemiş miyim* |
| *gitmişsin* | *gitmiş misin* | *gitmemişsin* | *gitmemiş misin* |
| *gitmiş* | *gitmiş mi* | *gitmemiş* | *gitmemiş mi* |

| | | | |
|---|---|---|---|
| *gitmişiz* | *gitmiş miyiz* | *gitmemişiz* | *gitmemiş miyiz* |
| *gitmişsiniz* | *gitmiş misiniz* | *gitmemişsiniz* | *gitmemiş misiniz* |
| *gitmişler* | *gitmişler mi* | *gitmemişler* | *gitmemişler mi* |

## INDEFINITE TENSE

| Affirmative | Interrogative | Negative | Interronegative |
|---|---|---|---|
| I (etc.) will | Will I (etc.) go | I (etc.) will | Will I (etc.) not |
| go or I (etc.) | or do I (etc.) | not go, I (etc.) | go or do I (etc.) |
| go | go | do not go | not go |
| | | | |
| *giderim* | *gider miyim* | *gitmem* | *gitmez miyim* |
| *gidersin* | *gider misin* | *gitmezsin* | *gitmez misin* |
| *gider* | *gider mi* | *gitmez* | *gitmez mi* |
| *gideriz* | *gider miyiz* | *gitmeyiz* | *gitmez miyiz* |
| *gidersiniz* | *gider misiniz* | *gitmezsiniz* | *gitmez misiniz* |
| *giderler* | *giderler mi* | *gitmezler* | *gitmezler mi* |

## FUTURE TENSE

| Affirmative | Interrogatioe | Negative | Interronegative |
|---|---|---|---|
| I (etc.) will | Will I (etc.) | I (etc.) will | Will I (etc.) not |
| go | go | not go | go |
| | | | |
| *gideceğim* | *gidecek miyim* | *gitmeyeceğim* | *gitmeyecek miyim* |
| *gideceksin* | *gidecek misin* | *gitmeyeceksin* | *gitmeyecek misin* |
| *gidecek* | *gidecek mi* | *gitmeyecek* | *gitmeyecek mi* |
| *gideceğiz* | *gidecek miyiz* | *gitmeyeceğiz* | *gitmeyecek miyiz* |
| *gideceksiniz* | *gidecek misiniz* | *gitmeyeceksiniz* | *gitmeyecek misiniz* |
| *gidecekler* | *gidecekler mi* | *gitmeyecekler* | *gitmeyecekler mi* |

# THE NARRATIVE MOOD (HİKÂYE KİPİ)

(79) The *Narrative Mood* is used when one person is giving to another an account of an action of which either he has been the "*doer*" or *has actaally been a witness.*

He will narrate this occurrence *in exactly the same tense and mood as it was in at the time of happening,* but will then *add* the word *idi* = was (this being the past attestative of the auxiliary verb *imek*) thereby showing that time is now past.

If he had not actually witnessed the occurrence he would use the **Reportative Mood** (see 81).

(79a) The *Narrative Mood* gives us all the actions of the respective tenses of the *Indicative Mood.* It gives among many the past *progressive, pluperfect, perfect,* and the *future in the past,* and *past* and *present* in the future.

(79b) **Note:** Study the examples below:

> *Her     gün     eve          saat     beşte     geliyor.* (Pres. Tense, Indic. Mood)
> (every   day     home to      hour     five at    comes he)
> = He comes home at five o'clock every day

> *Ankara'ya          gidecek.* (Future Tense, Indic. Mood)
> (Ankara **to**       will go he)
> = He will go to Ankara.

> *Sınavlarını          geçen ay          bitirdi.* (Past Tense, Indic. Mood)
> (examinations his     last month        finished he)
> = He finished his examinations last month.

The same sentences in the narrative mood will be:

> *Her gün     eve          saat beşte     geliyor     idi.*
> (every day   home to      hour five at   comes he    was)
> = He would come home at 5 o'clock every day.     or
> = He was coming home at 5 o'clock every day.

> *Ankara'ya     gidecek     idi.*          = He was going to Ankara.
> Ankara to     go will      was he)

> *Sınavlarını          geçen ay          bitirdi     idi.*
> examinations his     last month        finished    he was
> = He had finished his examinations the previous month.

(80) The *NARRATIVE MOOD* is obtained by placing next to, or by adding idi or its Abbrev. and mutated equivalents (*dı, di, du, dü* (62a and 62aa) or *ydı, ydi, ydu, ydü* (62b) or the assimilated *tı, ti, tu, tü* (62d) to the 3rd person of each tense of the *Indicative* mood.

*To obtain the other five persons in each tense the respective Personal suffixes must be added to the 3rd person singular (see 57eee).*

**Note:** In the following we have shown the 3rd person plural in two ways. The second one, i.e., adding *idi* (not changeable) to each person of each tense of the Indicative Mood is not so much in use for the first five persons, the form we have shown being the most used one. The two 3rd person plural forms, however, are equally used, hence the reason of our reproducing the second one as well.

## Narrative Mood of *kalmak* = to stay

### PRESENT TENSE

| **Affirmative Form** | | **Negative Form** | |
|---|---|---|---|
| I (etc.) was staying | | I (etc.) was not staying | |
| *kalıyor idim* or | *kalıyordum* | *kalmıyor idim* or | *kalmıyordum* |
| *kalıyor idin* or | *kalıyordun* | *kalmıyor idin* or | *kalmıyordun* |
| *kalıyor idi* or | *kalıyordu* | *kalmıyor idi* or | *kalmıyordu* |
| *kalıyor idik* or | *kalıyorduk* | *kalmıyor idik* or | *kalmıyorduk* |
| *kalıyor idiniz* or | *kalıyordunuz* | *kalmıyor idiniz* or | *kalmıyordunuz* |
| *kalıyor idiler* or | *kalıyordular* | *kalmıyor idiler* or | *kalmıyordular* |
| or *kalıyorlar idi* or *kalıyorlardı* | | or *kalmıyorlar idi* or *kalmıyorlardı* | |

### PAST TENSE (ATTESTATIVE)

| **Affirmative Form** | | **Negative Form** | |
|---|---|---|---|
| I (etc.) have stayed, or | | I (etc.) have not stayed, or did | |
| I (etc.) stayed | | not stay | |
| *kaldı idim* or | *kaldıydım* | *kalmadı idim* or | *kalmadıydım* |
| *kaldı idin* or | *kaldıydın* | *kalmadı idin* or | *kalmadıydın* |
| *kaldı idi* or | *kaldıydı* | *kalmadı idi* or | *kalmadıydı* |

| | | | |
|---|---|---|---|
| *kaldı idik* or | *kaldıydık* | *kalmadı idik* or | *kalmadıydık* |
| *kaldı idiniz* or | *kaldıydınız* | *kalmadı idiniz* or | *kalmadıydınız* |
| *kaldı idiler* or | *kaldıydılar* | *kalmadı idiler* or | *kalmadıydılar* |
| or *kaldılar idi* or *kaldılardı* | | or *kalmadılar idi* or *kalmadılardı* | |

## PAST TENSE (The English "Pluperfect")

**Affirmative Form**
I (etc.) had stayed

**Negative Form**
I (etc.) had not stayed

| | | | |
|---|---|---|---|
| *kalmış idim* or | *kalmıştım* | *kalmamış idim* or | *kalmamıştım* |
| *kalmış idin* or | *kalmıştın* | *kalmamış idin* or | *kalmamıştın* |
| *kalmış idi* or | *kalmıştı* | *kalmamış idi* or | *kalmamıştı* |
| *kalmış idik* or | *kalmıştık* | *kalmamış idik* or | *kalmamıştık* |
| *kalmış idiniz* or | *kalmıştınız* | *kalmamış idiniz* or | *kalmamıştınız* |
| *kalmış idiler* or | *kalmıştılar* | *kalmamış idiler* or | *kalmamıştılar* |
| or *kalmışlar idi* or *kalmışlardı* | | or *kalmamışlar idi* or *kalmamışlardı* | |

The above is not a "repeatative" tense. It is formed with the past participle of the verb.

## INDEFINITE TENSE

**Affirmative Form**
I (etc.) used to, or would have, stayed

**Negative Form**
I (etc.) used not to or would not have, stayed

| | | | |
|---|---|---|---|
| *kalır idim* or | *kalırdım* | *kalmaz idim* or | *kalmazdım* |
| *kalır idin* or | *kalırdın* | *kalmaz idin* or | *kalmazdın* |
| *kalır idi* or | *kalırdı* | *kalmaz idi* or | *kalmazdı* |
| *kalır idik* or | *kalırdık* | *kalmaz idik* or | *kalmazdık* |
| *kalır idiniz* or | *kalırdınız* | *kalmaz idiniz* or | *kalmazdınız* |
| *kalır idiler* or | *kalırdılar* | *kalmaz idiler* or | *kalmazdılar* |
| or *kalırlar idi* or *kalırlardı* | | or *kalmazlar idi* or *kalmazlardı* | |

# FUTURE TENSE

| **Affirmative Form** | **Negative Form** |
|---|---|
| I (etc.) was going to stay | I (etc.) was not going to stay |

| | |
|---|---|
| *kalacak idim* or *kalacaktım* | *kalmayacak idim* or *kalmayacaktım* |
| *kalacak idin* or *kalacaktın* | *kalmayacak idin* or *kalmayacaktın* |
| *kalacak idi* or *kalacaktı* | *kalmayacak idi* or *kalmayacaktı* |
| *kalacak idik* or *kalacaktık* | *kalmayacak idik* or *kalmayacaktık* |
| *kalacak idiniz* or *kalacaktınız* | *kalmayacak idiniz* or *kalmayacaktınız* |
| *kalacak idiler* or *kalacaktılar* | *kalmayacak idiler* or *kalmayacaktılar* |
| or *kalacaklar idi* or *kalacaklardı* | or *kalmayacaklar idi* or *kalmayacaklardı* |

# THE REPORTATIVE MOOD (RİVAYET KİPİ)

(81) The verb is used in the *Reportative Mood* when one is speaking of things which have taken place but have not been actually witnessed by the speaker, he only repeating information obtained from another source thereby sometimes causing doubt. It also is used when there is intention of *slight, consternation* or *contempt*. As in the Narrative Mood the action of the verb may have been brought to completion, but this fact is not definite. The action is enacted in the past and as in the *narrative mood* in the respective tenses of the time of completion.

(82) The *Reportative Mood* is obtained by placing next to or by adding *imiş* or its abbrev. and mutated equivalents *mış, miş, muş, müş* (62a), to the 3rd person of each tense of the *Indicative Mood*.

To obtain the other five persons in each tense the respective suffixes must be added to the 3rd person singular (see below) (see 57d and 57ee).

## Reportative Mood of *gelmek* = to come

### PRESENT TENSE

| **Affirmative Form** | **Negative Form** |
|---|---|
| (It is said) that I (etc.) used to come | (It is said) that I (etc.) used not to come |
| (It is said) that I (etc.) was coming | (It is said) that I (etc.) was not coming |

*geliyor imişim* or *geliyormuşum*
*geliyor imişsin* or *geliyormuşsun*
*geliyor imiş* or *geliyormuş*
*geliyor imişiz* or *geliyormuşuz*
*geliyor imişsiniz* or *geliyormuşsunuz*
*geliyor imişler* or *geliyormuşlar*
or *geliyorlar imiş* or *geliyorlarmış*

*gelmiyor imişim* or *gelmiyormuşum*
*gelmiyor imişsin* or *gelmiyormuşsun*
*gelmiyor imiş* or *gelmiyormuş*
*gelmiyor imişiz* or *gelmiyormuşuz*
*gelmiyor imişsiniz* or *gelmiyormuşsunuz*
*gelmiyor imişler* or *gelmiyormuşlar*
or *gelmiyorlar imiş* or *gelmiyorlarmış*

## PAST TENSE (ATTESTATIVE)

Owing to the fact being "reported" there can be no attestation to it.

## PAST TENSE (REPEATATIVE)

**Affirmative Form**
(It is said) that I (etc.) had,
or have, come

*gelmiş imişim*
*gelmiş imişsin*
*gelmiş imiş*
*gelmiş imişiz*
*gelmiş imişsiniz*
*gelmiş imişler*

**Negative Form**
(It is said) that I (etc.) had
or have not come

*gelmemiş imişim*
*gelmemiş imişsin*
*gelmemiş imiş*
*gelmemiş imişiz*
*gelmemiş imişsiniz*
*gelmemiş imişler*

## INDEFINITE TENSE

**Affirmative Form**
(It is said) that I (etc.) used
to come, would come

*gelir imişim* or *gelirmişim*
*gelir imişsin* or *gelirmişsin*
*gelir imiş* or *gelirmiş*
*gelir imişiz* or *gelirmişiz*
*gelir imişsiniz* or *gelirmişsiniz*
*gelir imişler* or *gelirmişler*

**Negative Form**
(It is said) that I (etc.) used not
to come, would not come

*gelmez imişim* or *gelmezmişim*
*gelmez imişsin* or *gelmezmişsin*
*gelmez imiş* or *gelmezmiş*
*gelmez imişiz* or *gelmezmişiz*
*gelmez imişsiniz* or *gelmezmişsiniz*
*gelmez imişler* or *gelmezlermiş*

# FUTURE TENSE

**Affirmative Form Negative Form**
(It is said) that I (etc.) will (It is said) that I (etc.) will not
be coming be coming

| | | | |
|---|---|---|---|
| *gelecek imişim* or | *gelecekmişim* | *gelmeyecek imişim* or | *gelmeyecekmişim* |
| *gelecek imişsin* or | *gelecekmişsin* | *gelmeyecek imişsin* or | *gelmeyecekmişsin* |
| *gelecek imiş* or | *gelecekmiş* | *gelmeyecek imiş* or | *gelmeyecekmiş* |
| *gelecek imişiz* or | *gelecekmişiz* | *gelmeyecek imişiz* or | *gelmeyecekmişiz* |
| *gelecek imişsiniz* or | *gelecekmişsiniz* | *gelmeyecek imişsiniz* or | *gelmeyecekmişsiniz* |
| *gelecek imişler* or | *gelecekmişler* | *gelmeyecek imişler* or | *gelmeyecekmişler* |
| or *gelecekler imiş* or | *geleceklermiş* | or *gelmeyecekler imiş* or | *gelmeyeceklermiş* |

# THE POTENTIAL MOOD (OBLIGATION)
## ZORUNLULUK KİPİ

(83) The Potential Mood is used to express *obligation* or *necessity*. It is translated with *"must"* or *"ought"*.

(84) There are three tenses: INDEFINITE, PAST ATTESTATIVE, PAST REPEATATIVE.

(85) It is obtained by affixing *malı* (Hard), *meli* (Soft) to the VERB ROOT:

(a) To form the "INDEFINITE" tense the personal suffix is then added (see 57ee, 57f, 57ff).

(6) To form the "*PAST ATTESTATIVE*" tense *idi* or its mutated equivalents, or (*ydı, ydi, ydu, ydü*) is then added followed by the personal suffix (see 57eee).

(c) To form the *PAST REPEATATIVE* tense *imiş* or its mutated equivalents; or (*ymış, ymiş, ymuş, ymüş*) is then added, followed by the personal suffix (see 57ee).

## potential (obligation) mood of *görmek* = to see

### INDEFINITE TENSE

| Affirmative Form | Negative Form |
|---|---|
| I (etc.) must see | I (etc.) must not see |

| | |
|---|---|
| *görmeliyim* | *görmemeliyim* |
| *görmelisin* | *görmemelisin* |
| *görmeli* | *görmemeli* |
| *görmeliyiz* | *görmemeliyiz* |
| *görmelisiniz* | *görmemelisiniz* |
| *görmeliler* | *görmemeliler* |

### PAST TENSE (ATTESTATIVE)

| Affirmative Form | Negative Form |
|---|---|
| I (etc.) ought to have seen | I (etc.) ought not to have seen |

| | | | |
|---|---|---|---|
| *görmeli idim* or | *görmeliydim* | *görmemeli idim* or | *görmemeliydim* |
| *görmeli idin* or | *görmeliydin* | *görmemeli idin* or | *görmemeliydin* |
| *görmeli idi* or | *görmeliydi* | *görmemeli idi* or | *görmemeliydi* |
| *görmeli idik* or | *görmeliydik* | *görmemeli idik* or | *görmemeliydik* |
| *görmeli idiniz* or | *görmeliydiniz* | *görmemeli idiniz* or | *görmemeliydiniz* |
| *görmeli idiler* or | *görmeliydiler* | *görmemeli idiler* or | *görmemeliydider* |

### PAST TENSE (REPEATATIVE)

| Affirmative Form | Negative Form |
|---|---|
| (It is said) that I (etc.) should, or ought to have seen | (It is said) that I (etc.) should, or ought not to have seen |

| | | | |
|---|---|---|---|
| *görmeli imişim* or | *görmeliymişim* | *görmemeli imişim* or | *görmemeliymişim* |
| *görmeli imişsin* or | *görmeliymişsin* | *görmemeli imişsin* or | *görmemeliymişsin* |
| *görmeli imiş* or | *görmeliymiş* | *görmemeli imiş* or | *görmemeliymiş* |
| *görmeli imişiz* or | *görmeliymişiz* | *görmemeli imişiz* or | *görmemeliymişiz* |
| *görmeli imişsiniz* or | *görmeliymişsiniz* | *görmemeli imişsiniz* or | *görmemeliymişsiniz* |
| *görmeli imişler* or | *görmeliymişler* | *görmemeli imişler* or | *görmemeliymişler* |

Actually there is no Present nor Future Tense in this mood the action in these two times being represented by the *indefinite* tense (see 73).

## THE SUBJUNCTIVE MOOD (DİLEK KİPİ)

(86). The *Subjunctive Mood* serves to express *supposition, doubt,* or *anxiety to obtain*. There is a vast difference between this mood and the *conditional mood*.

(87) There are three tenses: INDEFINITE, PAST ATTESTATIVE, and PAST REPEATATIVE.

(88) It is obtained by affixing "*sa*" (Hard), "*se*" (Soft) to the *VERB ROOT*:

(a) To form the "*INDEFINITE*" tense, the personal suffix is then added (see 57eeeee).

(b) To form the "*PAST ATTESTATIVE*" tense "*idi*" is then added followed by the personal suffix (see 57eee).

(c) To form the "*PAST REPEATATIVE*" tense "*imiş*" is then added, followed by the personal suffix (see 57ee).

(89) **Note:** The "*PRESENT*" and "*PAST*" tenses of the *English Subjunctive Mood* find their true equivalents in the "*INDEFINITE*" and "*PAST ATTESTATIVE*" tenses of the Turkish *Subjunctive Mood*.

### Subjunctive Mood of *almak* = to take
### INDEFINITE TENSE

| **Affirmative Form** | **Negative Form** |
|---|---|
| Would that I, | Would that I, or if |
| or if I (etc.) take | I (etc.) take not |
| | |
| *alsam* | *almasam* |
| *alsan* | *almasan* |
| *alsa* | *almasa* |
| *alsak* | *almasak* |
| *alsanız* | *almasanız* |
| *alsalar* | *almasalar* |

## PAST TENSE (ATTESTATIVE)

**Affirmative Form**
Would that I,
or if I (etc.) took

**Negative Form**
Would that I, or if
I (etc.) took not

| | | | |
|---|---|---|---|
| *alsa idim* or | *alsaydım* | *almasa idim* or | *almasaydım* |
| *alsa idin* or | *alsaydın* | *almasa idin* or | *almasaydın* |
| *alsa idi* or | *alsaydı* | *almasa idi* or | *almasaydı* |
| *alsa idik* or | *alsaydık* | *almasa idik* or | *almasaydık* |
| *alsa idiniz* or | *alsaydınız* | *almasa idiniz* or | *almasaydınız* |
| *alsa idiler* or | *alsaydılar* | *almasa idiler* or | *almasaydılar* |
| or *alsalar idi* or | *alsalardı* | or *almasalar idi* or | *almasalardı* |

**Note:** This tense is also used to express "If I had taken," etc. and "If I had not taken", etc.

## PAST TENSE (REPEATATIVE)

**Affirmative Form**
(It is said) if I (etc.) had
taken

**Negative Form**
(It is said) if I (etc.) had
not taken

| | | | |
|---|---|---|---|
| *alsa imişim* or | *alsaymışım* | *almasa imişim* or | *almasaymışım* |
| *alsa imişsin* or | *alsaymışsın* | *almasa imişsin* or | *almasaymışsın* |
| *alsa imiş* or | *alsaymış* | *almasa imiş* or | *almasaymış* |
| *alsa imişiz* or | *alsaymışız* | *almasa imişiz* or | *almasaymışız* |
| *alsa imişsiniz* or | *alsaymışsınız* | *almasa imişsiniz* or | *almasaymışsınız* |
| *alsa imişler* or | *alsalar imiş* | *almasa imişler* or | *almasalar imiş* |
| or *alsaymışlar* | | or *almasaymışlar* | |

A few examples are given below:

(89a) The action is taken into the past. Examples:

*Keşke erken gelse idi vapuru kaçırmazdık.*
(Would that he/she came early, the boat would not have missed we.)
= Would that he had come early we would not have missed the boat.

214

(90) Both verbs must be in the same tense. Example:

*Gelse*           *de*    *gitsek.* = We wish he/she would come so that we could go.
would that he comes also   would that we go

(91) A peculiar manner of using the "Indefinite" tense is to have the first verb in the "Affirmative" form followed by that of the "Negative" and the adverb "de" = also placed after each form. Example:

*Gelse*      *de*      *gelmese*        *de*     *ben*     *gideceğim.*
(if he comes    also    if he does not come   also    I     will go)
= Whether he comes or not I will still go.

(91a) **Note:** The other tenses are obtained with the help of the auxiliary verb *olmak*. Some tenses of the conditional mood are also used for this purpose.

## THE CONDITIONAL MOOD (KOŞUL KİPİ)

(92) The *Conditional Mood* is the mood used to express "condition" and "fear".

(93) There is a vast difference between this mood and the *subjunctive mood*.

(94) The *Conditional Mood* is obtained by placing next to or by adding *"ise"* or its abbrev. and mutated equivalents *"sa"* (Hard), *"se"* (Soft) or (*ysa, yse*) to the 3rd person of each tense of the *"indicative"* mood.

(94a) To obtain the other five persons in each tense the respective suffixes must be added to the 3rd person singular (see 57eeeee).

### Conditional Mood of *kalmak* = to remain

### PRESENT TENSE

| **Affirmative Form** | **Negative Form** |
|---|---|
| If I (etc.) remain or if I am remaining | If I (etc.) do not remain, if I am not remaining |
| *kalıyor isem* or    *kalıyorsam* | *kalmıyor isem* or     *kalmıyorsam* |

## PAST TENSE (ATTESTATIVE)

**Affirmative Form**
If I (etc.) remained, or if
I (etc.) have remained

*kaldı isem* or    *kaldıysam*

**Negative Form**
If I (etc.) did, or have,
not remained

*kalmadı isem* or    *kalmadıysam*

## PAST TENSE (REPEATATIVE)

**Affimative Form**
(It is said) If I (etc.) had
remained

*kalmış isem* or    *kalmışsam*

**Negative Form**
(It is said) If I (etc.) had
not remained

*kalmamış isem* or *kalmamışsam*

## INDEFINITE TENSE

**Affirmative Form**
If I (etc.) will remain

*kalır isem* or    *kalırsam*

**Negative Form**
If I (etc.) will not remain

*kalmaz isem* or *kalmazsam*

## FUTURE TENSE

**Affirmative Form Negative Form**
If I (etc.) will remain If I (etc.) will not remain

*kalacak isem* or    *kalacaksam*

*kalmayacak isem* or *kalmayacaksam*
or *kalmıyacak isem* (see 70d and 591)

## CONDITIONAL OBLIGATION
## PRESENT TENSE

**Affirmative Form**
If I (etc.) must remain

*kalmalı isem* or    *kalmalıysam*

**Negative Form**
If I (etc.) must not remain

*kalmamalı isem* or    *kalmamalıysam*

(95) The verb in the conditional mood is subordinate to another verb, which is either in the future or the indefinite tense. Example:

| *Vaktinde* | *gelirse* | *gideriz.* = If he arrives in time we will go. |
|---|---|---|
| in time | if he arrives | we will go |

(96) *da, de,* or *dahi* can be added to the phrase when the second verb is placed in the negative, and is translated as "though" or "even". Example:

| *Vaktinde* | *gelirse* | *de* | *faydası* | *olmaz.* |
|---|---|---|---|---|
| (time in | comes he if | though | benefit | will be not) |

= Though he arrives in time, there will be no benefit.
( = Though he would arrive in time it would do no good.)

(97) When the conditional is used without the main verb it denotes great anxiety or *fear:*

| *Aman,* | *bak* | *yağmur yağıyorsa* | *(gidemeyiz).* |
|---|---|---|---|
| O, | look | if it is raining | (we cannot go). |

*we cannot go* is not placed there, but it is understood to be there.

| *Ya yağmur yağarsa* | *(ıslanırız).* |
|---|---|
| Oh, if it rains | (we shall get wet). |

*we shall get wet* is not placed there, but it is understood to be there.

## THE IMPERATIVE MOOD (EMİR KİPİ)

(98) This Mood is used to *command,* to *forbid,* or as an *injunction.* It is used only in the 2nd person, sing. or plural. It may be "**PRESENT**" or "**ABSENT**", **PRESENT** meaning that the addressee is actually receiving the command for himself direct from the speaker, and **ABSENT** meaning that the addressee, *who is NOT in the presence of the addressor*, is receiving the command through the medium of a person who **IS**.

(99) *It is formed from the "INFINITIVE" MOOD (MASTAR).*

(100) To obtain the 2nd person singular **PRESENT,** the INFINITIVE ending *mak* (Hard), *mek* (Soft) is dropped. No further suffix is necessary (1).

(101) To obtain the remaining "persons" the following suffixes are added to the verb root (see also chart 57eeeeee):

*ın (in, un, ün), yın (yin, yun, yün) ınız (iniz, unuz, ünüz), yınız (yiniz, yunuz, yünüz)*
for the 2nd pers. plural PRESENT.
*sın (sin, sun, sün)* for the 2nd pers. sing. ABSENT (2).
*sınlar (sinler, sunlar, sünler)* for the 2nd pers. plural ABSENT (3).

(101a) As shown above there is only *one* form of address in the *present* singular, but *two* forms in the *present* plural. In chart 57eeeeee, and above, I have shown the three forms under nos. 1, 2, and 3, and hereunder show how they are each employed.

(1) Among friends, from a superior to an inferior, for all commands.

(2) For polite address to an inferior person, or persons, polite conversation among acquaintances.

(3) To a superior, in general use to many persons, for polite conversation between two persons, never for a military command.

## Imperative Mood of *kalmak* = to remain

### INDEFINITE TENSE

| Affirmative Form | Negative Form |
|---|---|
| **"Present"** | **"Present"** |

**2nd person** (used when addressee is in presence of addressor)

| | | | |
|---|---|---|---|
| **SING.:** *kal* | = remain you | *kalma* | = remain you not |
| **PLUR.:** *kalınız* | = remain you | *kalmayınız* | = remain you not |

| "Absent" | "Absent" |
|---|---|

**2nd person** (used when command conveyed through medium)

| | | | |
|---|---|---|---|
| **SING.:** *kalsın* | = let him remain | *kalmasın* | = let him not remain |
| **PLUR.:** *kalsınlar* | = let them remain | *kalmasınlar* | = let them not remain |

(102) It is also used in the 2nd person plural (*present* or *absent*) with or without a supplicative adverb for supplication, or courtesy. It is a very mild command.

Example:

*bu işimi lütfen yapınız* = please do this my work
(please attend to my affairs)

Courtesy : *geliniz* = come, do come

(102a) Compare this with the 2nd person of the present tense of the "*Optative Mood*".

Example:

*bakasın* = I wish you to look (with your free will)

(102b) It is also used in the 2nd person singular (*pres.*) when offering prayers to Allah.

Example:

*Yarab, beni affet.*
O God, absolve me.

(102c) The 2nd person singular or *plural (absent)* in the negative form denotes also *fear* and *contempt*.

*(103) The 2nd pers.* **ABSENT,** sing. or plural, can be used in the *interrogative* and *interronegative* forms when a question concerning the *addressee* is put by the "medium" to the *addressor* whose sense of authority is recognized.

Example:

*Gelsin mi?* = Should he come?
*Gelmesin mi?* = Ought he not to come?

219

# THE OPTATIVE MOOD (SOLICITOUS)
# (İSTEK KİPİ)

(104) The "Optative" Mood is the mood of the action where the doer is an absolutely free agent of his action. All other tenses or gerunds where the doer is in the same capacity, will be created out of the OPTATIVE MOOD.

(104a) It is the mood denoting *"desire"* and *"anxiety to realize."* Examples:

*Kalkayım        işime        bakayım.*
(I will get up        to my work    I will look)
= I will get up and attend to my work.

*Şimdi    gideyim,    tekrar    gelirim.*
(now    I will go    again        will come I)
= I will go now, I will come again.

*Bu sefer    gene    dediğini    yapayım.*
(this time    again    what you say    let me do)
= Again I will carry out your wishes.

*Bahçeyi    sulayayım.*
(the garden  let me water)
= Let me water the garden.

(104aa) The OPTATIVE MOOD is created by adding to the *VERB ROOT: a, e* to *verb roots* ending with a consonant and *ya, ye* (the "*y*" being inserted) where the *verb root* ends with a vowel.

Examples:

| | | | | |
|---|---|---|---|---|
| *bakmak* | = to look | | *baka* | = looking |
| *görmek* | = to see | | *göre* | = seeing |
| *okumak* | = to read | | *okuya* | = reading |
| *yürümek* | = to walk | | *yürüye* | = walking |

(104aa) **Note:** Owing to the fact that *negation suffixes have to be placed next to the verb root,* (see 59 and 59d) the Optative suffixes (*a, e*) are *removed* and *replaced after the negation suffix* when placing the Optative Mood in the Negative form.

As the negation (*ma, me*) ends with a vowel a "*y*" is inserted between the two vowels, if it had not already been inserted when first putting the verb in the optative mood.

(105) There are three tenses : INDEFINITE, PAST ATTESTATIVE, and PAST REPEATATIVE:

(a) To form the indefinite tense the personal suffix is added to the optative root as created above. (See 57eeee).

(b) To form the past attestative tense "*idi*" is added to the optative root, followed by the personal suffix (see 57eee).

(c) To form the past repeatative tense *imiş* is added to the optative root followed by the personal suffix (see 57ee, 62a, 62b).

(105d) This mood is conjugated with or without the interjection "*keşke*" "*would that*" which marks regret.

## Optative Mood (Solicitous) of *sevmek* = to love
### INDEFINITE TENSE

| Affirmative Form | Negative Form |
|---|---|
| I (etc.) wish to love | I do not wish to |
| Let (me, etc.) love, | love |
| be loving | (see also 59l) |

| | | |
|---|---|---|
| 1st Pers. Sing. : | *seveyim* | *sevmeyeyim* |
| 2nd Pers. Sing. : | *sevesin* | *sevmeyesin* |
| 3rd Pers. Sing. : | *seve* | *sevmeye* |
| 1st Pers. Pl. : | *sevelim* | *sevmeyelim* |
| 2nd Pers. Pl. : | *sevesiniz* | *sevmeyesiniz* |
| 3rd Pers. Pl. : | *seveler* | *sevmeyeler* |

### PAST TENSE (ATTESTATIVE)

| Affirmative Form | Negative Form |
|---|---|
| Would that I (etc.) | Would that I (etc.) |
| loved or had loved | had not loved |

| | |
|---|---|
| *seve idim* or *seveydim* | *sevmeye idim* or *sevmeyeydim* |
| *seve idin* or *seveydin* | *sevmeye idin* or *sevmeyeydin* |
| *seve idi* or *seveydi* | *sevmeye idi* or *sevmeyeydi* |
| *seve idik* or *seveydik* | *sevmeye idik* or *sevmeyeydik* |
| *seve idiniz* or *seveydiniz* | *sevmeye idiniz* or *sevmeyeydiniz* |
| *seve idiler* or *seveydiler* | *sevmeye idiler* or *sevmeyeydiler* |

In some cases the latter is also translated as:

| | |
|---|---|
| If I (etc.) loved or | If I (etc.) did not love or |
| had loved | had not loved |

## PAST TENSE (REPEATATIVE)

| **Affirmative Form** | **Negative Form** |
|---|---|
| (It is said) If I (etc.) had | (It is said) If I (etc.) had not |
| loved or if I should | loved or if I should not have |
| have loved | (see 591) loved |

| | |
|---|---|
| *seve imişim* or *seveymişim* | *sevmeye imişim* or sevmeyeymişim |
| *seve imişsin* or *seveymişsin* | *sevmeye imişsin* or sevmeyeymişsin |
| *seve imiş* or *seveymiş* | *sevmeye imiş* or sevmeyeymiş |
| *seve imişiz* or *seveymişiz* | *sevmeye imişiz* or sevmeyeymişiz |
| *seve imişsiniz* or *seveymişsiniz* | *sevmeye imişsiniz* or sevmeyeymişsiniz |
| *seve imişler* or *seveymişler* | *sevmeye imişler* or sevmeyeymişler |

**Note:** Only the 1st. pers. (singular and plural) is placed in the *interrogative form.*
Examples:

| | |
|---|---|
| *yazayım mı?* = shall I write? | *yazalım mı?* = shall we write? |

**There is no 2nd. pers., and for the 3rd. pers. see 103.**

(106) This mood can be qualified by another verb. It is then placed before the Infinitive of that verb and forms a "COMPOUND" VERB (see also 170). Examples:

| | | |
|---|---|---|
| Optat. Mood | : *baka* | = looking |
| Stupefactive | : *bakakalmak* | = to stand aghast |
| Facultative | : *bakabilmek* | = to be able to look |

(106a) It may also qualify a second verb, when the 3rd person singular of the Indefinite tense of this mood is placed in a repetitive form in front of the verb to be qualified (see also 173). Example :

*Ağlaya      ağlaya      anlatıyordu.*
(crying,      crying      he/she was narrating)
= He/she was narrating while he/she was crying.

(106b) The 2nd person singular of the Indefinite tense is also used as a supplicative demand or a very considerate command. Example:

*Ben      isterim ki    bu işe          sen bakasın.*
I          desire that   to this work    you should see)
= I wish you to see to this work (with your free desire.

These forms of commands are seen in the fermans of sultans to their commanders or governors.

(106c) It is definitely different from the 2nd person singular of the imperative mood.

# THE CONJUGATION OF COMPOUND VERBS
## POTENTIAL MOOD (FACULTATIVE)
(can = *bilmek*)

(107) This compound form of the verb is obtained through the help of the primitive verb *bilmek* (to know). Example:

*sevmek*    = to love              *sevebilmek*   = to be able to love (can love)
                                                     to know how to love

There is a great similitude in meaning between this verb in Turkish and the Verb "can love" in English. CAN = *bilmek* (to know) gives the meaning that the doer has the knowledge as to how to carry out the action of the VERB in question.

(107a) bilmek becomes an *auxiliary* verb to the verb *sevmek*. The optative *seve* can be placed in any of the other senses: *sevişe* (Participative, 178), *sevile* (Non-App., 156), *sevine* (Reflexive, 175).

223

(107b) It corresponds to the *potential mood* (ability) in English.

(107c) It is obtained by joining the *optative mood* of the primitive verb to the verb *bilmek* = to know (see 170a (3)). The conjugation of this mood will comprise all the *Moods* of the *Primitive* verb *bilmek* = to know, except the *Imperative Mood*, which is used in the negative form only.

(107d) Throughout the conjugation this feature (the state of free will) (see 104) is noticed in all the four forms.

**Note:** As there is a certain similarity, especially in the *negative form*, care must be taken not to confuse some tenses or forms of this mood with the same tenses and forms of other moods, the *Future* of the Indic. mood, for instance, as:

    *göremeyeceğim*   (Fut. tense, Pot. Fac. mood)
    *görmeyeceğim*   (Fut. tense, Indic. mood).

The Negative is formed by the suppression of the Root Word and all other suffixes of the Primitive Verb *bilmek* and the addition of the respective negative suffixes together with the tense, mood, and person suffixes to the *Optative Root* of the verb in question, i.e. (*seve*) as it is in this case.

The *Interronegative* is formed from the negative form (see Interro. 61).

## (107dd) INDICATIVE MOOD
## (FACULTATIVE)

### PRESENT TENSE

| affirmative | negative | interrogative |
|---|---|---|
| *sevebiliyorum* | *sevemiyorum* | *sevebiliyor muyum* |
| (I can love) | (I cannot love) | (can I love?) |

### PAST TENSE (ATTESTATIVE)

| affirmative | negative | interrogative |
|---|---|---|
| *sevebildim* | *sevemedim* | *sevebildim mi* |
| (I was able to love) | (I was not able to love) | (was I able to love?) |

## PAST TENSE (REPEATATIVE)

| affirmative | negative | interrogative |
|---|---|---|
| *sevebilmişim* | *sevememişim* | *sevebilmiş miyim* |
| (it is said I was able to love) | (it is said I was not able to love) | (is it said I was able to love?) |

## INDEFINITE TENSE

| affirmative | negative | interrogative |
|---|---|---|
| *sevebilirim* | *sevemem* | *sevebilir miyim* |
| (I will be able to love) | (I will not be able to love) | (will I be able to love?) |

## FUTURE TENSE

| affirmative | negative | interrogative |
|---|---|---|
| *sevebileceğim* | *sevemeyeceğim* | *sevebilecek miyim* |
| (I will be able love love) | (I will not be able to love) | (will I be able to love?) |

(107e) This class of *compound verb* has all the usual moods of the Verb.

(107f) Other *compound verbs* are conjugated in the same manner as the one above. They are:

> The **Stapefactive** (see 170a (1)).
> The **Precipitative** (see 170a (2)).
> The **Continuative** (see 170a (4)).

# THE CONJUGATION OF THE NON-APPARENT VERB

108) The conjugation of the Turkish Verb in the *Passive Voice* (Non-apparent) is the same as the conjugation of the *Primitive Verb*.

108a) The position and function of this verb in the sentence is exactly the same as in English. Hereunder a short synopsis is given and the student can build up the rest.

| I am being called | = *çağrılıyorum* | (Pres. tense Ind Mood) |
|---|---|---|
| I will be called | = *çağrılırım* | (Indef. tense Ind. Mood) |
| I have been loved | = *sevildim* | (Past tense Attest. Ind. Mood) |
| I had been loved | = *sevilmiş idim* | (Past tense of *imek* and Past Participle) |
| I will be called | = *çağrılacağım* | (Future tense Ind. Mood) |
| I was being sought | = *aranılıyordum* | (Pres. tense Nar. Mood) |
| I have been loved | = *sevildi idim* | (Past tense Attest. Nar. Mood) |
| I had been loved | = *sevilmiş idim* | (Past tense of imek and Past Part.) |
| I was going to be loved | = *sevilecek idim* | (Future tense Nar. Mood) |
| I must be called | = *çağrılmalıyım* | (Ind. tense Pot. Obl. Mood) |
| I ought have been called | = *çağrılmalı idim* | (Past tense Pot. Obl. Mood) |
| If I am loved | = *sevilsem* | (Ind. tense Subj. Mood) |
| If I were loved | = *sevilse idim* | (Past tense Subj. Mood) |
| If I am being loved | = *seviliyorsam* | (Pres. tense Cond. Mood) |
| If I will be loved | = *sevilir isem* | (Indef. tense Cond. Mood) |
| If I have been loved | = *sevildi isem* | (Past tense Cond. Mood) |
| If I will be loved | = *sevilecek isem* | (Future tense Cond. Mood) |
| If I must be loved | = *sevilmeli isem* | (Present tense (oblig.) Cond. Mood) |
| be you loved | = *sevil* | (2nd per. of Imp. Mood) |
| let me be loved | = *sevileyim* | (Ind. tense Opt. Mood) |
| I can be called | = *çağrılabilirim* | (Pres. tense Pot. Facult. Mood) |
| I could have been called | = *çağrılabilirdim* | (Past tense Pot. Facult. Mood) |

(109) As the Tenses and Moods in Turkish are different in some cases from the English, I am hereunder giving a chart showing to which tense the student should refer when he wants to express himself in any given manner. He will find it useful till he is well acquainted with the Turkish verb.

| I love, am loving | = *seviyorum* / Pres. tense, Indic. Mood |
|---|---|
| I am loving | = *sevmekteyim* / Pres. tense, Indic. Mood, prog. form of Verbal Noun (113a) |
| I do love (matter of habit) | = *severim* / Indef. tense, Indic. Mood |
| I have loved | = *sevdim* / Past tense Attest. Indic. Mood |
| I have been loving | = *seviyordum* / Present tense, Narr. Mood |
| I loved | = *sevdim* / Past tense Attest. Indic. Mood |
| I was loving | = *seviyor idim* / Present tense, Narr. Mood |
| I had loved | = *sevmiş idim* / Past tense Attest. Narr. Mood |
| I had been loving | = *sevmiş oldu idim* /Past tense Attest., Narr. Mood(Past Part. with verb *olmak*) |
| I will love (sense of future) | = *seveceğim* / Future tense, Indic. Mood |
| I will be loving (continuous) | = *sevmekte olacağım* / Future tense, Indic. Mood, prog. form of Verbal Noun (113a) |
| I will be loving (progressive) | = *seveceğim* / Future tense, Indic. Mood |
| I will have loved | = *sevmiş olacağım* / Future tense (Past Part. with verb *olmak*) |

| | |
|---|---|
| I will have been loving | = *sevmiş olacaktım* / Future tense Narr. Mood (Past Part. with verb *olmak*) |
| I might have been loving | = *belki seviyordum* / Past tense, Narr. Mood, Pot. |
| I can love | = *sevebilirim* / Indef. tense, Poten. Mood, Facul. |
| I could love | = *sevebilirdim* / Past tense, Poten. Mood Facul. |
| I could be loving | = *sevebilirim* / Indef. tense, Poten. Mood Facul. |
| I could have loved | = *sevebilir idim* / Past tense Poten. Mood Facul. |
| I could have been loving | = *sevmiş olabilir idim* / Indef. tense Poten. Mood Facul. (Past Part. with verb *olabilmek*) |
| I must love | = *sevmeliyim* / Indef. tense, Poten. Mood Oblig. |
| I must be loving | = *sevmeliyim* / Indef. tense, Poten. Mood Oblig. |
| I must have loved | = *sevmiş olmalıyım* / Indef. tense Poten. Mood Oblig. of *"sevmiş olmak"* |
| I must have been loving | = *sevmiş olmalı imişim* / Past tense rep. Poten. Mood Oblig. of *"sevmiş olmak"* |
| I would love | = *severim* / Indef. tense, Indic. Mood |
| I would have loved | = *sever idim* / Indef. tense, Narr. Mood |
| I would have been loving | = *sevmiş olacak idim* / Future tense, Narr. Mood of *"sevmiş olmak"* |
| I am loved | = *seviliyorum* / Pres. tense, Indic. Mood of *"sevilmek"* |
| I was loved | = *sevilmiştim* / Past tense (Past Part. with verb *"imek"*) |
| I have been loved | = *sevildim* / Past tense, Indic. Mood of *"sevilmek"* |
| I had been loved | = *sevilmiş idim* / Past tense (Past Part. with verb *"imek"*) |
| if I should have been loved | = *sevilmiş olsa idim* / Past tense, Condit. Mood, (Past Part. of Non-app. verb with verb *olmak*) |
| if I be loving | = *sevsem* / Indef. tense, Subj. Mood |
| if I loved | = *sevse idim* / Past tense, Subj. Mood |
| if I love | = *seversem* / Indef. tense, Cond. Mood |
| if I were loved | = *sevilecek olursam* / Indef. tense, Condit. Mood, (Non-app. form of adj. (see 32) with verb *olmak*) |
| if I am loving | = *seviyorsam* / Pres. tense, Cond. Mood |
| if I am being loved | = *seviliyorsam* / Pres. tense, Cond. Mood, Non-app. verb |
| if I had loved | = *sevmiş idiysem* / Past tense, Condit. Mood, Past Part. with *imek*) |
| if I have loved | = *sevdi isem* / Past tense, Cond. Mood |
| if I am loved | = *sevilirsem* / Indef. tense, Cond. Mood, Non-app. verb |
| if I will have loved | = *sevmiş olacak isem* / Future tense, Cond. Mood (Past Part. with *olmak*) |
| if I have been loved | = *sevilmiş olsa idim* / Past tense, Subj. Mood of olmak with Past Part. of *sevilmiş* |
| I may love | = *belki severim* / Indef. tense, Poten. Mood |
| if I had been loved | = *sevilmiş olsa idim* / Past tense, Subj. Mood, Past Part. with verb *olmak*) |
| I may be loving | = *belki seviyorum* / Present tense, Potent. Mood |
| I will be loved | = *sevileceğim* / Future tense, Indic. Mood of *"sevilmek"* |
| I should have been loved | = *sevilmiş olacaktım* / Future tense, Narr. Mood of *"sevilmiş"* with verb *"olmak"* |
| if I should be loved | = *sevilmiş olacak olursam* / Indef. tense, Condit. Mood of *sevilmiş* with verb *"olmak"* |
| I may have loved | = *belki sevmiş olurum* / Indef. tense, Poten. Mood (Past Part. with verb *olmak*) |
| I may have been loving | = *sevmiş olabilirim* / Indef. tense Pot. Mood (Facult.), Past Part. with verb *olmak* |
| I might love | = *belki severim* / Indef. tense Poten. Mood |
| I might be loving | = *belki seviyorum* / Pres. tense, Pot. Mood |
| I might have loved | = *belki sevdim* / Past tense Attest. Pot. Mood |

**Note:** Though I give this chart, I certainly advise the student to master as quickly as possible the fundamentals of the Turkish verb, the Tenses and Moods:

(a) The two Past Tenses, where in one the action was actually witnessed, and in the other one the action has only been intimated.

(b) The Indefinite Tense used when the action is of an habitual or a volitional character, both in the Present and in the Future, i.e., which is the "Future in the Present" and the "Present in the Future".

(c) All the actions of the Past (now being spoken of, and therefore forming the Narr. Mood) are revived in the actual Tense of the time of the action, to which *"idi"* (Narra.) or *"imiş"* (Report) is added, to recall that the action was carried out in the Past.

(d) The completion of the action of the verb is emphasized by placing it in the Past Participle, and conjugating it with the Auxiliary verbs *imek, olmak,* and *bulunmak.*

(e) That generally the form of the Turkish verb is an "assertive" form.

## PRESENT PARTICIPLE

(110) The *present participle* is that part of the verb which is active without being limited by manner, time, person, or number. It denotes action at the time of mention, this action being local and limited in time to the *present* or *past* according to the time of the verb in the phrase following. It is also used as an adjective (see 30) and as a gerund (see 124).

## PAST PARTICIPLE

(111) The *past participle* is that part of the verb which denotes the *completion* of the verb in the most definite manner. It is obtained by adding *mış (miş, muş, müş)* to the verb root. This *past participle* must never be confused with *mış* (72a). and *miş* (82).

(111a) It is also used as an adjective. (see 31 and 31a)

(111b) It is also used with the *present participle* of the verbs *olmak* or *bulunmak* when it represents the *perfect* form of the *present participle* of the primitive verb. Examples:

| | |
|---|---|
| *bitiren adam* | = the man **who finishes** |
| *bitirmiş olan adam* | = the man **who has finished** |

The English tenses showing the *completion of the action* have been shown in (66) where we have explained the *emphasis* put on the act of *completion.*

I will give here just the usual tenses as they are shown in the English grammar:

| IN ENGLISH | IN TURKISH |
|---|---|
| **Present Perfect** | **Past Tense** |
| I have loved | *sevdim* |
| | |
| **Pluperfect** | **Past Tense Narr. M.** |
| I had loved | *sevmiştim* |
| | |
| **Future Perfect** | **Future Tense** |
| I will have loved | *sevmiş olacağım* |

**Note:** All the other tenses are obtained by conjugating the past participle with the auxiliary verb *olmak* (see 66).

# THE CONJUGATION OF THE VERBAL NOUN

(112) The verb in the Infinitive, as a *"verbal noun"*, as we have seen in the chapter of nouns is the verb abounding in all its resourcefulness *not being limited* by *time, mood,* or *person.*

(112a) It actually denotes the "ACT OF". (See 12, a, b, c.). Examples:

| (Infin. verb) | *yazmak* | = to write |
|---|---|---|
| (verbal noun) | *yazmak* | = writing |

Out of the four principal *verbal nouns* the first one (see 12) as mentioned, when put in any one of the verbal cases shows us the part this *verbal noun* plays in cases where we would in English use the verb in the *infinitive* as a *noun phrase* or the *present participle* of the verb (which course must be avoided in Turkish).

I love writing (to write) you letters.

| = *Size* | *mektup* | *yazmayı* | *severim.* |
|---|---|---|---|
| (to you | letter | writing | I love) |
| (dat. case) | | (obj. case) | |

I take the liberty of WRITING you this letter.

| = *Size* | *bu mektubu* | *yazmaya* | *cesaret* | *ediyorum.* |
|----------|-------------|-----------|-----------|-------------|
| (to you | this letter | writing | courage | I am having) |
| (dat. case) | (obj. case) | (dat. case) | | |

I am (actually) WRITING you this letter.

| = *Size* | *bu mektubu* | *yazmakta* | *bulunuyorum.* |
|----------|-------------|------------|----------------|
| to you | this letter | in writing | I am in a state of |
| | (obj. case) | (loc. case) | |

I refrain FROM WRITING him a letter or (letters).

| = *Ona* | *mektup* | *yazmaktan* | *çekiniyorum.* |
|---------|----------|-------------|----------------|
| (to him | letter | from writing | I refrain) |
| | (nom. case) | (abl. case) | |

I have great pleasure IN WRITING (this) letter to you.

| = *Size* | *bu mektubu* | *yazmakla* | *çok* | *hoşnutum.* |
|----------|-------------|------------|-------|-------------|
| (to you | this letter | with writing | very | I pleased) |
| (dat. case) | (obj. case) | (instr. case) | | |

I endeavoured much to WRITE you a letter.

| = *Size* | *mektubu* | *yazmak* | *için* | *çok* | *uğraştım.* |
|----------|-----------|----------|--------|-------|-------------|
| (to you | letter | writing | for | much | I endeavoured) |
| (dat. case) | | | | | |

(112b) Studying in the above examples the INFINITIVE as a verbal noun (act of writing) in any of the verbal cases, we note the contrast in the manner of the expressing of these phrases in English and Turkish.

## PROGRESSIVE FORM OF THE VERBAL NOUN

(113) The verbal noun (12) when placed in the locative case ( = in) and conjugated with the auxiliary verbs *imek* and *bulunmak* provides the progressive form of the verb of the verbal noun in question.

(verbal noun in Nom. C.) *yazmak*     = writing
(verbal noun in Loc. C.) *yazmakta*    = in writing (in the course of writing)

(113a) To obtain the complete conjugation and meaning of the tenses and moods of *imek* and *bulunmak* (62) and (64) must be well studied. To conjugate, the *verbal noun* is first placed in the *locative* case and then treated as a single word. (See *imek* and *bulunmak*.)

## INDICATIVE MOOD

### Present Tense

*yazmakta bulunuyorum* = I am in the course of writing
(I'm writing) (very little used)

### Indefinite Tense

*yazmaktayım* = I am writing (much used)
*yazmakta* bulun*urum* = I will be in the course of writing
(I will be writing) (very little used)

### Past Tense (Attestative)

*yazmakta idim* or *yazmaktaydım* = I was in the course of writing
(I was writing) (much used)

### Past Tense (Repeatative)

*yazmakta imişim* or *yazmaktaymışım (see 62)*
= It is said that I was in the course of writing
(that I was writing)

### Future Tense

*yazmakta bulunacağım* = I will be in the course of writing
(I will be writing)

## INITIATORY FORM OF THE VERBAL NOUN

(114) When the Doer is about to commence an action the word *üzere* = *on the point of (about to)* is placed after the verbal noun, to this the necessary tense, mood and personal suffixes being added.

(114a) It is conjugated with the help of the verbs *imek* and *bulunmak* in the following tenses. This form of the verb denotes a STRONG DESIRE or a DEFINITE DECISION to *begin* the *action*.

## INDICATIVE MOOD

### Present Tense

*yazmak üzere bulunuyorum* = I am about to write
*yazmak üzereyim* (Ind. tense *imek*) = I am about to write

### Past Attestative

*yazmak üzere idim* = I was just writing

### Indefinite Tense

*yazmak üzere bulunurum* = I will be about to write (not much used)

### Future Tense

*yazmak üzere bulunacağım* = I will be about to write

## NARRATIVE MOOD

### Present Tense

*yazmak üzere bulunuyordum* = I was about to write

## CONDITIONAL MOOD

*yazmak üzere isem* = If I am about to write

(114b) It is a matter of practice which is going tó teach the student where to use *imek* and where to use *bulunmak*.

Note: These examples are in different cases from those shown above:

| *sizi* | *rahatsız etmekten* | maksadım | = my object in troubling you |
| you to | disturb from | my object | |
| (obj.case) | | | |

| *söylenmekte* | *bir fayda* | *yoktur* | = It is of no use grumbling |
| grumbling in | a benefit | there is not | |

232

## GERUNDIAL MOODS AND FORMS

(115) So far we have seen throughout the grammar the modificatory part the *Verb, Noun,* and *Adjective* play in their turn. It is of greater importance to understand the special function of the Turkish GERUND, i.e. interpreting the *Turkish expression of thought* in an easier and more *concise manner*, and in a style much akin to the English.

*The chapters on Gerund and Phrase construction (190) should be studied together.*

# GERUNDS

(116) In the various examples we have seen how far the verb as a verbal adjective, in its role of governing the noun, extends its influence to, or maintains its relationship with the noun, through its qualificative power coupled with EXTENSIBILITY of VERBAL TIME (tense) and MANNER (mood) (30 a, b), (31 a, b, c), (32 a, b, c, d).

(117) The verb also as a verbal adjective maintains the *passive consequence* created by this qualificative resultance in its full effectiveness as seen in adjectives (29 a, b, c, d) and in nouns (12 a to k).

(118) A GERUND is that part of the Verb which becomes active, as one word with the flexibility of the verb. Though the limitation of *Time, Mood,* or *Person* may be little or not at all shown by the actual form of the GERUND, yet it is comprehensive of mood, time, and person this being determined by the Verb which immediately follows it (bearing in mind that in Turkish the main sentence is placed *last*).

In other words it is a form of two actions being carried out:

(119) *Either (a) concurrently* where the verb of one of the actions is placed in one of these gerundial forms (see 127, 128, 129a, 136 WHERE THEY ARE TREATED FULLY):

*ıp (ip, up, üp), rak, (rek), iken, d- (ığ, iğ, uğ, üğ)ım,* etc.

Examples:

*Her gün*     *gelip*     gider.
(every day    comes he    goes he)
= Every day he comes and goes.

*Gülerek*     *ayrıldık.*
(laughing     parted we)
= We left each other while laughing. (in a laughing mood)

*Ona*     *ayrılırken*     *söyledim.*
(him to    we parted when    told I)
= I told him when we parted.

*Geldiğinde*     *ona*     *söylerim.*
(arriving his on,    to him    tell I)
(Loc. C.)     (dat. case)
= I tell him on his arrival. (when he arrives)

(120) *Or (6) consecutively* where the commencement of one action being subject to the commencement or termination of the other, the verb of one action is placed in one of these gerundial forms (see 130, 131, 132, 135 WHERE THEY ARE TREATED FULLY).

**madan önce, ıncaya kadar, dıktan sonra**
**meden önce, inceye kadar, dikten sonra**

Examples:

*İşimi siz gelmeden önce bitirdim.*  =  I finished my work before you arrived.
*Siz geldikten sonra işimi bitirdim.*  =  I finished my work after you arrived.
*Siz gelinceye kadar beklerim.*  =  I will wait till you arrive.

(121) *Or (c)* where one action has commenced on the termination of another one, the verb of the first action being placed in one of these gerundial forms (see 133-133b, WHERE THEY ARE TREATED FULLY).

*lı, li* or *lıberi, liberi*

*Example:*

| Londra'ya | geleliberi | rahatsızım. |
|---|---|---|
| (London to | since arrival | indisposed am (I)) |

= I am ill since I arrived in London.

(122) *And finally* (d) where the *resultance* of two actions enacted at different times is being explained in the usual simple manner, when the verb of one of the actions is placed in the following *gerundial form*. Example:

| Eve | geldiğimde | mektubunu | buldum. |
|---|---|---|---|
| (house to | arrival my on | letter your | found I) |
| dat. c. | | obj. c. | |

= On my arrival home I found your letter.

(123) The advantage of a gerund is that in some cases it eliminates the conjunction, in others it prevents their repetition, and thus helps to build up a more concise phrase.

## PRESENT PARTICIPLE AS A GERUND

*(Verb Root + an, en = (who, which) (whom, which) (that))*

(124) As a gerund this plays a very important part, in various capacities.

| Mektubu | getiren adam | siz | misiniz? |
|---|---|---|---|
| (the letter | who is bringing man | you | ? you are) |
| (obj. case) | | | |

= Are you the **man who brought** this letter?

In the above example it is necessary to study the position of *getiren*. It has the dual function of (a) being the subject of the transitive verb *getirmek* and (b) qualifying the *noun adam* = (man). This is the main feature which distinguishes a *gerund* from an *adjective* or a *noun*.

The tense of the GERUND with regard to the completion of the action, i.e. Present or Past (see 118), depends on the tense of the verb which follows it. Therefore, the gerund, according to the verb which follows it may have its meaning in the past or present sense. *Some more examples:*

(1)  **Gelen**              *adam*        *kimdir?*
     (who comes or came      the man       who is)
     = Who is the man who is coming?

(2)  **Gelenleri**                *tanıyor*      *musunuz?*
     (those who come or came know          ? you)
     (obj. c.)
     = Do you know those who are coming?

(3)  **Geleni**                      *görmedim.*
     (that which comes or came    seen not have I)
     = I have not seen the one who came.

(4)  **Gelen**                  *mektuplar*   *nerede?*
     (which comes or came        letters      where)
     = Where are the letters which came?

The meaning of this gerund is comprehensive of the *present* and *past* only.

(125) The future sense is obtained by using the Gerund formed from the 3rd person singular of the future tense of the verb (see 32).

> *Gidecek*        *adam*      *nerededir?*
> (who will go      man        where is)
> = Where is the man who is going?

> *Söyleyecekleri*   *sözleri*    *bilirim.*
> (saying their      the words    know I)
> = I know what they will be saying.

> *Gidecek*        *adamları*   *yarın*      *göreceğim.*
> (that will go     men         tomorrow     see will I)
>                   (obj. c.)
> = Tomorrow I will see the men who are going.

(126) In the above examples *gelen* is in the simple form and the general verbal translation is that it represents the action taking place in the present and being completed, the time of completion remaining local.

We can say it is of the capacity of a verb in every respect, the time being understood to be in conjunction with the time and mood of the main sentence.

(126a) It can be in the nominative case.

*Ankara'dan*     *gelen*                    *adam*     *gitti.*
(Ankara **from**   who comes or came   man       went)
= The man who came from Ankara has gone.

(126aa) **Note:** In (3) above, *"gelen"* is translated (which came) because the verb which follows is in the past tense (118).

(126b) It can be placed in the objective case. Example:

*Hırsızlardan*          *kaçanı*                *tuttular.*
(the thieves from    which ran away       caught they)
                              (obj. c.)
= They caught the one of the thieves who ran away.

**Note:** The auxiliary verbs *olmak* and *bulunmak* are of great assistance as a similar gerund (see 65).

Compare the following phrases. It will be found that the gerundial sentences are clearer and that the two actions are interdependent.

**Co-ordinating Phrase:**
*Havada leylekler uçuyorlardı ve onları gördüm.*
= Storks were flying in the air and I saw them.

**Gerundial Phrase:**
*Havada uçan leylekleri gördüm.*
= I saw the storks (which were) flying in the air.

**Co-ordinating Phrase:**
*Havada kartallar uçuyorlar ve onları görüyorum.*
= The eagles are flying in the air and I see them.

**Gerundial Phrase:**
*Havada uçan kartalları görüyorum.*
I see the eagles (which are) flying in the air.

**Co-ordinating Phrase:**

*Uçak kayboldu ve onu daha bulamadılar.*

= The airplane got lost and they haven't found it yet.

**Gerundial Phrase:**

*Kaybolan uçak daha bulunamadı.*

= The aeroplane which got lost has not yet been found.

(126c) **Note:** It is essential to study the following examples to see the nuances between the two verbal nouns (12 a, and c).

We must not confuse the above examples with any of these shown hereunder. Examples:

*Havada uçan kelebekleri gördüm.*
= I saw the butterflies which were fluttering in the air.
(while they were fluttering)

*Uçakların havada uçtuklarını gördüm.*
= I saw the aeroplanes flying in the air.

*Uçakların havada uçmalarını seyrettim*
= I looked at the **flying** of the aeroplanes in the air.

*Uçakların havada uçuşlarını gördüm.*
= I saw the **way** in which the aeroplanes were flying in the air.

## RAK (hard) REK (soft) = WHILE ... ING
(active or continuous progressive form)

(127) The verb in the first sentence is put in the "*Continuous Progressive*" form when:

(i) The first action has been *completed* BEFORE the *commencement* of the *second one,* but where in the meantime the *first action completes* or *explains* the *action* of the verb in the *second sentence.*

(ii) The first action is independently undertaken BEFORE the *commencement* of the *second one,* but is essentially IN ACCORD with the action of the *second one* which is about to *commence.*

Both together will now be SIMILTANEOUSLY active and progressive, the first one, in the meantime, explaining or describing the *continuative action* of the second verb.

This Gerund, in both forms, is OBTAINED by adding *rak* (hard) and *rek* (soft) to the verb IN THE OPTATIVE MOOD. Examples:

| infinitive | | root | final root | + | opt. suf. | + | ger. suf. | |
|---|---|---|---|---|---|---|---|---|
| *kalmak* | = to stay | Cons. *l* | *kal* | + | *a* | + | *rak* | = while staying |
| *gelmek* | = to come | Cons. *l* | *gel* | + | *e* | + | *rek* | = while coming |
| *korumak* | = to protect | Vowel *u* | *koru* | + | *ya* | + | *rak* | = while protecting |
| *yürümek* | = to walk | Vowel *ü* | *yürü* | + | *ye* | + | *rek* | = while walking |

Note: It is the same for all 6 persons.

(127a) These Gerunds, simple or complex, are actually, as explained, replacing sentences.

Hereunder are some *simple phrases* or sentences together with some *Gerundial phrases*, so that the student can actually see what is meant by the part the Gerunds play in phrase building in the Turkish language.

Co-ordinating Phrase:
*Eşyalarımı aldım ve otelden çıktım.*
= I took my luggage and came out of the hotel.

Gerundial Phrase:
*Eşyalarımı alarak otelden çıktım.*
= Taking my luggage I left the hotel.

Co-ordinating Phrase:
*Otomobile bindi ve gitti.*
= He got into the car and drove away.

Gerundial Phrase:
*Otomobile binerek gitti.*
Getting into the car he drove away.

**Co-ordinating Phrase:**
*Bağırıyordu ve koşuyordu.*
= He was shouting and running.

**Gerundial Phrase:**
*Bağırarak koşuyordu.*
= He shouted as he ran.

| *İKEN* | (separate) | to closed and open syllables |
| *KEN* | (contracted) | to open syllables |
| *YKEN* | (contracted) | to open syllables |

*İken, ken, yken* = while, during the time that, though ... not, instead of

## ACTIVE AND PROGRESSIVE FORM

(128) This is another gerund which has the PROGRESSIVE POWER. It is used when a *second action* will take place during the *performance* of a *first one*. This first action may be completed, active, or continuative and progressive.

This gerund is OBTAINED by placing:
*"iken"* as a separate word or
*"ken"* joinid on to the THIRD PERSON SINGULAR of the *present, indefinite* and *future* tenses of the *indicative mood* and the past participle of the verb, for both hard (Ph. 8) and soft (Ph. 9) Verbs. It is not subject to graduation. Examples:

**Co-ordinating Phrase:**
*Eve gidiyordum ve Nevin'i gördüm.*
= I was going home and I saw Nevin.

**Gerundial Phrase:**
*Eve giderken Nevin'i gördüm.*
= I saw Nevin as I was going home.

**Co-ordinating Phrase:**
*Çocuk bahçede oynayacak idi fakat sokağa çıktı.*
= The child was going to play in the garden but he went out.

**Gerundial Phrase:**
*Çocuk bahçede oynayacak iken sokağa çıktı.*
= The child went out instead of playing in the garden.

**Co-ordinating Phrase:**
*Güven hem kitap okur hem dinlenir.*
= Güven both reads and rests.

**Gerundial Phrase:**
*Güven kitap okurken dinlenir.*
= Güven rests while reading.

(128a) It is also added to *nouns, adjectives, definitive combinations* and the noun in the *locative case*.

(128aa) It is translated as *"while ... being"* when it is placed after a *noun* or *adjective*. It is the same for both hard and soft words:

| | |
|---|---|
| *iken* | as a separate word, or as |
| *ken* | joined to consonant-ending words, and |
| *yken* | joined to vowel-ending words. |

*ken* is not subject to *graduation* of *sound*.

(128aaa) **Note:** Though in form gerunds in general are in the 3rd person singular, *being the same for all 6 persons*, they are understood to be of the same person as that of the second action (see 118). This rule applies to all gerunds.

(128b) The two actions can be *performed* by two *different doers*. Example:

| *Kırda* | *dolaşırken* | *yağmur* | *başladı.* |
|---|---|---|---|
| (the countryside in | walking while | rain | started) |

= While walking in the countryside it started raining.

This gerund is also added to the past participle of any verb in the *affirmative* and *negative* form. It is translated as "though not", with a negative verb or adjective. Examples:

*Gelmiş iken söyleyeyim.*      = While I have come let me speak (I will speak)
*Görmemiş iken bunu söyleyemem.* = I could not say this while I have not seen

**Hard**
closed syllables : *ıp, up*

**Soft**
closed syllables : *ip, üp*

open syllables  : *yıp, yup*

open syllables  : *yip, yüp*

(129) Where two sentences are in a co-ordinating relationship and in the same tense, mood, and person, the first one is placed in the above gerundial form and the conjunction AND, etc., removed. It will retain all the limitations (tense, mood, and person, number) of the verb of which it has taken the place, this generally being understood to be that of the verb which follows (see 118).

(129a) In the ordinary way the doer of the verb and of the gerund is the *same person.*

This gerund is obtained by adding:

*ıp, ip, up, üp* to consonant-ending (closed syllable) verb roots a "*y*" (*yıp, yip, yup, yüp*) is inserted between the verb root and the suffix when the verb root ends with a vowel (open syllables).

**closed syllables**

| | | |
|---|---|---|
| *kalmak* | = to stay |
| *gelmek* | = to come |
| *bulmak* | = to find |
| *görmek* | = to see |

**open syllables**

| | | |
|---|---|---|
| *yakalamak* | = to catch |
| *lekelemek* | = to stain |
| *korumak* | = to protect |
| *yürümek* | = to walk |

Examples:

**Co-ordinating Phrase:**
*Annemi göreceğim ve İzmir'e gideceğim.*
= I'll see my mother and go to İzmir.

**Gerundial Phrase:**
*Annemi görüp İzmir'e gideceğim.*
= (After) seeing my mother I'll go to İzmir.

**Co-ordinating Phrase:**
*İstanbul'a geldi ve Ankara'ya gitti.*
= He came to Istanbul and went to Ankara.

**Gerundial Phrase:**
*İstanbul'a gelip Ankara'ya gitti.*
= Coming to İstanbul he went to Ankara.

**Co-ordinating Phrase:**
*Kuşlar havada uçtular ve bir saat sonra kayboldular.*
= The birds flew in the sky and disappeared after an hour.

**Gerundial Phrase:**
*Kuşlar havada uçup bir saat sonra kayboldular.*
= Flying in the sky the birds disappeared after an hour.

(129b) The two actions can, however, have *two different doers*. Examples:

*Ortalığı       sis       basıp       arabalar       gidemez       oldu.*
(the surrounding the fog covering       the cars       go could not became)
= The fog coming down, the cars could not move.

*Gidip       gelenlerin       adedi       çoğalıyor*
(going       coming those of       the number       increasing is)
= The number of those coming and going is increasing

(129c) The gerund can be put in the *negative* form when it takes the place of a *verb in the negative*. It is obtained by first placing *ma, me,* next to the verb root, then adding *yıp yip.*

**Note:** The changes of the harmony are subject to graduation. Examples :

| *kalıp* | *gelip* | *bulup* | *koruyup* | *yürüyüp* |
| *kalmayıp* | *gelmeyip* | *bulmayıp* | *korumayıp* | *yürümeyip* |

*Söz dinlemedi ve sokağa çıktı. /*
*Söz dinlemeyip sokağa çıktı.*
= He did not obey and went out.

(129d) All verbs of various voices, and of the infinitive mood can be placed in this gerund. Examples:

| | | | |
|---|---|---|---|
| *görüşüp* | *çekinip* | *gelmek* | *gelmemek* |
| *görüşmeyip* | *çekinmeyip* | *gelip* | *gelmeyip* |

*Londra'ya gitmek ve gelmek masraflı olur.*
*Londra'ya gidip gelmek masraflı olur.*
= It would cost a lot to go to and return from London.

(129e) It is very much used in every tense and mood of the verb. Even *present* or *past participles* and *infinitives* can be replaced by this gerundial form. Examples:

| | |
|---|---|
| *Gidip gelen oldu mu?* | = Has anybody called? |
| *Oraya gidip gelmiş bir adamdır.* | = He is a man who has been there. |
| *Artık gidip gelmekte anlam yoktur.* | = It is no use going any more. |

**Note:** There is necessity in Turkish to mention that the person had gone and come back.

| **Hard** | **Soft** |
|---|---|
| *madan önce, madan* = before | *meden önce, meden* = before |

## CONDITIONAL AND PREFERENTIAL FORM

(130) When the *occurrence* of the second action is subject to the *completion* of the *first action* the verb of the first action is placed in the above gerundial form and the second verb placed in the *negative form*. This usually marks commencement and motion of a second action.

(130a) This gerund is obtained by adding *madan* or *meden önce,* or simply *madan (meden)* to the verb root. **Study examples.**

**Note:** It is the same for all 6 persons.

(130b) When the second action is placed in the *affirmative* it then means that the *second action* will commence irrespective of the *first action being completed.*

| **Plain Phrase:** | *Dersimi bitiririm öyle gelirim.* |
| | I'll finish my lesson then I'll come |
| **Gerundial Phrase:** | *Dersimi bitirmeden önce gelmem.* |
| | I won't come before finishing my lesson. |

| **Plain Phrase:** | *Bu işi bitiririm öyle dersimi yaparım.* |
| | I'll finish this work then I'll do my lesson. |
| **Gerundial Phrase:** | *Bu işi bitirmeden önce dersimi yapmam.* |
| | I won't do my lesson before finishing this work. |

| **Plain Phrase:** | *Dersimi bitirmem ve gelirim.* |
| | I won't finish my lesson and I'll come. |
| **Gerundial Phrase:** | *Dersimi bitirmeden önce gelirim.* |
| | I'll come before I finish my lesson. |

| **Plain Phrase:** | *Bu işi bitirmem ve dersimi yaparım.* |
| | I won't finish this work and I'll do my lesson. |
| **Gerundial Phrase:** | *Bu işi bitirmeden önce dersimi yaparım.* |
| | I'll do my lesson before I finish this work. |

**Note:** This gerund is actually the verbal noun (12a) meaning "state of action," placed in the *Ablative case* and followed by *önce* = before.

**Note:** DO NOT confuse *ma, me* the verbal noun suffix with *ma, me* the negative particle.

(130c) The verbal noun can also be placed in the Dative case or in any of the other cases, and can carry out any of the other functions of the noun, the "Definitive Combination", for instance. It is only when this verbal noun has the function of the verb that it is a gerund: (See also (190) Phrase construction.) Examples:

*Bu işi çabuk bitirmede büyük hizmetiniz olur.*
= You will have accomplished great service in finishing this work quickly.

*Bu işi çabuk bitirmenin lûzumu meydandadır.*
= The necessity of finishing this work quickly is obvious.

| Hard | Soft |
|------|------|
| closed syllables: *ınca, unca* | closed syllables : *ince, ünce* |
| open syllables: *yınca, yunca* | open syllables : *yince, yünce* |

English translation : on ...ing, directly, when

Examples:

*Eve gelince bir mektup bulduk.*
We found a letter on arriving home.

*Ses duyunca ayağa kalktım.*
I stood up (directly) on hearing a voice.

(131) When the *commencement of the action in the second sentence depends on the realization or completion of the action in the first sentence,* the verb in the first sentence is placed in this Gerundial form, and the consequent action placed in the second sentence. This form is mostly used when the second action will immediately follow the completion of the first one. The second action may be continuative or may also be completed.

This Gerund is obtained by adding:

*ınca* (hard) or *ince* (soft) to consonant-ending verb roots.
*yınca* (hard) or *yince* (soft) to vowel-ending verb roots.

Note: *It is the same for all 6 persons. Examples:*

| | |
|------|------|
| *Vapura girdim ve hareket ettik* | *Vapura girince hareket ettik.* |
| I entered the boat and we sailed. | On embarking we sailed. |
| *Beni gördü ve kaçtı.* | *Beni görünce kaçtı.* |
| He saw me and ran away. | He ran away on seeing me. |
| *Uyanırım ve yataktan çıkarım.* | *Uyanınca yataktan çıkarım.* |
| I wake up and get out of bed. | On waking up I get out of bed. |

The Gerund can be placed in the negative form, the second verb then being placed (i) in the affirmative to mark "preference" and (ii) in the negative to mark "conditional."

Examples:

(i) *Gelmeyince*          *gideriz.*          = We will go if he does not come.
   (on not coming    we will go)

**Note:** This example would actually be better expressed as:

   *Gelmezse*                      *gideriz.*    = If he does not come we will go.
   (come shall not he if    will go we)

(ii) *Zeki gelmeyince*          *gitmeyiz.* = We will not go if Zeki does not come.
    (Zeki on not coming    go will not we)

**Note:** This example would actually be better expressed as:

   *Zeki    gelmedikçe*          *gitmeyiz.* = We will not go until Zeki has arrived.
   (Zeki    has come not till    will go not we)

For consonant ending verb roots:

   **Hard** = *ıncaya kadar, uncaya kadar*
   **Soft** = *inceye kadar, ünceye kadar*

For vowel ending verb roots:

   **Hard** = *yıncaya kadar, yuncaya kadar*
   **Soft** = *yinceye kadar, yünceye kadar*

English translation = until, up to the time that (conditional continuative)

## SUBSEQUENTIAL FORM

(132) This form of Gerund is used when the verb in the first sentence denotes *the time or fact of the commencement or completion of the action of the verb in the second sentence.*

It is formed by adding to the verb root:

247

*ıncaya kadar* to hard verb roots ending with a consonant (Ph. 8).
*inceye kadar* to soft verb roots ending with a consonant (Ph. 9).

A "y" (*yıncaya, yinceye*) is inserted when the verb root ends with a vowel.

The action of the second verb is *continuous* until the *commencement* or *completion* of the first one.

The verbs of both sentences are placed in the affirmative. This is a form of emphasis.

| | |
|---|---|
| **Simple Phrase:** | *Mektup almak ümidiyle* bekle*dim*. |
| | I waited with the hope of receiving a letter. |
| **Gerundial Phrase:** | *Mektup alıncaya kadar bekledim.* |
| | I waited till I received a letter. |
| | |
| **Simple Phrase:** | *Mektup almak için bekleyeceğim.* |
| | I'll wait to receieve a letter. |
| **Gerundial Phrase:** | *Mektup gelinceye kadar bekleyeceğim.* |
| | I'll wait till a letter arrives. |

## LI, Lİ = SINCE, FROM THE TIME THAT
(continuative - progressive)

For all words:      **LI** (hard)
                    **Lİ** (soft)

(133) To denote that the *occurrence* of an action or the *progressive* of *continuative* state of an action which began since the commencement or after the completion of a first action, this first action is placed in the above gerundial form.

This is obtained by placing the verb in the optative mood and adding "*lı*" or "*li*". *It is the same for all 6 persons.* Examples:

| | |
|---|---|
| **Simple Phrase:** | *İstanbul'a geldim fakat kimseyi görmedim.* |
| | I came to İstanbul but I didn't see anybody. |
| **Gerundial Phrase:** | *İstanbul'a geleli daha kimseyi görmedim.* |
| | I haven't seen anybody since my arrival in İstanbul. |

248

(133a) **Note:** This Gerund has that peculiar position of being an adjective determining the meaning of the second verb and yet holding all the potentialities of a verb.

*lıdan beri* = hard, for all words = since, from the time that
*liden beri* = soft, for all words = since, from the time that

(133b) This Gerund is practically the same as (133), but is in a more emphatic and precise form. The first sentence can also determine when the action of the second sentence will begin, or give reason for the commencement of the second action. It is formed exactly as (133) but is then placed in the ABLATIVE case, to which suffix *"beri"* is added (adverb meaning "this side" (of time)). Examples:

| | |
|---|---|
| **Simple Phrase:** | *İstanbul'a geldim ve çalışıyorum.* |
| | I arrived in İstanbul and I am working. |
| **Gerundial Phrase:** | *İstanbul'a geleli beri çalışıyorum.* |
| | I've been working since I came to İstanbul. |
| | |
| **Simple Phrase:** | *Londra'dan ayrıldım ve evden mektup bile almadım.* |
| | I left London and I haven't received even a letter from home. |
| **Gerundial Phrase:** | *Londra'dan ayrılalı beri evden mektup bile almadım.* |
| | I haven't received even a letter from home since I left London. |

## DIKÇA, DUKÇA

*dıkça, dukça (hard); dikçe, dükçe (soft)*
= for vowel and flat consonont ending verb roots

*tıkça, tukça (hard); tikçe, tükçe (soft)*
= for sharp consonont ending verb roots

English translation: as long as, so long as, while, during the time that (marking occurence of actions)

(134) When the prolongation or duration of the second action is subject to the duration of the action of the first verb the first verb is placed in the above gerundial mood.

This is obtained by adding:

*dıkça, dukça*     to hard verb roots (Ph. 8)
*dikçe, dükçe*     to soft verb roots (Ph. 9)

(134a) The "*d*" is changed to "*t*" when the verb root ends with any of the sharp consonants (see Ph. 29).

**Note:** *ça* (or *çe*) is the actual ending of this gerund, the "*dik*", etc. being the suffix of the 1st person plural of the past tense attestative of the indicative mood to which the *ça* *(çe)* is added. **It is the same for all 6 persons.** Examples:

| | |
|---|---|
| **Simple Phrase:** | *Siz orada kalırsanız ben burada kalırım.* |
| | (I will stay here if you stay there.) |
| **Gerundial Phrase:** | *Siz orada kaldıkça ben burada kalırım.* |
| | (I will stay here as long as you stay there) |

| | |
|---|---|
| **Simple Phrase:** | *İnsan çalışırsa ileri gider.* |
| | (Man progresses if he works.) |
| **Gerundial Phrase:** | *İnsan çalıştıkça ileri gider.* |
| | (Man progresses as long as he works.) |

(134b) **The Gerund can be placed in the Negative.** Examples:

| | |
|---|---|
| **Simple Phrase:** | *Siz buraya gelmezseniz biz bu işi bitiremeyiz.* |
| | (We cannot finish this work if you do not come here.) |
| **Gerundial Phrase:** | *Siz buraya gelmedikçe biz bu işi bitiremeyiz.* |
| | (We cannot finish this work as long as you do not come here.) |
| | (We cannot finish this work unless you come here.) |

*dıktan sonra, duktan sonra* (hard); *dikten sonra, dükten sonra* (soft)
= for vowel and flat consonant ending verb roots

*tıktan sonra, tuktan sonra* (hard); *tikten sonra, tükten sonra* (soft)
= for sharp consonant ending verb roots

English translation: after, subsequent to, as the result of
(actions are subsequential)

(135) When the *occurrence* of the action of *the verb* in the second sentence is

subsequent to the completion of the action of the verb in the first sentence this verb is placed in the above *gerundial* form.

This is obtained by adding to vowel and flat consonant-ending verb roots: *dıktan/duktan sonra* (hard), *dikten/dükten sonra* (soft).

The "*d*" is changed to "*t*" when the verb root ends with any of the sharp consonants.

(135a) **Note:** *tan,* etc. is the actual ending of this Gerund, the *dık* etc., being the suffix of the 1st person plural of the past tense attestative of the indicative mood, to which the *tan,* etc., is added. **It is the same for all 6 persons.** Examples:

**Simple Phrase:** *Kitabı okurum sonra onu iade ederim.*
= I will read the book and afterwards return it.
**Gerundial Phrase:** *Kitabı okuduktan sonra iade ederim.*
= I will return the book after I have read it.

**Simple Phrase:** *Evi geçtim sonra Osman'ı gördüm.*
= I passed the house and afterwards I saw Osman.
**Gerundial Phrase:** *Evi geçtikten sonra Osman'ı gördüm.*
= I saw Osman after I passed the house.

**Simple Phrase:** *Hırsız kaçtı fakat onu bir saat sonra yakaladılar.*
= The thief escaped but they caught him after an hour.
**Gerundial Phrase:** *Hırsızı kaçtıktan bir saat sonra yakaladılar.*
= They caught the thief an hour after he escaped.

(135b) The negative form of this gerund is also used. Examples:

**Simple Phrase:** *Kitabı okumadınız, bir şey anlamazsınız.*
= You haven't read the book, you won't understand anything.
**Gerundial Phrase:** *Kitabı okumadıktan sonra bir şey anlayamazsınız.*
= You cannot understand anything unless you have read the book.

Some typical Turkish expressions in this form:
*Gelmedikten sonra ne yapayım?*
What shall/can I do if he/she doesn't come?

*Ben istedikten sonra ona söz düşmez.*
If I am willing he/she has no right to interfere.

*İstemedikten sonra zorlayamazsınız.*
If he/she isn't willing you can't force him/her.

*Gittikten sonra ne yapabilirsiniz?*
If he/she has gone, what can you do?

**Note:** The part before *tan* is also an adjective (see 31c).

### The Relative Gerund

**singular**

| | | |
|---|---|---|
| 1st person | : | *D : or T : I, İ, U, Ü Ğ : I, İ, U, Ü M* |
| 2nd person | : | *D : or T : I, İ, U, Ü Ğ : I, İ, U, Ü N* |
| 3rd person | : | *D : or T : I, İ, U, Ü Ğ : I, İ, U, Ü* |

**plural**

| | | |
|---|---|---|
| 1st person | : | *D : or T : I, İ, U, Ü Ğ : I, İ, U, Ü M : I, İ, U, Ü, Z* |
| 2nd person | : | *D : or T : I, İ, U, Ü Ğ : I, İ, U, Ü N : I, İ, U, Ü, Z* |
| 3rd person | : | *D : or T : I, or U, KLAR : I, - - -* |
| | | *D : or T : I, or Ü KLER : İ --* |

(136) In this particular case it is necessary to remember that a gerund is that part of the verb which when placed in front of a noun has the qualificative function of an adjective and the extension of time of a verb. A careful study of the plain phrases we have given in contrast to the Gerundial ones will show that, although it seems that the thought could be expressed either way, the Gerundial form has that particular force of bringing home the point in mind for which the Gerund stands.

(136a) This Gerund is used where the *object* of the *first verb* (gerund) is also the *object* of the *second verb*. The two verbs may, or may not have a *common "doer"*. Example:

| *Okuduğum* | *kitabı* | *okudun mu?* |
|---|---|---|
| reading my | the book (obj. case) | you read? |
| (which I read) | | |

= Have you read the book I read?

252

This Gerund is nothing but the *verbal adjective* (i.e. 1st Pers. Plural of the *Past Tense Attestative* of the Primitive verb, similar to that shown in (31c) placed in a Definitive Combination where the first word is a *personal pronoun* in the *possessive case*. This personal pronoun, as usual, is omitted, only being used when there is need for emphasis. *It is a form, where the adjective qualifying the noun instead of the noun itself, is placed in the Possessive case. Note meaning in both Trans. and Intrans. verbs.* This Gerund is used when the completion of the action is in the *past* or *present*. It is formed as follows: The suffix of the *1st Person* plural of the *Past Attestative, Indicative mood, dık, (dik, duk, dük)* is added to the verb root. To obtain the six persons the suffixes as shown in chart 50h will be added. (See also (50j) to (50lll).) The *"k"* being a sharp consonant changes to *"ğ"* when coming in contact with the vowel of this suffix. The *"d"* is changed to *"t"* when the verb root ends with any of the sharp consonants (see Ph. 29).
*Note difference of meaning in Trans. and Intrans. verbs.*

| Pers. pron. | *görmek* = to see (Trans. verb) | |
|---|---|---|
| (omitted) | *gördük* = seen (31c) | |
| | | |
| (*Benim*) | *gördüğüm* | = seen by me, or my seeing |
| (*Senin*) | *gördüğün* | = seen by you, or your seeing |
| (*Onun*) | *gördüğü* | = seen by him etc., or his/her/its seeing |
| (*Bizim*) | *gördüğümüz* | = seen by us, or our seeing |
| (*Sizin*) | *gördüğünüz* | = seen by you, or your seeing |
| (*Onların*) | *gördükleri* | = seen by them, or their seeing |

| | *gelmek* = to come (Intrans. verb) | |
|---|---|---|
| | *geldik* = coming (31c) | |
| | | |
| (*Benim*) | *geldiğim* | = my coming |
| (*Senin*) | *geldiğin* | = your coming |
| (*Onun*) | *geldiği* | = his/her/its coming |
| (*Bizim*) | *geldiğimiz* | = our coming |
| (*Sizin*) | *geldiğiniz* | = your coming |
| (*Onların*) | *geldikleri* | = their coming |

**Simple Phrase:**  *Bir adamı arıyordu onu buldu.*
= He was looking for a man, he found him.

**Gerundial Phrase:**  *Aradığı adamı buldu.*
= He found the man he was looking for.

| **Simple Phrase:** | *Bir mektup gönderdim, onu aldı.* |
| | = I sent a letter, he received it. |
| **Gerundial Phrase:** | *Gönderdiğim mektubu aldı.* |
| | = He received the letter I sent. |

(136aa) *In the 3rd person sing. or plural, a noun, proper or common, can be the first word of the Def. Combination, instead of the pronoun. The meaning will vary with the sense of the verb. Compare the following sentences:*

| *(Onun)* | *söylediği* | *doğrudur.* | = What he said is correct. |
| (he of) | saying his | correct is | |

| *Adamın* | *söylediği* | *doğrudur.* | = What the man said is correct. |
| the man of | saying his | correct is | |

| *Ahmet'in* | *söylediği* | *doğrudu.r* | = What Ahmet said is correct. |
| Ahmet of | saying his | correct is | |

| *(Onların)* | *geldiklerini* | *biliyorum.* | = I know that they have come. |
| they of | coming their know I | | |

| *Gemilerin* | *geldiklerini* | *gördüm.* | = I saw the boats come. |
| the boats of | coming their saw I | | |

(136b) Whether the Doer of the action in the *gerundial phrase* is different from that of the verb in the second sentence or is the same, the person and number of the gerund is marked by the respective personal pronoun suffixes (see 50h).

(136c) The time inherent in this Gerund is reserved to the past and present, with the clear understanding that the action is completed.

(136cc) **Note:** When *mere reference* to the action in the past, present and future is made, the verbal noun (12a) is used instead of the Gerund. The verbal noun has a direct connection with this Gerund. It is translated as the "action or state of, or fact of the action". Examples:

*Adamın buraya gelmesi gerekir.*
= It is necessary for the man to come here.

*Gemilerin gelmeleri yakındır.*
= The boats will shortly arrive.

(136d) To extend the time of this Gerund to the *future*, with the object of stating the expected realization of the action in a time to come (see 136a) the 3rd pers. sing. of the Future of the Indicative Mood is taken. When a statement is made as to the *definite completion of the action in the future* then the action will be expressed with the *past participle* used with the *future tense of the verbs olmak or bulunmak* (see 136p). Example:

*Dükkân kapanmış bulunacağından artık yarın giderim.*
= As the shop will be closed I will go tomorrow.

(136e) This form of gerund is subject to the same variations as the previous one.

(136f) The object of the Gerund can also be the *Subject* or *Object* of the second verb.

(136ff) When it is the *Subject* it is used as it is, but when it is the *object* it is put in the *Objective* case (see 50lll). Examples:

*Aldığınız haber* (subject) *doğrudur.*
(past)
= The news you received is correct.

*Verdiği haber* (subject) *uydurmadır.*
(past or present)
= The news he is giving is false.

*Alacağın tedbirleri* (object) *unutma.*
(future)
= Don't forget the measures you are going to take.

*Gördüğün ev* (subject) *benimdir.*
(present)
= The house you are seeing is mine.

*Göreceğim adam* (subject) *babamdır.*
(future)
= The man I'm going to see is my father.

*Vereceğimiz örnekleri* (object) *kaybetmeyiniz.*
(future)
= Don't lose the samples we are going to give.

*Dediklerini* (object) *hatırınızda tutunuz.*
(present or past)
= Keep in your mind what they have told you.

(136fff) This gerund is also placed in the various verbal cases when in some cases it forms some new kinds of gerundial forms.

## IN THE NOMINATIVE CASE

(136g) It is used as it is, i.e. in the Nominative Case (see 24aa), when it is the subject of a verb.

| *Dediğim* | *geç güç* | *çıktı.* |
|---|---|---|
| (said by me | late difficult | come out) |

= Whatever I said though late or difficult came to pass.

| *Dediğin* | *doğrudur.* | = What you say or said is correct. |
|---|---|---|
| (said by thee | is true) | |

| *Dediği* | *iyi* | *kötü* | *oldu.* |
|---|---|---|---|
| (said by him | good | bad | came to pass) |

= Whatever he said bad or good has come to pass.

| *Senin* | *bilmediğin* | *ne var?* | = What is there that you do not know? |
|---|---|---|---|
| (thou of | known not by thee | what is there) | |

| *Söylediğim* | *yeri* | *buldunuz mu?* |
|---|---|---|
| (told by me | the place | found have you?) |

= Have you found the place of which I have spoken to you?

(136gg) It is also followed by certain postpositions:

| takdirde | = in the event of | halde | = although |
|---|---|---|---|
| zaman | = when | gibi | = as |

256

*Dediğim gibi oldu.*　　　　　　　　= It happened as I foretold.

*Bildiğim halde gittim.*　　　　　　= I went though I knew of it.

*Gördüğüm zaman inanırım.*　　　　= I believe (it) when I see (it).

## IN THE OBJECTIVE CASE

(By add. *ı, i, u,* or *ü* to 1st and 2nd pers. sing. and plur. *nı, ni, nu,* or *nü* to 3rd pers. sing. and plur. see 50lll.)

(136h) When this gerund is the object of a verb it is placed in the objective case.

*Söylediğimi*　　*dinleyiniz.*　　　　　= Listen to what I am telling you.
(saying my　　　listen you)

*Ne*　　*söylediklerini*　　*biliyor musunuz?*　= Do you know what they are saying?
(what　saying their　　do know? you)

*Kapıcının*　　*geldiğini*　　*babama*　　　*bildir.*
(the porter of　coming his　father my to　　announce)
　= Inform my father that the porter has arrived.

## IN THE DATIVE CASE

(By add. *a* or *e* to 1st and 2nd pers sing. and plur; *na* or *ne* to 3rd pers. sing. and plur. see 50lll.)

(136hh) It is placed in the dative case when it is an object to an intransitive verb of the second class.

*Dediğime*　　*bakmayınız.*　　　　= Don't take any notice of what I am telling.
(saying my to　look don't you)

*Söylediğine*　　*önem*　　*veriniz.*　= Pay attention to what he says.
(saying his to　attention　pay you)

*Sorduklarıma    cevap    verir    misiniz?*
(askings my to    answer    give will    ? you)
= Will you give me an answer to what I am asking you)

(136hhh) **Note:** This gerund is also followed by the adverbs.

*göre* = according    ***nazaran*** = in view of    ***binaen*** = upon

*İşittiğime    göre    bu    sene    üzüm mahsulü    çok iyi    imiş.*
(Hearing my to    according    this    year    raisin crop    much good    is)
= According to what I have heard this year the raisin crop is very good.

*Söylediklerine    göre    İstanbul'da    soğuk    varmış.*
(sayings their to    in view    of Istanbul in    cold    there is)
= According to what they say it is cold in Istanbul.


## IN THE LOCATIVE CASE

(By add. *da* or *de* to 1st and 2nd pers sing. and plur.; *nda* or *nde* to 3rd pers. sing. and plur. see 50lll.)

(136i) When it is placed in the *locative* case it means *on,* or *at the time when,* and it completes the meaning of the verb in the main sentence.

*Eve geldiğimde İbrahim'i gördüm.*
= I saw İbrahim when I arrived home or on my arrival home.

*Sokağa çıktığımda hava açıldı.*
= It cleared up when I got out.

*Londra'ya vardığında size yazacaktır.*
= He will write to you when he arrives in London.

*İzzet'i gördüğünüzde benden selam söyleyiniz.*
= Give my regards to İzzet when you see him.

It can be placed in this case only when it is in the nominative case.

When *de* is found to be placed after the gerund in any of the other cases it is not the locative suffix but the adverb "also" = *de* (see 139c) and is written separately.

## IN THE ABLATIVE CASE

(By add. *dan* or *den* to 1st and 2nd pers. sing. and pl.; *ndan* or *nden* to 3rd pers. sing. and pl. see 50lll)

(136j) When this gerund is placed in the ablative case it forms the causal gerund, **or a causal case of a verb.** Examples:

*Rahatsız    olduğumdan    okula    gitmedim.*
(indisposed  being my from  school to  go not did I)
= I did not go to school as I was unwell.

*Sizi    gördüğüme    çok    sevindim.*
(you    seeing my    much    delighted was I)
= I am very happy as I have seen you.

*Geç    kaldığından    İbrahim'i    mazur    görünüz.*
(late    staying her from  İbrahim    excused    see you)
= Forgive İbrahim for being late.

*Bu işi    yaptığınızdan    memnun    musunuz?*
(this work    doing your from  content    ? you are)
= Are you pleased at having done this job?

(136k) This gerund is made more concise when the adverb *beri* meaning this *side (this side of time)* (since) is added to the above. It is merely making the time of the second action more precise. In other words it is the causal gerund in the emphatic form. Example:

*Buraya    geldiğimden    beri    rahatsızım.*
(here to    arrival my from  since    unwell am)
= I have been unwell ever since I arrived here.

This sentence can be replaced by (133a):

*Buraya geleli beri rahatsızım.*

# IN THE CAUSATIVE CASE *(için)*

(1361) The gerund can also be placed in the simple causative form by adding *(için* = for, as, since), **when it becomes a causal case to a verb.**

> *Gerçeği     bildiğim için     öyle     hareket ettim.*
> (the truth   knowing my as   like that   acted I)
> = I behaved like that for I knew the truth.

> *Uzaktan     geldiğim     için     beni     bekle.*
> (far from   coming my   for     me     wait)
> = As I have come from a long distance wait for me.

> *İnsanca hareket     ettiğiniz     için     sizi     tebrik ederim.*
> (man as behaving   your     for     you     congratulate I)
> = I must congratulate you on behaving like a man.

**Note:** It is seldom put in the Instrumentative Case:

> *Söylediğimle yetinme.*          = Don't be satisfied with what I say.

## POSSESSIVE CASE

(By add. *ın, in, un,* or *ün* to 1st and 2nd pers. sing. and pl.; *nın, nin, nun,* or *nün* to 3rd pers. sing, and pl. see 50lll.)

(136m) The *possessive* case of this gerund is best replaced by the verbal noun (12a) put in the *possessive (genitive)* case where it forms the first part of a definitive combinition (50h) and as such, (being the object of the second verb) will be placed in the objective case (see 24n and 50lll). Examples:

> *Çalışmamın     mükâfatını     isterim.*
> (labour my     of the reward   desire I)
> (gen. c.)     (acc. c. 24e)
> = I want the reward of my labour.

(136mm) **Note:** As part of a definitive combination this gerund can be put in all the variations of it (see 136nn). Example:

*geldiğimin* = my coming of  *sebebini* = the reason
  (gen. case)     (acc. c.) (obj. c.)

(136n) *When the completion of the action is to take place in the future it is formed as follows:*

By adding the Future Tense suffix *cak* (Hard) or *cek* (Soft) to the optative mood. To obtain the six persons, the suffixes as shown in chart 50h will be added. See also 50j to 50lll. The "*k*" being a sharp consonant changes to "*ğ*" when coming in contact with the vowel of the personal suffix (see Ph. 31). It is used in all the manners and forms of the Gerund in the past tense.

*gelmek* = to come  *kalmak* = to stay  *söylemek* = to say

| | | | |
|---|---|---|---|
| *geleceğim* | = my coming | *kalacağım* | *söyleyeceğim* |
| *geleceğin* | = your coming | *kalacağın* | *söyleyeceğin* |
| *geleceği* | = his/her/its coming | *kalacağı* | *söyleyeceği* |
| *geleceğimiz* | = our coming | *kalacağımız* | *söyleyeceğimiz* |
| *geleceğiniz* | = your coming | *kalacağınız* | *söyleyeceğiniz* |
| *gelecekleri* | = their coming | *kalacakları* | *söyleyecekleri* |

Examples:

*Gideceğim daha belli değildir.*
= It is not yet known whether I will be going.

*Nereye gideceğimi ben de bilmiyorum.*
= Neither do I, myself, know where I will be going.

*Bu işi yapacağına inanma.*
= Don't believe that he will do this job.

*Yapacağından emin misin?*
= Are you sure that he will do it?

(136nn) Note the difference between *this gerund* with the six personal suffixes affixed and the ordinary *future tense*. It is also interesting to study this gerund when placed in the verbal cases.

Hereunder two examples of (136a and 136n):

| Nom. | : | *geleceğim* | *gördüğüm* |
|------|---|-------------|------------|
| Obj. | : | *geleceğimi* | *gördüğümü* |
| Dat. | : | *geleceğime* | *gördüğüme* |
| Loc. | : | *geleceğimde* | *gördüğümde* |
| Poss. | : | *geleceğimin* | *gördüğümün* |
| Abl. | : | *geleceğimden* | *gördüğümden* |
| Cau. | : | *geleceğim için* | *gördüğüm için* |
| Instr. | : | *bildiğim ile* | *gördüğüm ile* |

(136p) *Both the PAST PARTICIPLE and also the 3rd PERSON of the FUTURE tense of any verb can be used with the verb "olmak" placed in this gerundial form, and the PAST PARTICIPLE of any verb with the verb "bulunmak" placed in this gerundial form. "olmak" and "bulunmak" can be subject to all the variations of this Gerund.* Examples:

*Enver Bey gitmiş olduğundan kendisini göremedim.*
= Enver Bey had gone I could not see him himself.

*Tamamen bitirmiş olduğu için artık bir şey yapılamazdı.*
As he had finished altogether nothing further could be done.

## CASINA, CESİNE

*casına* (hard); *cesine* (soft)
= for vowel and flat consonant ending (verbal) words
*çasına* (hard); *çesine* (soft)
= for sharp consonant ending (verbal) words

English translation:  as if + clause

## SUPPOSITIONAL FORM

(137) This gerund is used when comparison is made between a "REAL" state and a "SUPPOSITIONAL" one.

It is formed by adding:     *casına* or *çasına* (Hard) or *cesine* or *çesine* (Soft)

to the PAST PARTICIPLE Where "COMPLETION OF THE ACTION" is meant, and to the 3rd person singular of the INDEFINITE tense, where the "PROGRESSIVE" form of the verb is to be understood.
**Note:** It completes the meaning of the verb which follows. *It is the same for all 6 persons.*
Examples :

| | |
|---|---|
| *Koymuşçasına buldum.* | = I found it as if I knew where I had put it. |
| *Darılmışçasına hareket etti.* | = He behaved as if he were angry. |
| *Görmüşçesine anlatıyorsun.* | = You relatest it as if you had seen it. |
| *Bilmişçesine söyledi.* | = He spoke as if he knew of it. |
| *Bilircesine söylüyor.* | = He speaks as if he knows about it. |
| *Görürcesine buluyor.* | = He finds it as if he is seeing it. |

## MAZLIK, MEZLİK
(form used for indicating dissimulation)

*mazlık* (hard), *mezlik* (soft) / for all verbal nouns
English translation: ... not to ... or not to have ...

(138) This gerund is used to *expose the feignedness* of the negation of an action which in reality is being enacted or completed. It actually denotes the *dissimalative mood* of the verb. It is obtained by affixing to the *verbal noun* the negative suffix *maz, mez* and finally adding *lık, lik* (see also 13a). It is then placed in the necessary verbal case according to the verb with which it is used. The "*k*" changes to "*ğ*" when coming into contact with a vowel (see Ph. 31) (obj., dat., poss. cases). Examples:

| | |
|---|---|
| *Anlamamazlık taslıyorsunuz.* | = You pretend not to understand. |
| *Bilmemezlikten geliyor.* | = He feigns not to have known, or to know. |
| *İşitmemezlik taslıyor.* | = He pretends not to have heard or hear. |
| *Görmemezliği âdet edindi.* | = He has the habit of pretending not to have *seen (has made a habit of ...).* |
| *Tanımamazlıktan geliyor.* | = He pretends not to recognize. |

**Note:** Verbal case varies according to verb it is with.

# PHRASES JOINED BY *Kİ* = THAT

(139) Two *sentences can be joined* together by using the word *ki* (meaning *"that"*).

(139a) It must always be written separately.

(139b) The first verb can be used in any tense of any mood, but the verb in the second sentence must be in the *optative* mood, the *absent* person of the *imperative* mood, or the *future tense* of the indicative mood, according to the tense of the first verb. This latter is generally used in the 3rd person singular. Study the following examples:

| *Gönül* | *ister* | *ki* | herkes | memnun | ol*sun.* |
|---|---|---|---|---|---|
| (the heart | shall wish | that | everybody | satisfied | be) |

= One wishes (that) everybody could be happy.

| *Arzu* | *ederim ki* | *bu* | *işte* | *kazanasınız.* |
|---|---|---|---|---|
| (desire | will have I that | this | work at | would that win you) |

= I hope (that) you will succeed in this (affair).

| *Arzu* | *ederim ki* bu | *işte* | *siz kazanasınız.* |
|---|---|---|---|
| (desire | will have'I that | this work at | you would that win you) |

= I hope that you yourself (for emphasis on the person) will succeed in this (affair).

| *Eminim ki* | *davayı* | *siz* | *kazanacak*sınız. |
|---|---|---|---|
| (sure am that | the case | you | win will you) |

= I am sure (that) you (yourself = emphasis) will win your case.

| *Korkarım* | *ki* | *haksızsınız.* |
|---|---|---|
| (afraid am | that | wrong are you) |

= I am afraid (that) you are wrong.

**Note:** Do not confuse *ki* = (THAT) with *ki* = (WHICH) (see 51).


## USE OF *DA, DE* or *DAHİ* = ALSO (Adv.) and *DA, DE* = IN (Loc. suff.)

(139c) The adverb *da, de* = ALSO must not be confused with the locative *da, de* = IN.

(139d) *da, de* ( = in) is changed to *ta, te* when joined to a word ending with a sharp consonant (see Ph. 31).

(139e) *da, de* ( = also) never has the *d* changed to <F53t.

(139f) *da, de* ( = also) is always written separately and *da, de* ( = in) is joined on to the word.

(139g) *da* will follow a *hard* word, and *de* a soft one. *Dahi* follows both hard and soft. Examples:

*da, de* = in (locative case) (see 18a)

*Bizde böyle şeyleri sevmezler.*
In our place (or country) they don't like such things.

*Evdeki eşyaları gördünüz mü?*
Have you seen the furniture which is at home?

*Elinizdeki nedir?*
What have you in your hand?

*Neredesiniz?*
Where are you?

*Orada mısınız?*
Are you there?

*Ayakta durmayınız.*
Don't remain foot on (standing)

*dahi* or *da, de* = also (adv. see 56a)

*Biz de böyle şeyleri severiz.*
We, too, love such things.

*Ben de geleceğim.*
I also will come.

*Biz de orada olsaydık bir şey yapamazdık.*
If we had been there too, we could not have done anything.

*Bu işi yaptığınızdan da çok memnun olacaksınız.*
You will also be pleased at having done this job.

*Söylediğine de önem veriniz.*
Also pay attention to what he says

# CLASSIFICATION OF THE VERB

(140) The VERB is divided into two sections in respect of its action, namely *Transitive* and *Intransitive*.

(141) It is again sub-divided in respect of the presence or absence of its "doer" into *"cited"*, or *"apparent"* and *"uncited"* or *"non-apparent"* (see 155-156).

## THE TRANSITIVE VERB

(142) *TRANSITIVE.* A verb is *transitive* when the action carried out by the "doer" affects an object, definite or indefinite in a clear and direct manner. This object determines the extent of the action of the verb and is called the *"evident object"*.

(142a) *A verb is Transitive* when it can give an answer to the question *"kimi"* (whom), or *"neyi"* (which). (Note that the question is, itself, in the *objective case*).

(142b) In the sentence the *"evident object"* is placed in front of, and nearest, the verb.

## THE VERBAL CASE OF THE TRANSITIVE VERB

(142c) When the *"evident object"* is *definite* it is placed *in the objective case, this latter being the direct verbal case of a transitive verb*. Examples:

*adamı çağırmak* = to call the man
*tabağı temizlemek* = to clean the plate

(142d) When the "*evident object*" is *indefinite* it is placed in the *nominative case*. To find out if the object of the verb is indefinite the question (*ne* = what) is put. Examples:

| | |
|---|---|
| *adam görmek* | = to see a man |
| *tabak yıkamak* | = to wash a plate, or plates |

(142e) The object in either case can be in the plural if the objects are more than one. Examples:

| | |
|---|---|
| *çocukları çağırmak* | = to call the children |
| *adamlar görmek* | = to see many men |

(142f) The object can also be a clause or a sentence. Example:

*kitap okumayı sevmek* = to love to read a book

(143) An object is *definite* when it is a *proper noun,* a *pronoun,* a *definite demonstrative adjective,* a noun which the latter qualifies, or a noun preceded by any of the following prepositions denoting definiteness:

| | | | |
|---|---|---|---|
| *kimse* | = anybody, nobody | *her* | = every |
| *her* | = everyone | *her bir* | = every one |
| *herkes* | = everybody | *bütün* | = all |

Examples for definite objects:

| | |
|---|---|
| *İbrahim'i gördüm.* | = I have seen İbrahim. (Proper nonn) |
| *Sizi tanırım.* | = I know you. (Personal pronoun) |
| *Bu elbiseyi beğeniyorum.* | = I like this suit. (Noun qual. by Demons. Adj.) |
| *Bunu aldım.* | = I have taken this one. (Demons. Pro.) |
| *Kimseyi görmedim.* | = I have not seen anybody. |
| *Her şehri gezdim.* | = I have toured every town. |
| *Herkesi bilirim.* | = I know everybody. |
| *Her birini getirdim.* | = I have brought everyone. |
| *Bütün sözleri işittim.* | = I heard every word (all the words). |

(144) An **object is indefinite** when it is preceded by a preposition denoting **indefiniteness** as shown hereunder:

| *bir* | = an | *birçok* | = many | *birkaç* | = some |
|-------|------|----------|--------|----------|--------|
| *epey* | = many | *hiçbir* | = no, none | *nice* | = numerous |

Examples:

| *Bir kaplan avladım.* | = I have hunted down a tiger. |
|------------------------|-------------------------------|
| *Birçok kitap aldım.* | = I bought many books. |
| *Hiçbir adam görmedim.* | = I have seen no man. |
| *Birkaç adam isterim.* | = I want several men. |
| *Epey adam bilirim.* | = I know many men. |
| *Nice çocuklar büyüttüm.* | = I have reared up numerous children. |

## OTHER VERBAL CASES OF THE TRANSITIVE VERB

(145) In a sentence there are other nouns, phrases, or sentences which also qualify the action of the "doer", or explain the different phases of the action of the verb, such as the locality, instrument, cause, or purpose.

The nature of this relationship will be comprehended by noting the case in which the object has been put. These cases are usually known as the Declension of the Noun, but I refer to them as the "Verbal Cases" as they actually show the relationship between the verb and one or more words in the sentence. It is of very great importance to know the main case of each verb. It will play a very intricate part in phrase construction. (See 190d.)

(145a) This relationship is determined by putting the relevant question for each verbal case to each word in the sentence. To find out which noun is in the Locative Case, for instance, a question in the Locative Case is put, and the word which answers that question is the Locative Verbal Case.

The following are the questions:

| *nerede* | = where (Locative) |
|----------|--------------------|
| *nereye* | = whereto (Dative) |
| *nereden* | = where from, whence (Ablative) |
| *ne ile* | = with what (Instrumentative) |
| *ne için* | = for what (why) (Causative) |

(146) It is also necessary to know the other words which directly explain the various phases of the action of the verb (see 17, 18, 19 20, 21).

Examples showing these various verbal cases.

| | | |
|---|---|---|
| Dative | : *(bir eve) girmek* | = to enter (to a house) |
| Locative | : *(evde) kalmak* | = to remain (at home) (in the house) |
| Locative | : *(havada) uçmak* | = to fly (in the air) |
| Locative | : *(sandalyede) oturmak* | = to sit (on a chair) |
| Ablative | : *(yüksekten) atlamak* | = to jump (from a height) |
| Ablative | : *(akşamdan) yatmak* | = to go to bed (at nightfall) (from) |
| Instru. | : *(vatan için) çalışmak* | = to work (for the motherland) |
| Causat. | : *(namusla) yaşamak* | = to live (with honour) |

(147) Note that the Locative suffix is written in only one way in Turkish, *"da"* for hard words and *"de"* for soft, but is translated into English by various prepositions, **in, at, on**, etc. (see 18).

**The LOCATIVE stands for location in volume, space, and time.** It will be found to be the same with all the cases. It is advisable to learn the first one as the main one, for that will always be used in Turkish.

(148) **IMPORTANT NOTE: It is therefore essential when learning a Turkish verb that the case of the object qualifying or determining the action of the verb should be learnt with it, so that the object, which comes before the verb in the sentence, can be placed in the appopriate case.**

(149) The verb may have only one word or may have many words in various cases to define the different phases of its action, as:

*Sandalyede oturuyorum.*
    = I sit on the chair.

*Arkadaşımla çalışmak için akşamdan evde kaldım.*
    = I remained at home from the early evening to work with my friend.

# THE INTRANSITIVE VERB

(150) The *intransitive verb* is a verb whose action remains **within or with the "doer", its nature never altering,** and is complete without the help of any *other word*. It is enacted under any condition. It is then called a **true intransitive.** Example:

| | |
|---|---|
| *uyumak* | = to sleep |
| *gitmek* | = to go |

(151) A verb is a true intransitive when it can neither answer the questions *"whom"* (*kimi*) or *"what"* (*neyi*), which questions are usually put to, and are answered by a transitive verb, nor the questions *"to whom"* (*kime*) or *"to what"* (*neye*), which questions are usually put to and answered by an intra-transitive verb.

**The direct verbal case of the true intransitive verb is either the ablative or the locative.**

(152) There are some true *intransitive* verbs which are preceded by a noun, by a *descriptive adjective,* or by words *reproducing* the *sound* of the *action* of the verb, as:

| | |
|---|---|
| *yemek yemek* | = to eat food |
| *oyun oynamak* | = to play a play |
| *uyku uyumak* | = to sleep a sleep |
| *çalgı çalmak* | = to play an instrument |
| *çağıl çağıl çağlamak* | = water to fall murmuringly |
| *mışıl mışıl uyumak* | = to sleep peacefully |
| *hüngür hüngür ağlamak* | = to weep sobbingly |
| *parıl parıl parlamak* | = to shine beamingly |

(152a) This mode of expression (152) is used for emphasis and has a special value in the language. It is *frequently used.*

(153) The nature of a *TRUE INTRANSITIVE* verb can be altered by putting the verb in special senses, as will be explained in the chapter on verb formation (167).

# THE VERBAL CASE OF AN INTRANSITIVE VERB

(154) The *INTRANSITIVE VERB* has another aspect peculiar to the language, i.e. the action or the effect of the action of certain verbs *going out towards an object*. This object is exposed to the effect of the action without being actually under the direct influence of the "doer". *To mark this indirect relationahip the word denoting the object is placed in the Dative Case.* Examples:

| | |
|---|---|
| *(sokağa) çıkmak* | = to go out (to street) |
| *(adama) bağırmak* | = to shout (at a man) |
| *(adama) bakmak* | = to look (at a man) |
| *(eve) girmek* | = to enter (a house) |
| *(köylere) gitmek* | = to go (to villages) |

(154a) Briefly, an *intransitive* verb is either a *"true intransitive"* when the verb is complete in itself, the action of the *"doer"* being *passive* as shown in (150), in other words the *direct opposite* to a *transitive verb,* or is an *intransitive* verb with a *dual function,* which I shall call *"intra-transitive."*

(154b) Either the action is *passive*, when the verb will be *intransitive*, as:

*sokakta bağırmak* = to shout in the street

(154c) Or the action of the verb goes out *towards an object*, this object always being in the *Dative Case.* This verb is almost a *Transitive one,* the only difference being that a *Transitive verb* has its object in the *objective case* and the *Intra-Transitive* has also an *object*, but in the *dative case,* marking the direction of the action of the verb, as:

*bir adama bağırmak* = to shout to a man

Here the effect of the action of the verb is directed *towards the object.*

(154d) It is an *Intransitive* of the second category (*Intra-Transitive*) when it cannot answer the questions *kimi* = "whom" or *neyi* = "what" in the one sense (154b) but can answer the questions *kime* = "to whom" or *neye* = "to what" in the other sense (154c).

# OTHER VERBAL CASES OF THE INTRANSITIVE VERB

(154e) An Intransitive (*Intra-Transitive 154c*) would have the same verbal cases as a True Intransitive (150).

An Intransitive (*Intra-Transitive 154c*) would have one or all the verbal cases, in addition to the *Dative Case*, but cannot at the same time have the *Objective Case*.

## THE APPARENT VERB

(155) In both *Transitive* and *Intransitive* verbs the main feature is the aspect of the action of the verb and the definite presence of the "doer" in both cases. When the "doer" of the verb's action is known the verb is also *"Apparent"*. Examples:

| | | |
|---|---|---|
| (App. Trans.) | *Ahmet bir kitap aldı.* | = Ahmet took a book. |
| (App. Intrans.) | *Bebek uyuyor.* | = The baby is sleeping. |

## THE NON-APPARENT VERB

(156) A verb is called *Non-Apparent* when the action or result of the action is being witnessed without the identity of the "doer" being known. The Personal Verbal Pronoun suffixes represent the *object* of the verb, *but this object has no direct instrumentality in the function of the action.* Examples:

| | | |
|---|---|---|
| (Non-App.) | *Çağırıldım.* | = I have been called. |
| (Non-App.) | *Bebek uyutuldu.* | = The baby was made (put) to sleep. |

(157) This form is often used when there is no necessity nor desire to mention the "doer", or when an action is cited in a general manner. Great care should be taken not to confuse it with the **Reflexive verb**. It is obtained by:

(158) i. Inserting before the verbal ending a letter "*l*" (preceded by the necessary euphony letter) to all verb roots ending with a consonant as:

| | | | |
|---|---|---|---|
| *görmek* | = to see | *görülmek* | = to be seen |
| *süpürmek* | = to sweep | *süpürülmek* | = to be swept |

Examples:

*Şapkayı gördünüz mü?* = Have you seen the hat? (App. Trans.)
*Şapka görüldü mü?* = Has the hat been seen? (Non-App. Trans.)

*Odayı süpürdüler mi?* = Have they swept the room? (App. Trans.)
*Oda süpürüldü mü?* = Has the room been swept? (Non-App. Trans.)

(158a) ii. Inserting the letter **"n"** (preceded by the necessary euphony letter) to all verb roots ending with **"l"** or a vowel, as:

| | | | |
|---|---|---|---|
| *süslemek* | = to adorn | *süslenmek* | = to be adorned |
| *kovalamak* | = to pursue | *kovalanmak* | = to be pursued |
| *bulmak* | = to find | *bulunmak* | = to be found |

Examples:

*Gelini süslediler.* = They have adorned the bride. (App. Trans.)
*Gelin süslendi.* = The bride has been adorned. (Non-App. Trans.)
*Düşmanı kovaladılar.* = They have pursued the enemy. (App. Trans.)
*Düşman kovalandı.* = The enemy has been pursued. (Non-App. Trans.)
*Uçağı bulduk.* = We have found the aeroplane. (App. Trans.)
*Uçak bulundu.* = The aeroplane has been found. (Non-App. Trans.)

(158b) In certain cases, the **non-apparent** state of the verb is emphasized by inserting a second *l* preceded by *ı, i, u, ü*, after the *N*.

(159) **Note:** When the verb is in the Non-Apparent form, the author of the action may be one or many persons.

(160) The verb is usually put:

(160a) In the 3rd person singular when the object is in the singular or plural, and is put in front of the verb, as:

*Kurt vuruldu.* = The wolf was shot.
*Hırsızlar tutuldu.* = The thieves were caught.

(160b) In the 2nd person singular or plural when the object, singular or plural, respectively, is addressed, as:

*Okula gönderildin.* = You were sent to school.
*Okula gönderildiniz.* = You were sent to school.

(161) It is important to remember that a "NON-APPARENT" verb has no direct subject. In the 3rd per. sing. it forms a much used mode of expression.

The **non-apparent** verb is the verb in the **passive voice**, but it must not be compared too strictly.

(162) It must also be understood that the action was carried out by a *certain outside doer*.

(163) The object of a *"Non-Apparent"* verb, being indefinite, is in the *Nominative* and not in the *"Objective"* case.

(164) The *doer* of such a verb could be mentioned by putting the preposition *"tarafından"* (by) after the *doer*. Example:

*Türk Milleti Atatürk ve İsmet İnönü tarafından kurtarıldı.*
The Turkish nation was liberated by Atatürk and İsmet İnönü.

(165) This same phrase can also be explained with the verb in the *"Transitive"* form as hereunder:

(165a) *Türk Milletini Atatürk ve İsmet İnönü kurtardı.*
= Atatürk and İsmet İnönü liberated the Turkish nation.

(166) The *Non-Apparent* verb is conjugative in all the moods and tenses of the verb conjugation.

# VERB FORMATION

(167) *Verbs are formed in various ways.* There are verbs which are primarily so by structure, the root by itself having *in the current language,* no *adjectival or nounal*

274

meaning. There are also verbs obtained by way of affixing to *nouns* and *adjectives* the verbal suffixes *mak* or *mek* only or by affixing *l la, le, lan, len* or *laş, leş (sa, se; da, de; ar, er; sı, si; ımsa, imse)*, plus the final verbal suffix *mak, mek.* Examples:

| | | | | | |
|---|---|---|---|---|---|
| (Adj.) | SIK | = close together | sıkmak | = to squeeze |
| (Adj.) | EKŞİ | = sour | ekşimek | = to turn sour |
| (Noun) | AN | = mind | anmak | = to remember |
| (Noun) | BAĞ | = tie (link) | bağlamak | = to tie |
| (Noun) | PAY | = share | paylaşmak | = to apportion |
| (Noun) | SÜS | = adornment | süslemek | = to adorn |
| (Adj.) | MOR | = mauve | morarmak | = to turn mauve |
| (Noun) | SÖZ | = word | sözleşmek | = to arrange a meeting |
| (Adj.) | GÜZEL | = beautiful | güzelleşmek | = to become beautiful |
| (Noun) | NAZ | = coyness | nazlanmak | = to act coyly |
| (Noun) | EV | = house | evlenmek | = to get married |
| (Noun) | FISIL | = hissing sound | fısıldamak | = to whisper |
| (Adj.) | DİRİ | = alive | dirilmek | = to come to live |
| (Adj.) | AZ | = little | azımsamak | = to consider too little |
| (Adj.) | HAFİF | = light | hafifsemek | = to belittle |
| (Pron.) | BEN | = my | benimsemek | = to profess ownership |

(168) A *primary* verb can be placed in *various verbal senses* (Reflex, Caus., Reciproc., Particip. etc.) by the insertion of a servile letter, *l, n, t, ş,* or by placing a syllable, *dir (tir)*, between the root of the verb and the verbal suffix *mak* or *mek*, .

## THE COMPOUND VERB

(169) The **compound verb** is obtained chiefly by using one of the verbs *kalmak, olmak, bulunmak, etmek, eylemek, buyurmak, kılmak,* preceded by a noun or an adjective. Examples:

| | | | |
|---|---|---|---|
| mutabık kalmak | = to agree | yardım etmek | = to help |
| vuku bulmak | = to happen | ikram eylemek | = to proffer |
| razı olmak | = to consent | kabul buyurmak | = to accept |
| memnun olmak | = to be content of | af buyurmak | = to forgive |
| ihya kılmak | = to animate | hazır bulunmak | = to be present |

(169a) It is also obtained by using two verbs together the first one being placed in the OPTATIVE Mood (obtained by adding *a, e (ya* or *ye),* to the verb root, and adding the second one in the Infinitive Mood. The second verb only is subject to the usual conjugation. This form is very frequently used. A chart is shown under number (107dd).

(170) **Note:** The verb put in the *optative mood* has the special *function of modifying* the action of the second verb, at the same time showing that the two actions are being carried out *simultaneously*. In this form the two verbs are *joined*.

(170a) Hereunder we show some verbs together with the verbs which are affixed, the two together expressing a more concise and comprehensive meaning. These are the four most frequently used:

### STUPEFACTIVE

| (170a.1) | **kalmak** | = to remain | *bakmak* | = to look |
|----------|------------|-------------|----------|-----------|
|          | *bakakalmak* | = to remain looking, to stand aghast | | |

### PRECIPITATIVE

| (170a.2) | **vermek** | = to give | *bakmak* | = to look |
|----------|------------|-----------|----------|-----------|
|          | *bakıvermek* | = to give a hurried look | | |

### FACULTATIVE

| (170a.3) | **bilmek** | = to know | *yapmak* | = to do |
|----------|------------|-----------|----------|---------|
|          | *yapabilmek* | = to be able to do | | |

### CONTINUATIVE

| (170a. 4). | **durmak** | = to stand | *beklemek* | = to wait |
|------------|------------|------------|------------|-----------|
|            | *bekleyedurmak* | = to keep on waiting (to wait indefinitely) | | |

(171) The verb in the *optative mood* can also be used as an adverb, when it is placed in front of the verb. Example:

Çıka       geldi       = He/she came unexpectedly.
(he/she coming out   came)

(172) When it is intended to qualify the action of one verb by the action of another, the qualifying verb is placed in the *Optative Mood*, and placed in front of the verb to be qualified in a repetitive form, as:

| | |
|---|---|
| *güle güle anlatmak* | = to relate while laughing (with laughter) |
| *bağıra bağıra konuşmak* | = to talk shoutingly (Turkish mode of expression) |
| *koşa koşa geldi* | = she/he came while running |

(173) The repetitive form also denotes emphasis, duration, or continuation.

| | |
|---|---|
| *Göre göre aldı.* (emphasis) | = He bought (it) (with his eyes open). |
| *Bile bile yaptı.* (emphasis) | = He did (it) (knowingly). |
| *Çekişe çekişe aldı.* (emphasis) | = He bought (it) after much bargaining. |
| *Söylene söylene gitti.* (continuation) | = He went (away) grumbling. |
| *Düşüne düşüne deli oldu.* (duration) | = He went mad (through) continuous brooding. |

(173a) *bile bile* and *göre göre* are very frequently used for the purpose of **emphasis**.

(174) Two different verbs can be placed in the *optative* mood and then be placed in *front* of the verb. Examples:

*Düşe      kalka      yoluna      devam etti.*
(falling      getting up      journey his      to continued he)
= Each time he fell he got up, and in this manner continued his journey.

*Gide      gele      işini      bitirdi.*
(going      coming      work his      finished he)
= By a continuous going to and fro he finished his work.

*Bata      çıka      geldik.*
(sinking      getting out      arrived we)
= We had to trudge along.

Note: Any of the above examples could be phrased differently by putting each word in the optative mood, in the required tense and person, and yet it would not give the clarity and comprehensiveness which is found in the above examples. A lot is left to the Comprehension of the party addressed.

The student must make an extra study of this compound verb and the optative mood.

# THE REFLEXIVE VERB

(175) A verb is in the REFLEXIVE mood when:

(a) The "doer" of the action of the verb is directly affected by his action.

(b) Or when, through his own action, the "doer" causes himself to become the object of the action of a second party.

This is a form peculiar to the Turkish language, and is totally different from the non-apparent verb. Examples:

*Görüldüm.* = I have been seen.     *Göründüm.* = I have been seen.
(They saw me.)                   (I showed myself).

It is obtained by:

(175a) i. Inserting an *"n"* (preceded by the necessary euphony letter) between the verb root and the verbal suffix, in both consonant and vowel-ending words, as:

*dinlemek* = to listen     *dinlenmek* = to listen to oneself (to meditate)

(175b) ii. Also by inserting an *"l"* between the verb root and the verbal suffix (preceded by the necessary sound letter, when the word ends with a consonant), as:

*atmak* = to throw     *atılmak* = to throw oneself (to assail)
*boğmak* = to drown     *boğulmak* = to drown oneself (to be drowned)

Examples:

*Üzerine atıldım.*          = I threw myself on him.
*Az kaldı boğuluyordum.* = I nearly drowned myself
                         or I was nearly drowned.

(176) The verbal case of the noun accompanying such a verb is the ABLATIVE case as:
*İsraftan çekinmelidir.*
    = One must draw oneself away from spending.
    (One must refrain from extravagance.)

*Adamcağız kederinden dövünüyordu.*
= The poor man was frantic in his distress.

(177) **Note:** There is a great *structural* resemblance between a *reflexive verb* and a "non-apparent" verb but they differ in that whereas a reflexive verb always has a subject, a "non-apparent" verb has no subject, or if there is a subject it is in a special verbal case, the noun being in the Nominative case, and preceded by *"tarafından"* (by) (see 164).

### RECIPROCATIVE AND PARTICIPATIVE VERBS

(178) The *reciprocative* sense of the verb is obtained by inserting a "ş" (preceded by the necessary euphony letter) between the verb root and the verbal suffix, as:

| | | | |
|---|---|---|---|
| *görmek* | = to see | *görüşmek* | = to see each other |
| *bulmak* | = to find | *buluşmak* | = to find each other, to meet |

Examples:

*Yarın görüşelim.* = Let us have a chat tomorrow.
*Dün buluştuk.* = We met yesterday.

(179) The *"PARTICIPATIVE"* verb is formed in the same way as the *reciprocative* verb. It differs from that verb only in the meaning it gives to the verb. It designates *taking part in the same action.* Examples:

*kaçmak* = to run away       *kaçışmak* = to run away together

(180) The verbal case of this class of verb is the *Instrumentative* case, which in this instance also means "together" or "with one another". Examples:

| | |
|---|---|
| *bir adamla görüşmek* | = to have a talk with a man |
| *Kumandan ile görüştüm.* | = I had a chat with the commandant. |
| *Dün arkadaşı ile buluştu.* | = He met his friend yesterday. |

# THE CAUSATIVE VERB

(180) A *causative* verb is a verb formed from any one of the two classes of "*INTRANSITIVE*" verbs (154b, 154c) where the action is *being modified*.

(181) a. The action, instead of being created and remaining within the "doer" (True Intran. see 150) is transferred unto an object in a direct manner (Trans. 142), or in other words, the "doer" causes the action which was confined to himself to be carried out on another "object". Example:

| | | |
|---|---|---|
| *uyumak* = to sleep (cause *oneself to sleep*) | *uyutmak* = *to put to sleep* (cause another one to sleep) |

(181) b. The indirect impartibility to the object of the action or the effect of the action of the verb (Intransitive) is caused by the first "doer" to be done by the second "doer". Example:

| *bağırmak* | = to scream | *bağırtmak* | = to cause to scream |
|---|---|---|---|
| *bakmak* | = to look | *baktırmak* | = to cause to look |

(182) b. 1. These two forms are obtained by inserting a "*t*" (preceded by the necessary sound letter) between the verb root and the verbal suffix:

To verbs of **one syllable** (these are few, and are to be learned by heart) as:

| *kokmak* | = to smell | *kokutmak* | = to cause to smell, perfume, odour |
|---|---|---|---|
| *korkmak* | = to be afraid | *korkutmak* | = to frighten |

(182) b. 2. To verbs of several syllables ending with a vowel, or with the consonants *r* and *l*, as:

| *büyümek* | = to grow | *büyütmek* | = *to rear* |
|---|---|---|---|
| *öksürmek* | = to cough | *öksürtmek* | = *to cause to cough* |
| *söylemek* | = to say | *söyletmek* | = *to cause to say* |
| *yorulmak* | = to get tired | *yorultmak* | = *to cause to get tired* |

*(182) b. 3.* By inserting "*dır*" (*dir*, etc., *tır*, *tir* etc.) to verbs of one syllable as:

| | | | |
|---|---|---|---|
| *gülmek* | = to laugh | *güldürmek* | = to cause to laugh |
| *bilmek* | = to know | *bildirmek* | = to cause to know |
| *kapmak* | = to snatch | *kaptırmak* | = to cause to snatch |

(182) b. 4. To verbs of several syllables ending with any consonant except *r* and *l*, as:

| | | | |
|---|---|---|---|
| *çalışmak* | = to work | *çalıştırmak* | = to cause to work |

(183) c. There are certain verbs of *one syllable* which are made *causative* by the insertion of "*r*" only preceded by necessary euphony letter, the *d* or *t* as shown in 182 being dropped (Ph. 30d). They are to be learned through a teacher. Examples:

| | | | |
|---|---|---|---|
| *kaçmak* | = to run away | *kaçırmak* | = to cause to run away |
| *batmak* | = to sink | *batırmak* | = to cause to sink |
| *şişmek* | = to swell | *şişirmek* | = to cause to swell |

(184) d. There are certain other verbs which are not made according to any of these rules. These must be learned through a teacher. Examples:

| | | | |
|---|---|---|---|
| *görmek* | = to see (tran.) | *göstermek* | = to show |
| *gelmek* | = to come | *getirmek* | = to bring |
| *gitmek* | = to go | *götürmek* | = to take away |

(185) e. Causative verbs can be made causative for the second time, when the action is understood to be carried out by a third party through the instrumentality of a second party, who himself is subject to the influence of the first "doer".

The *verbal case* of the noun accompanying a *causative verb* is the *objective case*, hence the reason for calling a causative verb also a transitive verb, and as such making it causative.

(185) e. 1. By adding *dır, (dir, dur, dür), tır, (tir, tur, tür)* to a causative verb (already made causative by the insertion of "*t*"), as:

| | |
|---|---|
| *bir çocuğu büyütmek* | = to rear up a child |
| *bir çocuğu (çiftlikte) büyüttürmek* | = to cause to rear up a child |
| | (in a farm) (to have a child reared up on a farm) |

(185) e. 2. By inserting "*t*" between the Causative verb root (made Causative by the insertion of *ır, ir, dır, tır,* etc.) and the verbal suffix. Examples:

| | | |
|---|---|---|
| 1st deg. Caus. | *fırsatı kaçırmak* | = to cause a chance to go |
| 2nd deg. Caus. | *fırsatı kaçırtmak* | = to cause to let a chance go |

(186) f. A *reciprocative* and a *participative* verb can be made causative (as shown in 182) and as such made causative again (e. 1 and 2), as:

| | |
|---|---|
| *görmek* | = to see |
| *görüşmek* | = to see each other (Reciprocative) |
| *görüştürmek* | = to cause to see each other (Caus. 1st deg.) (to introduce) |
| *görüştürtmek* | = to cause to introduce (Caus. 2nd deg.) |
| *ermek* | = to attain |
| *erişmek* | = to reach together (Participative) |
| *eriştirmek* | = to cause to attain (Caus. of 1st deg.) |
| *eriştirtmek* | = to cause one to let reach (Caus. of 2nd deg.) |

(187) This *reciprocative* (186) Verb (2nd degree) directly controls the **objective case**. It may also control the *instrumentative* case, without necessarily being followed by any of the other cases. Example:

*Ahmet'i Mehmet'le görüştürmek*
= to cause Ahmet and Mehmet to see each other (to have a chat)

(188) To grasp the proper meaning of any of these verbs the original meaning of the primary verb must first be ascertained.

## CERTAIN HINTS

(189) When dealing with verbs, conjugation or gerund formation ascertain whether the ending letter of the verb root is a *sharp, flat,* or *neutral consonant* or whether it is a *vowel,* and in both cases whether the general structure of the word is a *hard* or a *soft* one.

Always make a point to find out the exact function of the word when it is ending with :

| | | | |
|---|---|---|---|
| *ı* (16a) *yı* (16b) | Example: | *Kadın odayı süpürdü.* | |
| | | = The woman swept the room. | |
| *sı* (24e) | Example: | *Çocuğun babası geldi* | |
| | | = The child's father arrived. | |
| *nı* (24n) | Example: | *Beyazını sen al.* | |
| | | = You take the white. | |
| *sını* (24e, 24n, 24p) | Example: | *Yarısını bana ver.* | |
| | | = Give me the half. | |
| *nı* (50h, 16a) | Example: | *Kitabını al* | |
| | | = Take your book. | |

| | | | |
|---|---|---|---|
| *mi* (50m, 50r) | Example: | *Kendimi tanıtmadım.* | |
| | | = I did not make myself known. | |
| *mi* (60) | Example: | *Kendi mi söyledi?* | |
| | | = Did he say (it) himself? | |

| | | | |
|---|---|---|---|
| *mı* (50h, 16a) | Example: | *Paramı aldınız.* | |
| | | = You have taken my money. | |
| *mı* (60) | Example: | *Para mı aldınız?* | |
| | | = Is it money you have taken? | |

as although in many instances the "endings" may be spelt and sound alike they have no connection with each other, as, for instance, in the last two examples (50h, 16a) *paramı*, being *para* (money) plus the 1st pers. personal suffix *m* plus the objective case suffix *ı*, and (60) *para mı* being *para* (money) followed by the Interr. suffix *mı*.

## CONSTRUCTION OF SENTENCES

(190) The general conditions of *sentence construction* are to a certain extent similar to those in the English language, i.e., main sentences, clauses, attributes, etc., etc. I am enumerating here the preliminaries of sentence construction and shall use the word "attribute" (simple or compound) for all accessories, such as phrases, clauses, etc.

The main features to note are:

(190a) The *SUBJECT* as well as the *VERB* or the *OBJECT* of the *VERB* may have an attribute (simple or compound).

283

(190b) The *sentence COMMENCES* with the *SUBJECT* or the *ATTRIBUTE* of the *SUBJECT*, and *ENDS* with the *VERB*.

The *ATTRIBUTE* of the *Subject* is placed **BEFORE** the *Subject*.

The *ATTRIBUTE* of the *Verb* or of the *Object* of the *Verb* is placed **BEFORE** the *Verb*.

(190c) The **SUBJECT** mentioned in (b) if in the form of a *personal pronoun* is usually omitted from the sentence. It is only put for emphasis (58). *The personal pronouns* are interpreted by the *personal verbal pronoun suffixes* (see 57ee etc.).

As the Transitive Verb requires its *direct object* in the *objective case* (see 142c) and the Intratransitive verb may also have its *direct object* in the *dative case* (see 154c) we can make a simple phrase, by putting the object belonging to every verb in the appropriate verbal case (see 140-150). Examples:

| | | |
|---|---|---|
| **1.** *Ahmet'i gördüm.* | = I saw Ahmet. |
| **2.** *Zeki Bey'e söyledim.* | = I told Zeki Bey. |

The various cases of either verb can be added. Examples:

**3.**     *Hayrullah'ı dün sokakta gördüm.*
       Yesterday I saw Hayrullah in the street.

**4.**     *Gazinoda Mehmet'in selamını Ahmet'e söyledim.*
       In the casino I gave Ahmet Mehmet's regards.

When two verbs are to be used *in the same person, tense and mood the first one* is placed in a gerundial form (see 129.) Example:

**5.**     *Ahmet Ankara'dan gelip İstanbul'a gitti.*
       Ahmet came from Ankara and went to İstanbul.

(190d) We have seen by now how to form plain phrases, and it would therefore seem easy to place two or three simple sentences side by side and link them together with conjunctions.

In the Turkish language however, although these simple sentences are not totally discarded, their repetition is usually avoided wherever possible.

284

The language requires that the dependent sentence and the conjunction be replaced by a gerundial sentence and used *as the direct object of the verb in the main sentence.*

A careful study of the Gerunds (127), (128), (129), (130), (132), (133), (133b), (134), (135), (137), and (138), will show that they are clauses made up of particles of verb, postposition, and adverb, etc., which are in some cases of an *adjectival* nature, and in others of an **adverbial** mood. Therefore when the gerund replaces a dependent sentence *it qualifies or modifies the action of the verb in the main sentence.*

Consequently it does not take a specific personal pronoun suffix, the person and number being usually understood to be *the same as that of the verb in the main sentence.* The conjunction which originally existed between the two sentences is now innate in the gerund.

The selection of any one of these gerunds is based on the relationship between the two actions, that of the main sentence, and that of the dependent sentence. It is therefore essential to ascertain the nature of this relationship, i.e. whether the action in the main sentence is dependent on (a) the *completion*, (b) the *duration*, or (c) the *commencement*, etc., of the action in the dependent sentence. Examples:

(1) "I will tell you when I see you."

will be understood as, and converted into:

(1) "I will tell you **on seeing** you."
*Sizi görünce söylerim.*

(2) "I will write my letter after I have seen you."

will be understood as, and converted into:

(2) "I will write my letter after **having seen** you."
*sizi gördükten sonra mektubumu yazarım. (135)*

In the chapter on gerunds we have seen the various phases of the relationship between the two actions. The sentences are interdependent and the relationship variable. There is, however, an aspect of relationship totally different from any explained above. It is *the direct connection between the main sentence and the dependent sentence* where the action of the dependent sentence is governed by the verb in the main sentence.

The selection of the gerund appertaining to this second aspect is where difficulty is sometimes experienced, for this is where the dependent sentence is condensed as much as possible, and reconstructed in such a way *as will enable it as a whole to be made the direct object of the verb in the main sentence.*

As the *direct object of a verb has to be in one of the verbal cases,* i.e. the *objective case* for a **transitive verb** (142c), the *dative case* for an *intra-transitive verb* (154c), the *ablative* or *locative case for an intransitive verb* (150), it is necessary that the verb should be placed in a form whereby it can be placed in one of these cases. This form is a *nounal form,* for this is the only form which can be declined.

To obtain the correct form there are two points to consider:

1.  Is the action completed?                  "After you have actually arrived."
2.  Is it only of a suggested state?       "On your arrival."

In the first case the verb in the dependent sentence will be replaced by an *adjective of the verb reduced to a noun* (Relative Gerund) (see (136)). In the second case it will be replaced by the *verbal noun* (12a), this being the same verb in a *nominal form*.

After the verb of the dependent sentence has been converted into a nounal form and the Pers. Verbal Pronoun suffixes, the subject of the verb, replaced by the Definitive Personal Pronoun suffixes, the relationship which existed between the two sentences prior to the elimination of the conjunction will be re-established by *putting the Gerund into the necessary verbal case required by the verb in the main sentence.*

It is of the utmost importance to remember that all gerunds, (in this case, the relative gerund (136) or the verbal noun (12a)) still retain their verbal potentialities, i.e. their relationship with all words governed by them, in the same manner as when they were verbs. In the process of converting the verb into a nounal form, its *person* and *number suffixes,* denoting the personal verbal connection between author and action, were temporarily lost. *This connection is re-instated by adding to the newly formed nounal verb, before adding the verbal case suffix, the respective definitive personal pronoun suffix.* To do this the nounal verb is placed in a definitive combination, the nounal verb being the second word (in the Accus. case), and the subject of the verb being the first word. If this latter is a noun, common or proper, it is placed in the genitive case. If it is a *pers. verbal pronoun suffix* (the personal pronoun itself having been dropped, as is customary) it is replaced by a *definitive personal pronoun suffix,* which is added to the verb now in a nounal form (see 50ll).

## SELECTION OF RELATIVE GERUND

*The adjectival form* (shown in (31c)) is selected if there is *suggestion of the completion of the action.* To establish the person and number of the verb it is placed in the definitive combination, and finally put in the necessary verbal case. Example:

"When you arrive home, see me!"

will be understood to be suggestive of the completion of the action,

"When you have arrived home, see me!"

and will be converted into:

On your arriving (having arrived) home, see me.

*Eve geldiğinizde beni görünüz.*

## SELECTION OF THE VERBAL NOUN

The verb in the dependent sentence will be replaced by the simple verbal noun (12a), when there is a suggestion that the action of the *verb is more a mood of the verb,* or *when simply mention of the action is made.*

It is subject to the same personal suffix rules as mentioned overleaf (see also (50h)). See also (126c), (130), (130c), (136m), (138). Examples:

(1)     "It is necessary for you to come to the office."

will be understood as, and converted into:

(1)     **"Your arrival** to the office is necessary."

*Yazıhaneye uğramanız lâzımdır.*

Owing to lack of space I am not able to give as comprehensive an explanation as I would wish, on a subject which is rather involved, but I feel sure that if the student makes a careful study of the foregoing explanations and examples and the chapters on gerunds and bears in mind the main rules enumerated above, he will be able to master the language and express himself in the correct Turkish manner. Study the following examples:

**6.**  *Melek Hanım geldi* = Melek Hanım came.

7.  *Ahmet'in babası geldi* = Ahmet's father came.

8.  *Rüştü Bey Ankara'dan İstanbul'a gitti.*
    Rüştü Bey left Ankara for Istanbul.
    (Rüştü Bey went from Ankara to Istanbul.)

9.  *Uğur Antalya'ya babasının yanına gitti.*
    Uğur went to his father's place in Antalya.

10. *Ali babasının arzusuna rağmen Ankara'ya gitmeyip İstanbul'a döndü.*
    Ali didn't go to Ankara but returned to İstanbul against his father's wishes.

11. *Güven annesiyle beraber Türkiye'ye gitti.*
    Güven went to Turkey with her mother.

12. *Adnan vapuru kaçırdı.*
    Adnan missed the boat.

13. *Tarık vapurun kaptanını tanıyor.*
    Tarık knows the captain of the boat.

14. *Polis vapurdaki yolcuları birer birer gözden geçiriyordu.*
    The policeman was taking stock of each passenger on the boat.

In No. 9 *Babası* (see 50h and 1) = (*his father*), is the second word of a *Definitive Combination* (where the first word, i.e. the 3rd *pers. pronoun* is omitted (*onun babası*).

In No. 9 the word *Yan* = (side) completes the meaning of "*babası*" (see 241) therefore it has been placed in the accusative case (*yanı*), being the second word of the new definitive combination of the two words, *baba* and *yan*. This definitive combination, completing the meaning of the verb "*gitti*" is placed in the dative case (24p) (*yanına*).

15. *Güven Ankara'dan yarın hareket ederek İzmir'e uğradıktan sonra İstanbul'a dönecektir.*
    Güven will leave Ankara tomorrow and after going to İzmir he will return to İstanbul.

16. *Neşe babasından mektup alıncaya kadar İzmir'de kalacaktır.*
    Neşe will remain in İzmir till she receives a letter from her father.

17. *Güven'in böyle birdenbire hareket etmesinin sebebini bir türlü anlayamadım.*
I could not understand at all the reason of Güven's sudden departure.

18. *Babasından mektup alır almaz hemen hareket etmesi için Kenan'a yazdım.*
I have written to Kenan to leave as soon as he receives a letter from his father.

19. *Bayan Jones kızından mektup almadığı için son derece üzülmektedir.*
Mrs. Jones is worrying very much at not having received a letter from her daughter.

20. *Birkaç defa gidip geldiğim halde hiçbir sonuç elde etmeyerek döndüm.*
Though I went several times I returned without having obtained any result.

21. *Ne günlere kaldık.*
Good gracious! What are we coming to?

22. *Aman bayıldım şuna (or şu işe)*
I would have died of laughter (about this affair).

23. *Şaşarım ben buna.*
Well! I am surprised.

24. *Aç karnına sokağa çıktı.*
He went out on an empty stomach.

25. *Oda karmakarışık idi.*
The room was upside down.

26. *Kavga olmasın diye ağzımı açmadım.*
I kept my mouth shut to keep the peace.

27. *Herhangi dükkâna isterseniz girebilirsiniz.*
You may go into any shop you like.

28. *Kim olursa olsun içeriye biletsiz giremez.*
Nobody can enter without a ticket.

29. *Vakti olsun olmasın her durumda beni gelip görsün.*
He must find time to come and see me.

30. *Âlemin evine öyle kolay kolay girilemez.*
You cannot get into a person's house so easily as that.

# ATATÜRK'ÜN GENÇLİĞE HİTABESİ

*Ey Türk gençliği! Birinci vazifen, Türk istiklâlini, Türk cumhuriyetini, ilelebet, muhafaza ve müdafaa etmektir.*

*Mevcudiyetinin ve istikbalinin yegâne temeli budur. Bu temel senin, en kıymetli hazinendir. İstikbalde dahi, seni, bu hazineden, mahrum etmek isteyecek, dahilî ve haricî, bedhahların olacaktır. Bir gün, istiklâl ve cumhuriyeti müdafaa mecburiyetine düşersen, vazifeye atılmak için, içinde bulunacağın vaziyetin imkân ve şeraitini düşünmeyeceksin! Bu imkân ve şerait, çok nâmüsait bir mahiyette tezahür edebilir. İstiklâl ve cumhuriyetine kastedecek düşmanlar, bütün dünyada emsali görülmemiş bir galibiyetin mümessili olabilirler. Cebren ve hile ile aziz vatanın, bütün kaleleri zapt edilmiş, bütün tersanelerine girilmiş, bütün orduları dağıtılmış ve memleketin her köşesi bilfiil işgal edilmiş olabilir. Bütün hu şeraitten daha elîm ve daha vahim olmak üzere, memleketin dahilinde, iktidara sahip olanlar gaflet ve dalâlet ve hattâ hıyanet içinde bulunabilirler. Hattâ bu iktidar sahipleri şahsî menfaatlerini, müstevlilerin siyasî emelleriyle tevhit edebilirler. Millet, fakr u zaruret içinde harap ve bîtap düşmüş olabilir.*

*Ey Türk istikbalinin evlâdı! İşte, bu ahval ve şerait içinde dahi, vazifen; Türk istiklâl ve cumhuriyetini kurtarmaktır! Muhtaç olduğun kudret, damarlarındaki asîl kanda, mevcuttur!*

- *Atatürk, 20 Ekim 1927*

## ATATÜRK'S ADDRESS TO THE TURKISH YOUTH

Turkish Youth, your first duty is forever to preserve and defend the Turkish Independence and the Turkish Republic.

This is the very foundation of your existence and your future. This foundation is your most precious treasure. In the future, too, there may be malevolent people at home and abroad, who will wish to deprive you of this treasure. If some day you are compelled to defend your independence and your Republic, you must not tarry to weigh the possibilities and circumstances of the situation before taking up your duty. These possibilities and circumstances may turn out to be extremely unfavourable. The enemies conspiring against your independence and your Republic, may have behind them a victory unprecedented in the annals of the world.

It may be that, by violence and ruse, all the fortresses of your beloved fatherland may be captured, all its shipyards occupied, all its armies dispersed and every part of the country invaded. And sadder and graver than all these circumstances, those who hold power within the country may be in error, misguided and may even be traitors. Furthermore; they may identify their personal interests with the political designs of the invaders. The country may be impoverished, ruined and exhausted.

Youth of Turkey's future, even in such circumstances, it is your duty to save the Turkish independence and Republic. You will find the strength you need in your noble blood.

Atatürk, 20 October 1927

## İSLAMIN BEŞ ŞARTI

*1. Allah'ın birliğine, Allah'tan başka tanrının olmadığına ve Hz. Muhammedin O'nun elçisi olduğuna inanmak. Buna inanmak, Hz. Muhammed'in söylediği her şeye inanmak anlamına gelir.*

*2. Günde beş vakit namaz kılmak; gün doğarken, öğleyin, ikindi vakti, akşam ve yatsı vakti.*

*Arapça'da yapılan her ibadete namaz denir. Bu ibadeti yöneten kişiye imam, kendisine yardımcı olana da müezzin adı verilir. Namaz vakti insanlara müezzin tarafından duyurulur. Eskiden ezanı müezzinler minareye çıkıp okurlardı, günümüzde bu iş hoparlör sistemleriyle gerçekleştirilmektedir.*

*Dünyanın her yerindeki Müslümanlar "kıble" adı verilen ve ruhsal birliği temsil eden Kabe yönünde namaz kılarlar. Kıble sözcüğü Kabe'den gelir, anılan yerde bir Kybele kültü bulunduğundan Kabe sözcüğü Anadolu'nun ana tanrıçası ile ilgilidir. Müslümanlar için Kabe İbrahim ile oğlu İsmail'in Tanrı adına inşa ettikleri bir sığınaktır. Kabe Tanrı'nın eşsizliğinin simgesidir.*

*Namazı camide kılmak daha makbuldür. Aslında camide kalma katı bir zorunluluk değildir. Kutsal günler dışında kadınlar genellikle evde ibadet ederler. Her bir namaz yaklaşık 10-20 dakika sürer.*

*Düzenli olarak günde beş kez camide namaz kılan insanların ortalama sayısı Türkiye'deki toplam erkek Müslümanların % 4-8'ini geçmez.*

*Müslümanlar için Cuma, Hıristiyanların Pazar ya da Yahudilerin Cumartesi günleri gibi kutsal gündür. İmamlar Cuma günleri öğle namazının ardından Türkçe vaaz verirler. Yasalar uyarınca vaazlarında siyasetten bahsetmeleri yasaktır. Erkeklerin Cuma namazına katılmaları farzdır, bu günlerde namaza katılım oranı % 30-40'a ulaşır. Birçok yerde Cuma günleri insanların namaza katılmak üzere dükkânlarını kapattıklarını görmek mümkündür.*

*İki dini bayramın (Şeker ve Kurban Bayramı) ilk günlerinde sabah erkenden kılınan namazlar erkekler için yılın en önemli namazlarıdır. Bu namazlara katılım oranı % 70-80'e ulaşabilir.*

*3- Oruç: Mübarek Ramazan ayı boyunca 30 günlüğüne oruç tutulur. Güneşin doğumundan günbatımına dek yemek, içmek, sigara, cinsel ilişkide bulunmak yasaktır; hastalar, güçsüzler, hamile kadınlar, nöbet tutan askerler, uzun yola gidenler ve çocuklar oruçtan muaftır.*

*Ramazan ayının gelişi ülke çapında büyük bir toplumsal olaydır. Kutlamak için minarelerin şerefeleri aydınlatılır; Ramazanı karşılamak üzere minareler arasına yüzlerce ampulden oluşturulmuş mahyalar asılır. Mahya şekilleri arasında çiçekler, kayıklar, köprüler ya da camiler sayılabilir. Ramazan ayı boyunca gazeteler, dergiler ve TV kanalları özel yayın yaparlar.*

*Oruç faaliyeti sokaklarda dolaşan davulcuların manili davul sesiyle sabah saat 3:00 civarında başlar. İnsanları oruca kaldırması için her mahallenin kendi davulcusu bulunur. Davulcunun tüm çabası bu ayın sonunda çevredeki evlerden toplayacağı bahşişler içindir.*

*Davulcu tarafından uyandırılan insanlar gün doğana dek yemek yiyebilirler, günün doğuşu o günkü orucun başlamasına işaret eder. Oruç süresince yasak olan tek şey yemek değildir. Küfretmek, yalan söylemek, başkalarına zarar vermek gibi kötü davranışlar da yasaktır.*

*Oruç tutan insanlar buna saygı gösterilmesini beklerler. Özellikle küçük kentlerde lokantalar kapanır ve insanlar umuma açık yerlerde bir şeyler yiyip içmezler.*

*Gün batarken, müezzinin akşam namazı için ezan okuması o günkü orucun bitişini gösterir. Orucu açmak için zeytin, tuz, hurma ve su makbul yiyeceklerden sayılır.*

*Kentsel bölgelerde insanların % 20-25'i oruç tutarken, kırsal bölgelerde bu oran %60-70'e kadar çıkar.*

*4. Hac: Mekke'ye hac ziyareti yapmak mali durumu uygun olanların görevidir. Bir yaş sınırı yoksa da, insanlar hac görevlerini genellikle 50-60 yaşlarına geldiklerinde yerine getirme eğilimindedir. Hacdan dönen kişi, dindarlığının göstergesi olarak adının önünde hacı sıfatını kullanmayı hak eder. Bir hacı yaşamının kalan süresinde günah işlememeye daha da özen gösterir.*

*5. Zekat: Her yıl servetinin 1/40'ını muhtaç kimselere vermektir. Uygulamada çok kişi fakirlere zekat verir ama bu her zaman belirtilen oranda olmayabilir.*

*Anadolu Destanı, Şerif Yenen, 1998, İstanbul - Turkey*

## THE FIVE CONDITIONS OF ISLAM

1- To say and to believe "I witness that there is no God but Allah and Mohammed is his prophet". When somebody believes in this, it means he believes and acknowledges everything declared by Mohammed.

2- To practice namaz 5 times a day; early in the morning, at noon, in the afternoon, in the early evening and at night.

Each prayer is called namaz in the Arabic language. The leader of the prayer is the imam and his assistant during the prayer is the müezzin. The time to pray is announced to people by the müezzin. In former times this took place from the top of a minaret, but now it is announced over loudspeakers.

All Moslems in the world pray in the Kaaba direction and call it "kıble" which represents a spiritual unity. The word kıble derives from Kaaba which is associated with Kybele (the mother goddess of Anatolia) as there was previously a cult of Kybele in Kaaba. For a Moslem the Kaaba is the sanctuary that Abraham and his son İsmail built for God. It is a symbol of God's uniqueness.

It is accepted as being more correct if people practice namaz in the mosque, although they are not obliged to do so. Women generally practice at home except the holy days. Each set of prayers is about 10-20 minutes long.

The average number of people practicing namaz in the mosque, regularly 5 times a day, is not more than 4-8 % of the total male Moslem population in Turkey.

293

For a Moslem, Friday is the holy day as is Sunday for a Christian or Saturday (Shabbat) for a Jew. The imam gives a sermon to the people in Turkish at the noon time prayers on Fridays. According to the law, they are not allowed to speak about politics in their sermons. For men, these noon time prayers on Friday have to be practiced in the mosque and the average number of people attending rises to 30-40 % of the total male population. In many places you may notice that shops close so that workers may attend the Friday noon time namaz.

Early morning prayers on the first days of the two religious holidays (Şeker and Kurban Bayramı) are the two most important prayer times for men in a year. Attendance at these times can rise to 70-80 % of the male population.

3. Oruç: To fast for 30 days during the holy month of Ramadan (Ramazan in Turkish). From sunrise to sunset eating, drinking, smoking and having sexual intercourse is forbidden for all except the sick, the weak, pregnant women soldiers on duty, travelers on necessary journeys and young children.

The coming of Ramadan is a big social event throughout the country. To celebrate it minaret balconies are lit as hundreds of lights (mahya) are stretched between the minarets of mosques with some figures, words and expressions to welcome or praise Ramadan. The figures are of flowers, boats, bridges or mosques. Papers, magazines and TV channels have special features and programs during Ramadan.

The process of fasting starts at about 3 o'clock in the morning with the street drummer's music. Each vicinity has its own drummer who makes music to wake people up each morning during the whole month. All his efforts are to make a living from the tips he collects at the end of the holy month from his neighborhood.

After being awakened by the drummer people have the opportunity to eat before sunrise as it is then which marks the beginning of fasting for the day. While fasting eating is not the only thing prohibited. Bad behavior, such as cursing, lying, doing harm to others are also forbidden.

People who fast expect respect from others. This means, especially in smaller cities, that restaurants will be closed during the daytime and people will not eat, drink or smoke in public.

At sunset, the müezzin's call for the early evening prayer marks the end of the day's fasting. Olives, salt, dates and water are religiously accepted as being the best foods to break the day's fasting.

About 20-25 % of Turkish people fast in Ramadan in urban areas and 60-70% in rural areas.

4. Hac: Visiting Mecca on a pilgrimage is only achievable for those who can financially afford it. Generally people prefer going to Mecca when they come to a certain age usually between 50-60 although there is no age restriction. The returning pilgrim is entitled to use the honorific hacı (pilgrim) before his name, a title that indicates his piety. He iş then more careful to refrain from any sin for the rest of his life.

5. Zekat: To give alms to the poor as a part of one's wealth that being 1/40 each year. In practice lots of people give alms to the poor, but sometimes not at the established rate.

Turkish Odyssey, Şerif Yenen, 1998, İstanbul - Turkey


## TÜRK HAMAMI

*Türk hamamında, ya her iki cins için ayrı bölümler ya da kadın ve erkeğe ayrılmış farklı günler vardır.*

*Bir hamamın ilk bölümüne ya da soyunma alanına girdiğinizde giysilerinizi çıkarır ve çizgili pamuk kumaş olan peştamalı üzerinize geçirirsiniz. Bu kumaş parçası kalçanın etrafına sarılır. Bazı insanlar altlarına mayolarını giyerler. Ayağa nalın giyilir.*

*Peştamal ve nalınları giydikten sonra mermer kurna ve musluklarla çevrelenmiş, ortasında alttan ısıtmalı mermer göbek taşının bulunduğu odaya geçersiniz. Burada kurnalardan birinin yanına oturup hamamtasını kullanarak üstünüze su dökersiniz. Cildiniz yumuşayıncaya kadar su dökmeye devam eder veya göbek taşının üzerine yatarsınız.*

*Tellak cildiniz hazır olduğunda sizi göbek taşına götürecek ve vücudunuzu keselemeye başlayacaktır. Vücudunuzdan çoğu insanın kir olduğunu düşündüğü küçük siyah parçalar çıkacaktır. Ama bu aslında derinizin ölü üst tabakasıdır. Bu aşamada isterseniz masaj da yaptırabilirsiniz. Sonra tellak sizi sabunlayacak ve deri gözeneklerinizin kapanması için sıcaklığı azalan suyla yıkayacaktır.*

*Artık soyunma alanına dönüp geleneksel ince belli bardaklarda çay içme zamanıdır.*

*Anadolu Destanı, Şerif Yenen, 1998, İstanbul - Turkey*

# THE TURKISH HAMAM

In a Turkish hamam there are either two separate sections for each of the sexes or different days and hours allocated to men and women.

When you enter the first section or the changing area of a hamam you begin by taking off your clothes and putting on a peştemal (sarong), which is a piece of striped cotton cloth. This is wrapped around the midriff and tucked into place. Some people choose to wear their bathing suits underneath. A kind of wooden clog called nalın are worn on the feet.

Dressed with peştemal and clogs, you go to the next room where a göbek taşı (navel stone), a marble heated table, is situated in the middle surrounded by marble sinks and taps. Here, you sit next to one of these sinks and start pouring lukewarm water over yourself with a hamam tası (bowl). You keep pouring water until your skin softens, meanwhile increasing the temperature of the water as your body gets used to it.

The hamam attendant, tellak, will take you to the göbek taşı when your skin is ready and start rubbing your body with a special glove, kese. Tiny black pieces will get rubbed off your body which most people think is dirt. This is in fact the top layer of dead skin. At this stage a massage is optional. Next, the tellak will give you a soapy rub down and wash you with water in decreasing temperature in order to make your pores close.

Now it is time to go back to the changing area to lie down and drink tea in the traditional tiny glasses.

Turkish Odyssey, Şerif Yenen, 1998, İstanbul - Turkey


## SÜNNET

*Sünnet penisin ön derisinin kesildiği bir ameliyattır. Kimi din grupları arasında, özellikle Yahudilerle Müslümanlar arasında dinsel önemi büyük bir uygulamadır. Sünnetin Tanrı'nın Hz. İbrahim ile yaptığı anlaşmadan çok önce eski Mısır'da uygulandığı bilinir. Müslümanlıkta ise sünnet Kuran'da yazılı değildir. Hz. Muhammed'den gelir. İslam'da Peygamberin yaptığı ya da söylediği her şeye sünnet denir; bu nedenle bu işlem çağdaş Türkçe'de sünnet olarak adlandırılır.*

*Sünnet işleminin riskleri de vardır. Sağlık açısından sağladığı avantajlara bakıldığında
bu riskler göze almaya değer niteliktedir. Ürologlara göre sünnetli erkekler sünnetsiz
erkeklere oranla çok daha az idrar yolları enfeksiyonu geçirirler ve cinsel yolla bulaşan
hastalıklara yakalanma riskleri daha azdır. Müslüman bir ülke olan Türkiye'de bütün
Müslüman erkek çocukları lisanslı sünnetçiler tarafından 2-14 yaşları arasında sünnet
edilir. Toplumsal bakış açısından sünnetin en önemli özelliği, bir çocuğun dinsel
topluluğuna yeni bir üye olarak tanıtılmasıdır. Bu da Müslümanlığa geçen insanların ilk
adım olarak neden sünnet edildiklerini açıklar. Çok küçük yaştan itibaren bir erkek
çocuğa sünnetin erkekliğe geçiş olduğu söylenir durur. Sünnet insanların yaşamındaki
önemli olaylardan biri olduğu için düğünle kutlanarak yapılır.*

*Bir ailede birden fazla erkek çocuk varsa hepsini birden sünnet etmek için uygun zaman
beklenir. Bu durumda küçük çocuk dört yaşından küçük olabilir. Kimi kırsal bölgede
köylüler işleri paylaştıkları gibi sünnet düğünü masraflarını da paylaşırlar. Zengin kişiler
de fakir çocukları ya da yetimleri kendi çocuklarıyla birlikte sünnet ederler. Hayırsever
kurumlar fakir çocuklar ve yetimler için toplu düğün törenleri yaparlar. Çocukların okul
dönemleri göz önünde bulundurulduğunda sünnetler yazın çocuklar tatildeyken
haziran-eylül aylarında hafta sonları yapılır.*

*Anadolu Destanı, Şerif Yenen, 1998, İstanbul - Turkey*

## CIRCUMCISION

Circumcision is an operation in which the foreskin of the penis is removed. It is a
practice of great religious significance among certain religious groups, notably the Jews
and the Moslems. Circumcision is known to have been practiced in ancient Egypt even
before it was introduced to the Jews as part of God's covenant with Abraham. In Islam,
however, the authority for circumcision came not from the Koran but from the example
of the Prophet Mohammed. In Islam, whatever the prophet does or says is called sünnet;
therefore this word stands for circumcision in modern Turkish.

Urologists claim that circumcised males have far fewer urinary tract infections and are
less at risk for catching sexually transmitted diseases than are uncircumcised males. On
the other side, pediatricians say that the medical risks attendant upon the surgery far
outweigh the possible future consequences of foregoing the operation.

As an Islamic country, in Turkey all Moslem boys are circumcised between the ages 2-14
by licensed circumcising surgeons. From the social point of view, the most prominent
feature of circumcision is the introduction of a child to his religious society as a new

member. This explains the reason for circumcision of people who convert into Moslems as a first step. It is impressed on a boy at a very early age that circumcision is a step for transition to manhood. As long as they are accepted as very important events in people's lives, circumcisions are generally made with big ceremonies in festive atmosphere.

If a family has more than one boy, they wait for an appropriate time to perform it altogether. In this case the younger child might be less than 4. In some rural areas, villagers sometimes share expenses of a circumcision feast like they do with the work. Wealthy people may take poor boys or orphans together with their children for circumcision. Charity organizations make collective ceremonies for poor boys and orphans. Considering school periods of children, circumcisions are held in summer months while the children are on vacation, from June through September at weekends.

Turkish Odyssey, Şerif Yenen, 1998, İstanbul - Turkey

## AYASOFYA

*Ayasofya, Mısır Piramitleri ve Çin Seddi dışında belki de dünyanın en büyük binasıydı. Yüzyıllar boyunca da dünyanın en büyük kilisesi olmuştur. Günümüzde ise Londra'daki Aziz Paulus, Roma'daki Aziz Petrus ve Milano'daki Duomo'dan sonra en büyük kilisedir. Büyük Osmanlı mimarı Sinan özyaşamöyküsünde hayatını Ayasofya'nın başarılı tekniğini aşmaya adadığını söylemiştir.*

*Ayasofya Hagia Sophia'ya adanmıştır; adının anlamı Hz. İsa'nın niteliklerinden biri olan İlahi Bilgelik'tir. Bugünkü Ayasofya aynı yerde inşa edilen üçüncü binadır.*

*Birinci bina İS 390'da inşa edilen ahşap çatılı bir bazilikaydı. Bu ilk kilise Megale Ekklesia (Büyük Kilise) 404 yılındaki bir ayaklanmada yanmıştır. Bunun yerine Theodosius masif bir bazilika yaptırmış ancak o da 532 yılında İustinianos'a karşı yapılan Nika Ayaklanması'nda yanmıştır. İustinianos aynı yıl Ayasofya'yı yeniden inşa ettirmeye başlamıştır. Mimarları iki Anadolulu dehadır: Trallesli mühendis ve matematikçi Anthemios ile Miletoslu mimar İsidoros. İmparatorluğun her yanından malzeme toplamış ve yapım sırasında yüz ustabaşının denetiminde on bin işçi çalışmıştır. İustinianos 537 yılında Ayasofya'yı "Süleyman (Şlomo) seni geçtim!" sözleriyle tekrar hizmete açmıştır.*

*Binanın deprem bölgesinde bir fay hattı üzerinde bulunması, kentin birçok ayaklanma ve yangına sahne olmasıyla, Ayasofya çoğu kez hasar görmüş ve birçok restorasyon geçirmiştir.*

298

*Bizans dönemindeki bir başka önemli olay, İkonoklazm döneminde kiliseden bütün dinsel resimlerin kaldırılmasıdır. 1204 yılındaki 4. Haçlı Seferi sırasında kilise yağmalanmış ve Ayasofya'da iğrenç olaylar meydana gelmiştir. 1453 yılında Konstantinopolis'i fethettikten sonra Sultan Mehmet ilk olarak Ayasofya'ya gitmiş ve binanın hemen camiye dönüştürülmesi emrini vermiştir. Bu da minare, mihrap ve minber gibi İslami unsurların eklenmesiyle yapılmıştır. Bunların hepsi binanın ana ekseninin 10 derece güneyine doğru Mekke yönünde yerleştirilmiştir. Mimar Sinan da restorasyon ve İslam unsurların eklenmesinde görev almıştır. Payandalar Osmanlı döneminde eklenmiştir. İki devasa mermer kap Pergamon'dan 16. yy'da getirilmiş ve kandiller için yağ depolamakta kullanılmıştır. Galerilerin seviyesindeki sekiz yuvarlak ahşap plaka, İslam hat sanatının güzel örneklerindendir. Bu plakalara yazılan adlar Allah, Hz. Muhammed, dört halife (Hz. Ebubekir, Hz. Ömer, Hz. Osman ve Hz. Ali) ile Hz. Muhammed'in torunları Hasan ve Hüseyin'e aittir.*

*Zaman içinde Ayasofya mezarlar, çeşmeler, kütüphaneler vb. gibi bölümlerden oluşan bir külliye haline gelmiştir. Binadaki Bizans dönemi mozaik ve fresklerin kilisenin Türkler tarafından camiye dönüştürülmesiyle kapatıldığı söylenir ama bu kısmen doğrudur. Gezginler Osmanlı döneminde Ayasofya'daki resimlerden söz ederler. Bu da resimlerin hepsinin kapatılmadığını gösterir.*

*Ayasofya 916 yıl kilise, 481 yıl cami olarak kullanılmıştır. 1934'te Mustafa Kemal Atatürk'ün emriyle müzeye çevrilmiş ve o günden bu yana da ziyaretçilere açılmıştır.*

*Anadolu Destanı, Şerif Yenen, 1998, İstanbul - Turkey*

## HAGIA SOPHIA

The Hagia Sophia was probably the largest building on the world's surface, barring the Egyptian Pyramids, or the Great Wall of China. For many centuries it was the largest church and today is the fourth largest in the world after St. Paul's in London, St. Peter's in Rome and the Duomo in Milan. The great Ottoman architect Sinan, in his autobiography, says that he devoted his lifetime in the attempt to surpass its technical achievements.

It was dedicated to the Hagia Sophia which means the Divine Wisdom, an attribute of Christ.

Today's Hagia Sophia is the third building built at the same place. The first one was a basilica with a wooden roof and was built in 390 AD. This original church Megale Ecclesia (Great Church) was burned down in a rumpus in 404. Theodosius replaced it with a massive basilica which was burned down in the Nika Revolt against Justinian in 532. Justinian began rebuilding the Hagia Sophia in the same year. The architects were two Anatolian geniuses, Anthemius of Tralles, an engineer and a mathematician and Isidorus of Miletus, an architect. They started collecting materials from all over the empire. In the construction ten thousand workers worked under the supervision of one hundred master builders. Justinian reopened it in 537 entering the Hagia Sophia with the words "Solomon, I have surpassed you!".

Because the building is on a fault line in an earthquake zone and the city passed through many riots and fires, the Hagia Sophia was destroyed and underwent restorations several times.

Another major event during the Byzantine period was the removal of all religious images from the church in the iconoclastic period. During the Fourth Crusade in 1204, the church was pillaged and some disgusting events took place in the Hagia Sophia. After conquering Constantinople in 1453, Sultan Mehmet immediately went to the Hagia Sophia and ordered that it be converted into a mosque. This was done by adding the Islamic elements such as minarets, the mihrab and the minber all of which were appropriately positioned to face toward Mecca, 10 degrees south of the main axis of the building. The architect Sinan was also assigned to make some restorations and add Islamic elements to the building. Buttresses were added in the Ottoman period. Two huge marble jars were brought from Pergamum in the 16 C and probably used to keep oil for candles. The eight round wooden plaques at gallery level are fine examples for Islamic calligraphy. The names painted on these plaques are Allah, Prophet Mohammed, the first four Caliphs Ebubekir, Ömer, Osman and Ali, and the two grandsons of Mohammed, Hasan and Hüseyin.

In time Ayasofya became a complex consisting of tombs, a fountain, libraries, etc. It has been thought that when Turks converted the church into a mosque, all the pictures were covered which is not correct. According to the narration of travelers, pictures were still standing but figures' faces were covered.

Ayasofya was used as a church for 916 years and as a mosque for 481 years. In 1934, by the order of Mustafa Kemal Atatürk, it was made a museum and has since been open to visitors.

Turkish Odyssey, Şerif Yenen, 1998, İstanbul - Turkey